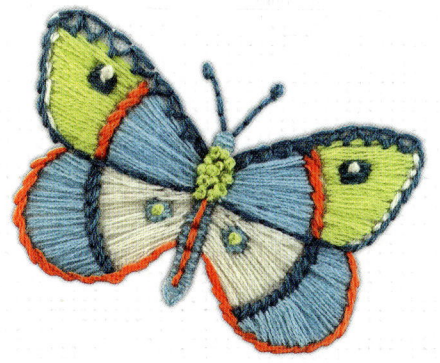

*This book is for anyone
seeking connection through craft.
I hope each stitch
inspires lasting memories and
brings you closer
to your creativity and community.*

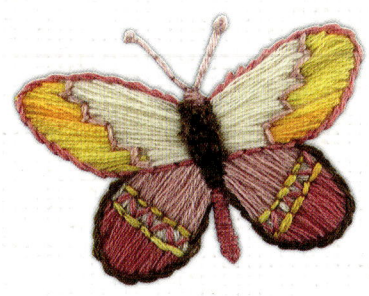

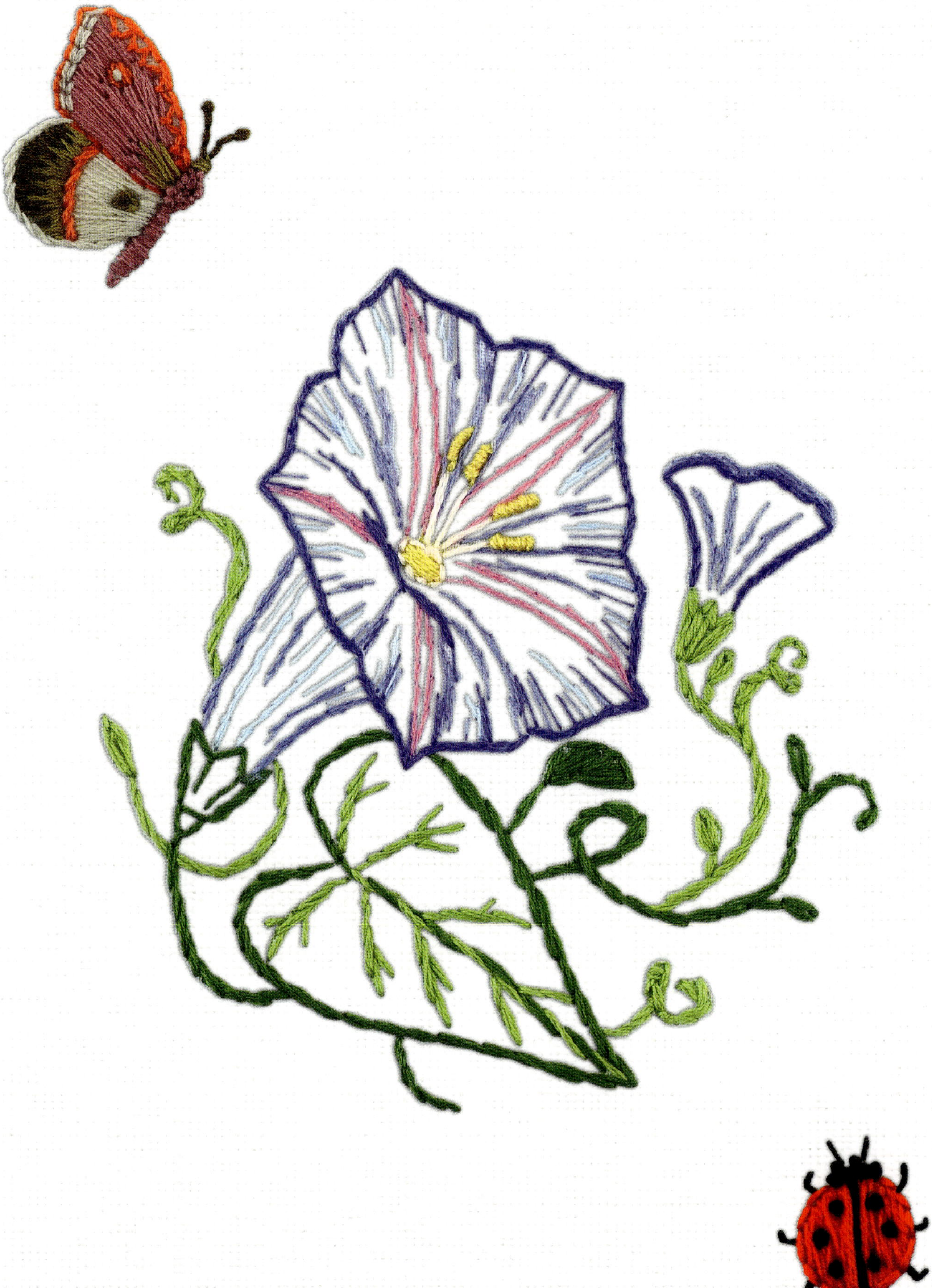

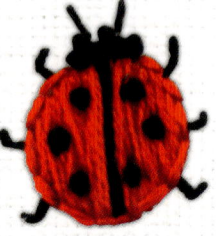

Birth Flower Embroidery

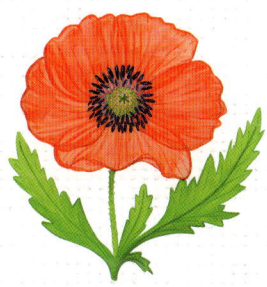

A Month-by-Month Celebration of Floral Embroidery

AMY L. FRAZER

Walter Foster

Contents

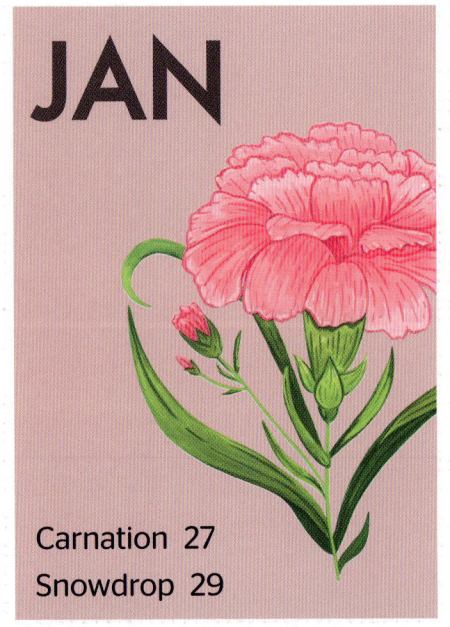

JAN

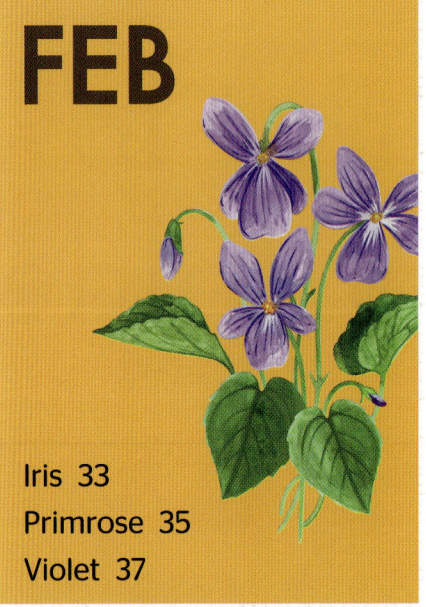

FEB

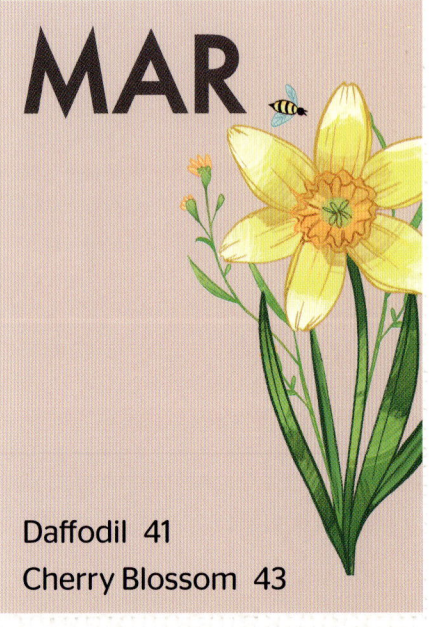

MAR

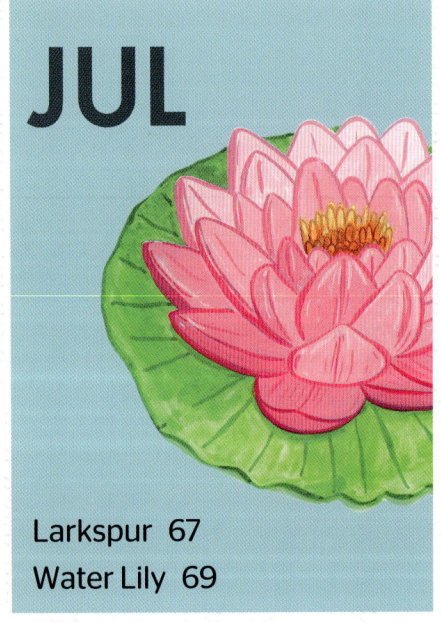

JUL

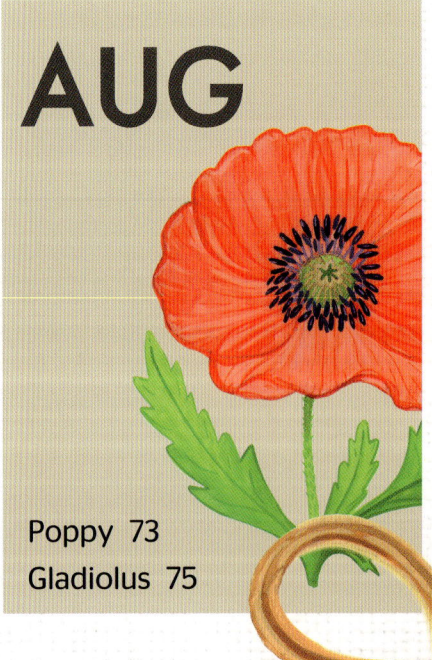

AUG

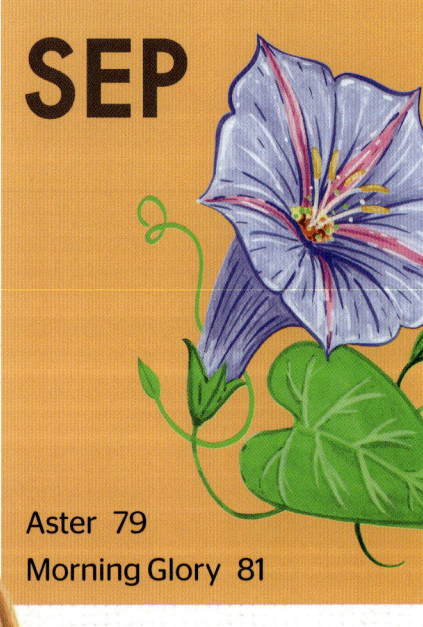

SEP

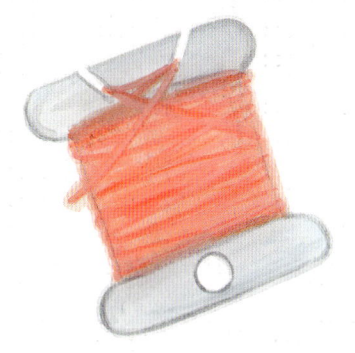

Welcome to the Beautiful World of Birth Flowers 7
Tools & Materials 8
Transfer Techniques 11
Stitch Guide 13

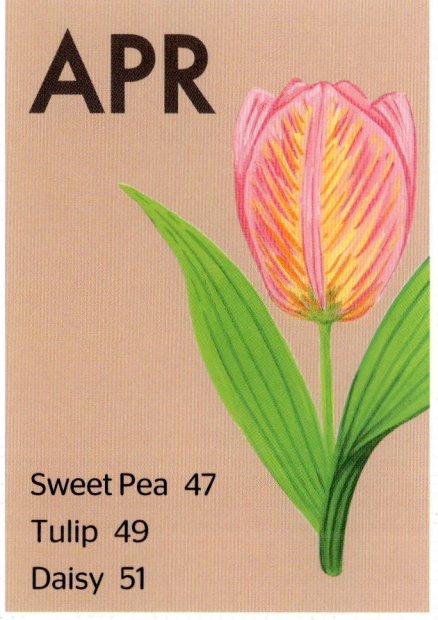

APR

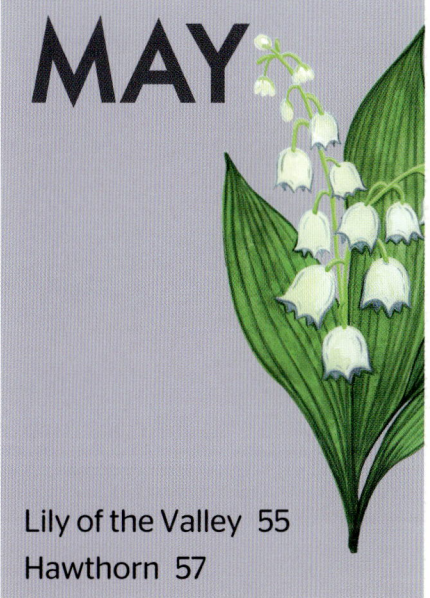

MAY

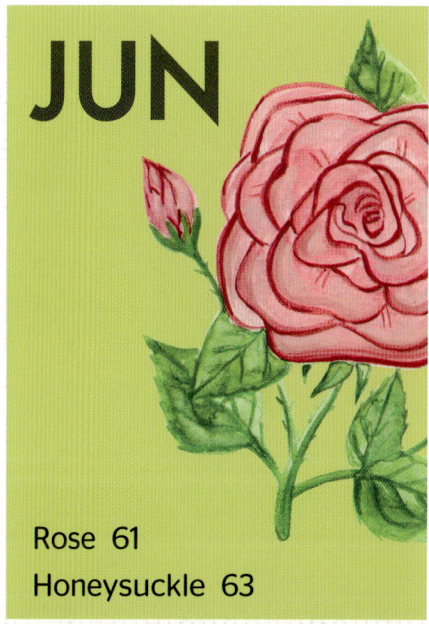

JUN

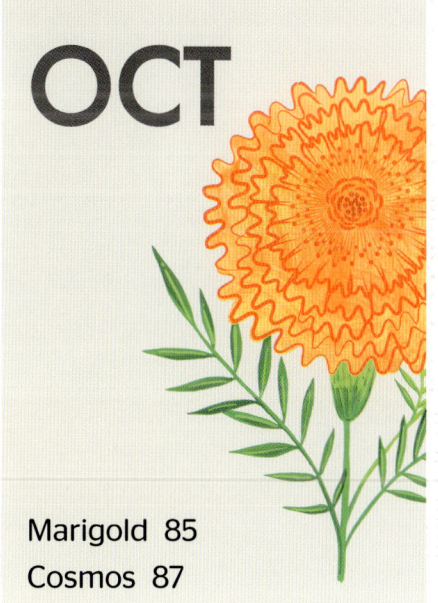

OCT

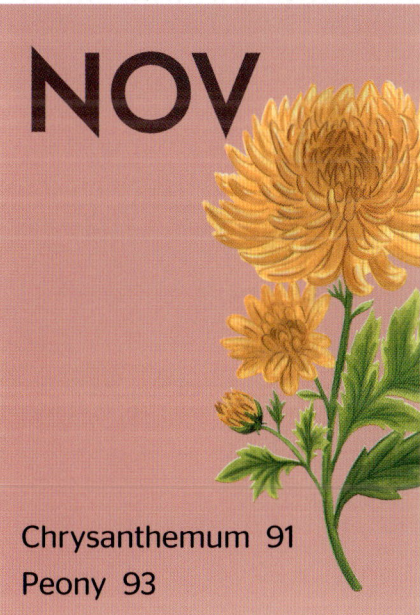

NOV

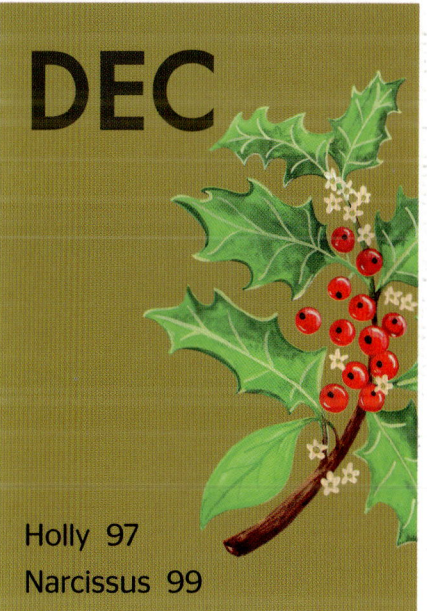

DEC

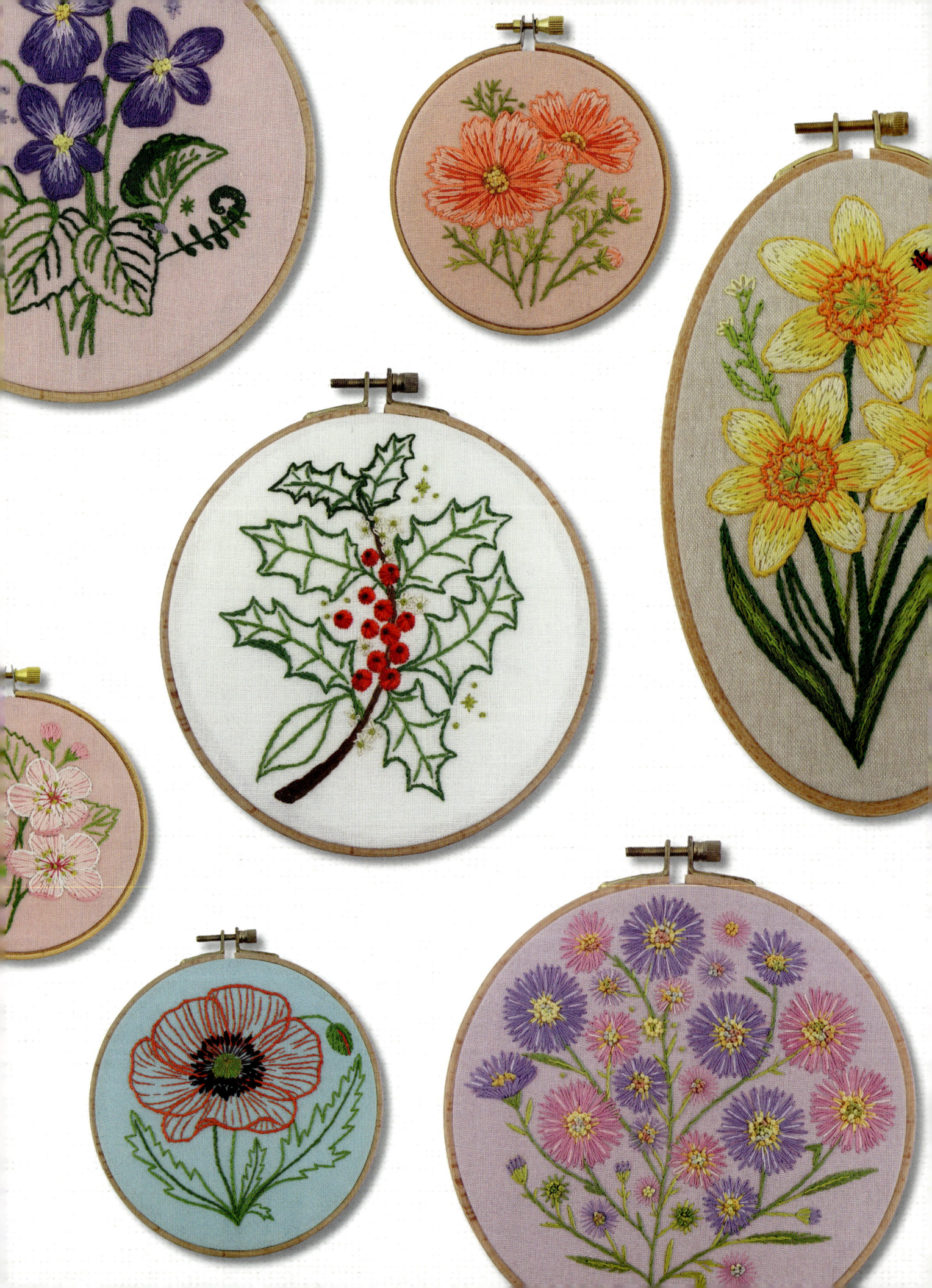

WELCOME

to the Beautiful World of Birth Flowers

Since ancient Roman times, when the tradition of celebrating birthdays first began, each month of the year has been paired with a representational flower. Today we recognize them as birth month flowers.

Over the centuries, the flowers assigned to each month evolved and expanded. Some are natural fits, like the daffodils that bloom in the early spring associated with the month of March. Or holly, a hallmark of the holiday season, paired with December. Others are the same color as their month's birthstone, such as the purple shades of violets that match amethysts in February.

But it doesn't stop there. During the Victorian era, books like *The Language of Flowers: An Alphabet of Floral Emblems* (1857) added new layers of meaning to flowers and their "secret" language.

It's fascinating to get to the root of these histories and discover what ties each flower to each month and what they symbolize. Here we're going to take it a step further and weave that knowledge with the timeless tradition of hand embroidery.

In this book, you'll find twenty-six beautiful birth month flowers to embroider. From January to December, each flower has been artfully illustrated and stitched with charming details. Use the step-by-step instructions and templates to stitch a special keepsake for yourself, friends, and family. Then, customize your floral designs with add-ons like butterflies, bumblebees, names, and dates, for memorable gifts crafted for the lucky recipient! If you're daring and up for a challenge, you can create a one-of-a-kind design that pairs several flowers together for a handstitched bouquet of your entire family's birth flowers!

By stitching these flowers, we not only capture their beauty but also create lasting keepsakes imbued with their meanings. Gather your materials, choose a flower that speaks to you, and let's begin stitching together the beauty of the seasons, one petal at a time.

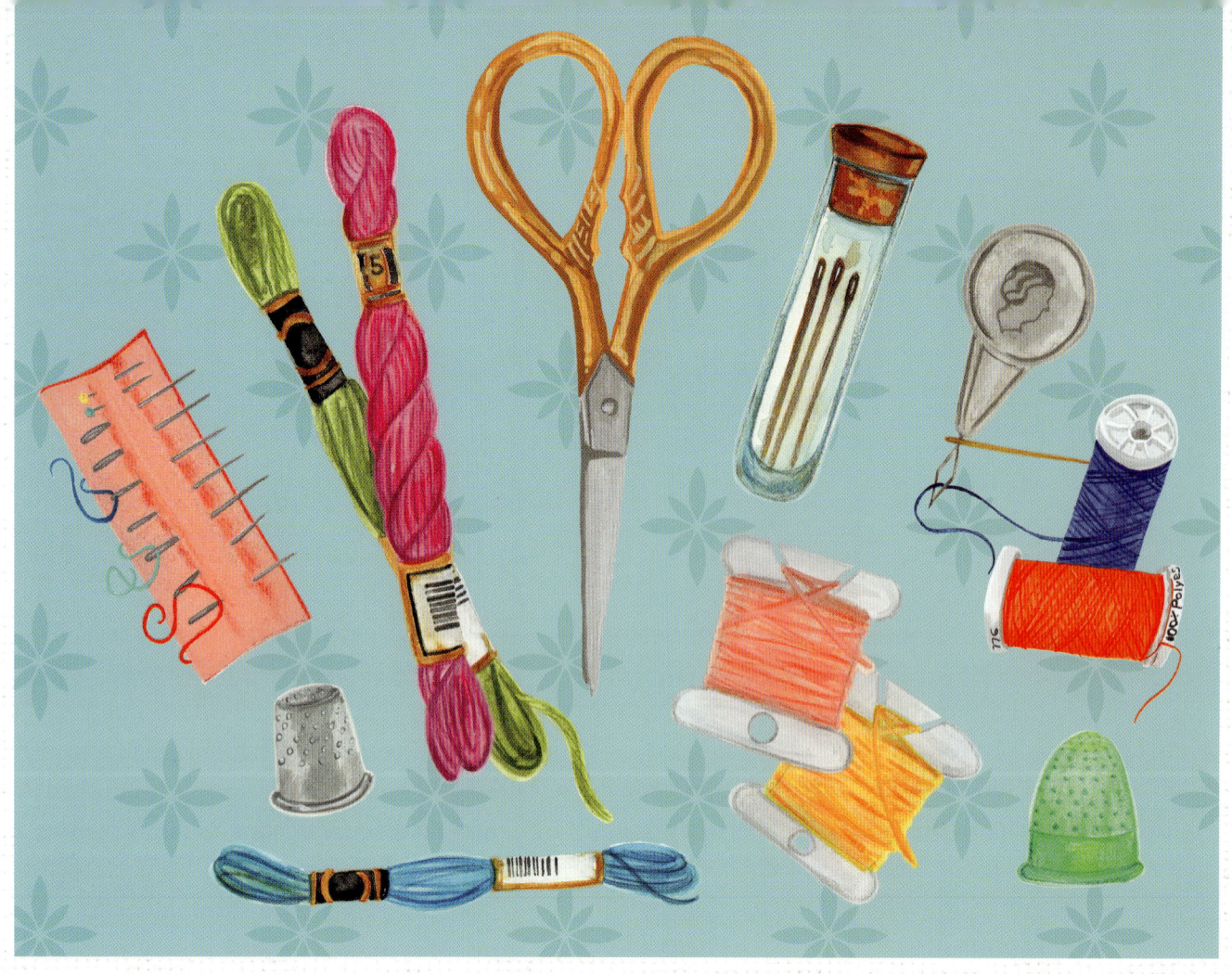

TOOLS & MATERIALS

If you're new to embroidery and were drawn to this book with the desire to learn to stitch, these first few sections are for you! As with any hobby, craft, or art practice, you will acquire all kinds of sewing notions, also known as supplies. Here, I share the basic toolkit you'll need as we work through the projects in this book. I encourage you to experiment and discover what types of fabric you prefer, which needles become your go-tos, and the perfect sewing scissors for your projects.

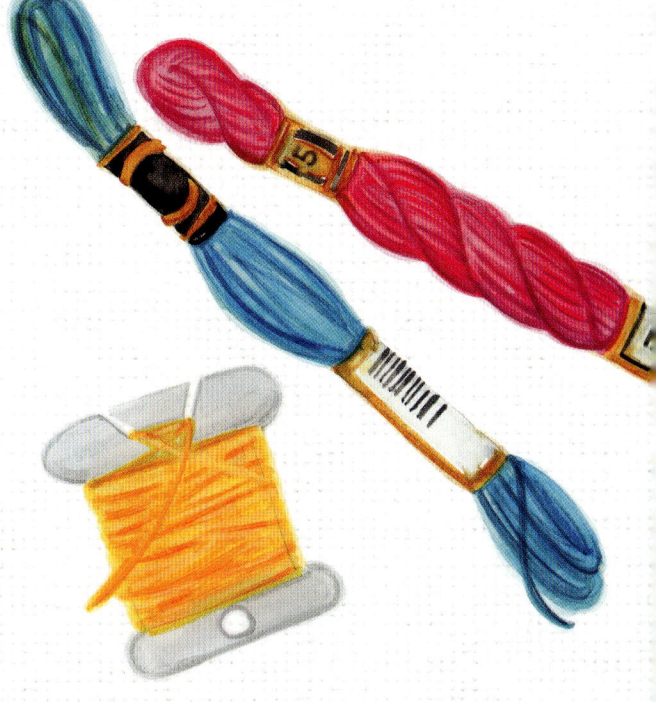

TOOLBOX ESSENTIALS

FABRIC

Fabrics that are best suited for embroidery, such as cotton and linen, are called "plain weave." This means that the warp and weft, or threads that run horizontally and vertically, are irregular and *don't* require you to pay particular attention to where your needle enters the fabric.

NEEDLES

The thickness of your needle should match the thickness of your thread. Pick a needle that's too big for your thread, and you'll leave holes in the fabric. Pick a needle that's too small, and the thread won't be able to pass through the eye. You'll also want a needle with a bigger eye if you use more strands of floss. Experiment with different sizes of threads and needles to find what works best for you. I usually sew with 3 strands of floss and a size 5 embroidery needle or a 22 or 24 chenille needle.

It's helpful to have a needle book or a piece of felt to keep your needles in one place. It's also a real time saver to load up several needles with thread and put them in your needle book so that they are ready to go for a project.

THREADS

There are so many different types of threads and yarns. For me, if it fits through the eye of a needle, I'll embroider with it. However, DMC six-strand cotton floss is the most commonly used embroidery thread and one that I use all the time. It's easy to find at your local craft or fabric store and comes in a wide array of colors. This thread is made up of six strands twisted together. It can be separated, allowing you to modify the thickness of the floss depending on the number of strands you use. You'll see the number of threads used in parentheses on the stitch diagrams. For example, the label BS (2) means to backstitch with two strands.

A few of the projects in this book use perle cotton, which cannot be separated. It is a mercerized, twisted single strand and comes in a range of colors and thicknesses. It has a beautiful sheen and is soft to sew with.

SCISSORS

Having the right scissors on hand for embroidering will make life so much easier for you! Keep them sharp and use them only for their intended purpose. It can be difficult to snip thin threads with scissors that are too large.

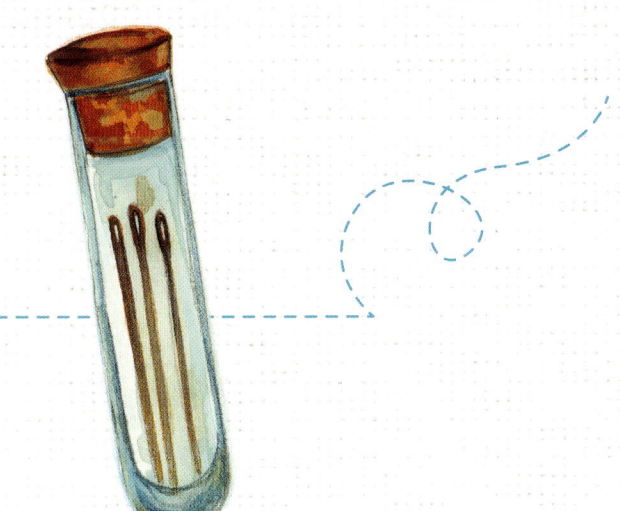

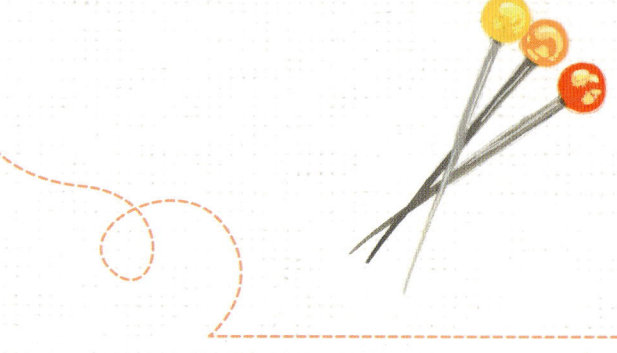

HOOPS AND FRAMES

To hoop or not to hoop? That is the question. I personally almost always use a hoop to keep my fabric flat and tight when stitching.

Hoops come in a wide range of sizes, from about 3 to 14 inches (7.5 to 35.5 cm) or larger in diameter. A quality hoop will maintain the fabric at an even tension and keep the grain straight. This will allow you to keep the stitches even and consistent. If the hoop seems loose, you can wrap the inner ring with a long ¼-inch (0.5 cm) strip of fabric to keep it nice and tight.

To assemble an embroidery hoop with fabric, separate the two rings of the hoop. After transferring the design to your fabric, center the fabric over the inner ring. Then place the outer ring over the fabric, tightening the screw to hold the frame together. Pull the fabric snug.

OTHER EMBROIDERY & SEWING SUPPLIES

These sewing supplies are nice to have but not essential to start embroidery. Look out for other materials specific to drawing and transferring images that I'll cover in later chapters.

- **Storage container:** Keep the threads and materials you use for each project in a small box so that you can pull it out when you want to work on a certain piece.

- **Thimbles:** These handy protectors are great to have in case you need to push your needle through a thick patch of stitches or a few layers of fabric.

- **Floss bobbins:** Either plastic or cardboard, these work well for keeping your thread organized.

- **Iron and ironing surface**

- **Thread conditioner:** You can swipe the end of your thread through this to help thread the needle, or you can pull your full length of thread through it to put a protective layer on the thread.

- **Needle threader**

- **Quilting pins:** When using a large piece of water-soluble stabilizer, it's sometimes helpful to pin it down in a few spots to keep it from shifting around.

- **Water-soluble pens or pencils**

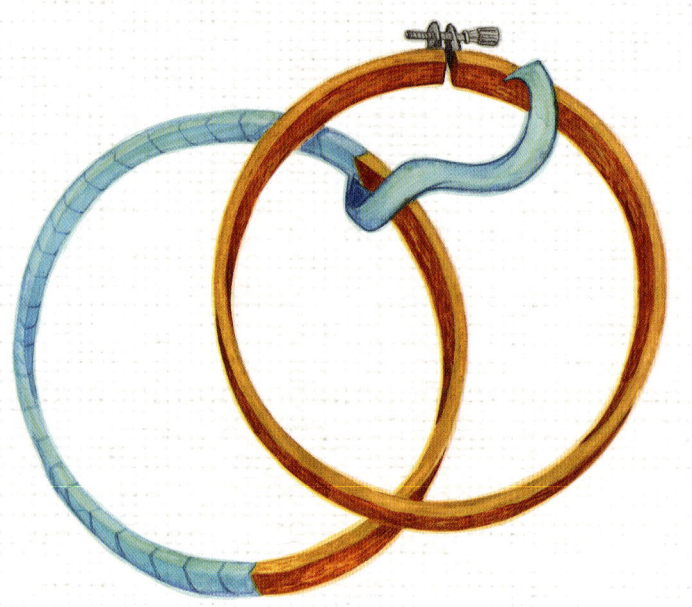

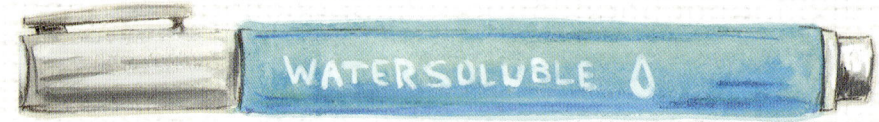

TRANSFER TECHNIQUES

There are quite a few methods to transfer your template to the surface of your fabric. The method you choose will depend on several factors including the size and detail of the project, the content and color of the fabric you are using, and the materials and tools you have available to you. Your experience or comfort level with embroidery can come into play as well.

Before committing to any of these transfer methods for your project, it's important to test them out on a scrap piece of the fabric you are using. Different types of fabrics will work differently with each transfer method and this will save you time, money, and maybe some heartache, in the long run.

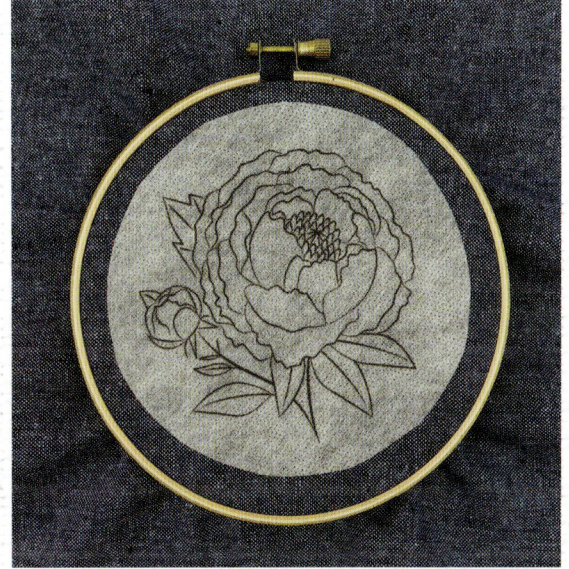

METHOD 1:
WATER-SOLUBLE STABILIZER

This is my go-to method for transferring designs to fabric, especially if they are complex and detailed. With this material, you can copy, trace, or print the pattern directly onto the stabilizer, then place that on your fabric. I prefer the sticky-back version that adheres to the fabric instead of pinning it down. When you're done with your project, remove the stabilizer by running it under water.

Tip: Remember this is water-soluble, so any water drops will start to dissolve it. If this happens, let it dry before continuing. Very high humidity will also affect the stabilizer, so store in a cool, dry place.

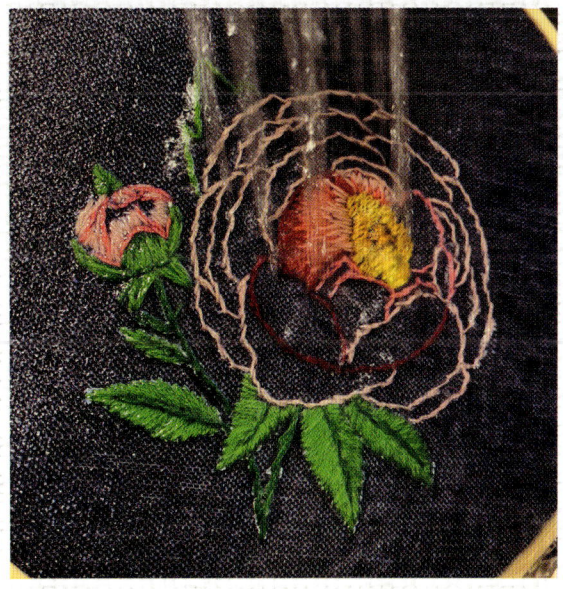

Method 1

METHOD 2: DIRECT TRACING

Depending on your tracing pen, this method of directly tracing the pattern onto the fabric is removable. Using a bright window or lightbox, simply place the fabric over the template and trace it with a Frixion (heat-soluble) or water-soluble pen. When finished stitching, use heat or water to remove any visible linework. Note that some stitchers like to use a sharp graphite pencil. However, this doesn't always wash out. Be sure to test the method you choose on scrap cloth before transferring to your fabric.

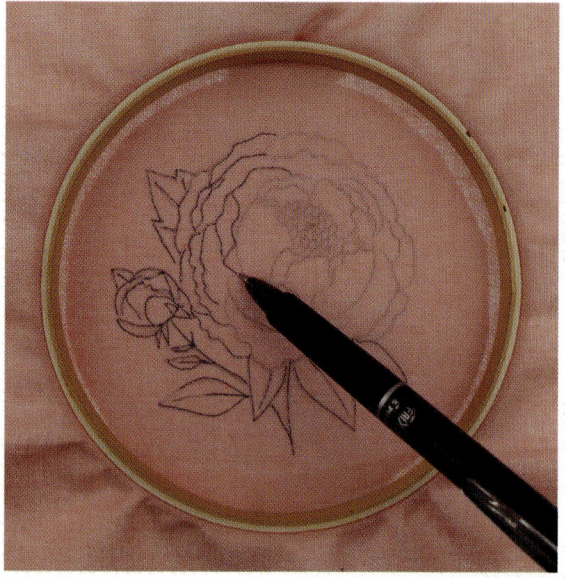

Method 2

METHOD 3: HOT-IRON TRANSFER

This transfer method works well but creates a permanent transfer that won't wash away after stitching. There are many hot iron transfer pens and pencils available, but my absolute favorite is the Fine Point Transfer Pen from Sublime Stitching. They come in a variety of colors, and you can use the transfer multiple times! The most important detail with this technique is you must trace the *reverse* image of the design, especially if it has writing. Otherwise, your design will transfer backwards. Once traced, follow the manufacturer's instructions on how to iron and transfer the template to the fabric.

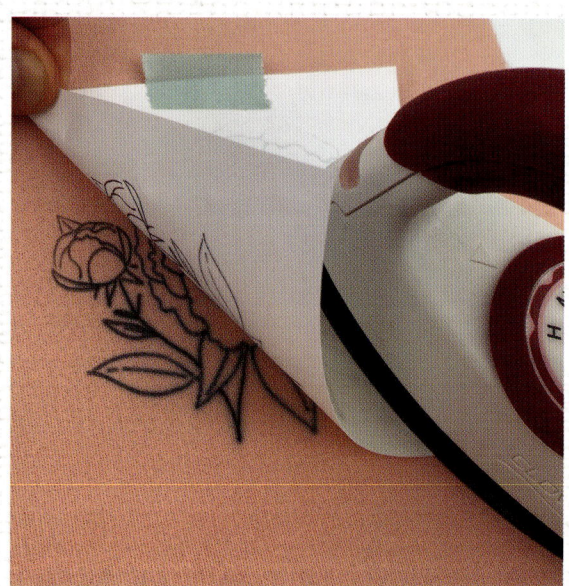

Method 3

OTHER METHODS

Variations and methods of transferring patterns to fabric include carbon transfer paper, printing directly to fabric, stencils, and prick and pouncing. I've outlined the three techniques that I think best suit the projects in this book and that are easiest to use. Experiment and see which methods you like best!

STITCH GUIDE

Whether you're new to embroidery or an experienced stitcher, mastering and practicing basic stitches is key to creating beautiful designs. This book emphasizes simplicity, using a few fundamental stitches to achieve striking effects.

THREAD AND NEEDLE PREP

A crucial part of the creative process is preparing your tools. I like to load up a few needles with the colors I'm using and place them in a small piece of felt. This saves some time when stitching.

STARTING AND FINISHING

With the threaded needle, bring the tip through the back of the fabric at the starting point. This is referred to as "up 1." The next step, unless you're making a knot, is "down 2." Insert the needle into the fabric and push it through, pulling the thread until it catches on the front. Continue stitching.

As you stitch, the thread will inevitably become knotted. Don't worry! Try to unknot it, and if after a few tries it isn't working, tie it off on the back and start with a freshly threaded needle.

To finish stitching or to change colors, tie a small knot on the back side, close to the fabric. Run the thread under a few stitches before snipping it. Make sure that when you end a thread, you have enough length to finish it off—generally about 5 to 6 inches (12.5 to 15 cm).

STITCH LEGEND

Stitches used in the embroideries and their abbreviations:

Backstitch (BS)
Whipped Backstitch (WBS)*
Threaded Backstitch (TBS)*
Bullion Stitch (BUL)
Chain Stitch (CS)
Detached Chain Stitch (DCS)*
Couching Stitch (CH)
Fly Stitch (FLY)
French Knot (FK)
Leaf Stitch (LF)
Long and Short Stitch (L+S)
Satin Stitch (SAT)
Shaded Satin Stitch (SHSAT)*
Split Backstitch (SPLBS)
Star Stitch (STR)
Straight Stitch (SS)
Stem Stitch (STM)

*Indicates a variation of the basic stitch.

READING THE STITCH DIAGRAMS

The projects in this book are presented with stitch diagrams showing you the stitch, floss, and number of threads to use. For example, a green dot with "STM (2)" means you use 2 strands of the green color indicated and work stem stitch.

To make the project exactly as you see it, follow the stitch guide. You can also make your own choices! Change the colors or stitches for a truly one-of-a-kind creation.

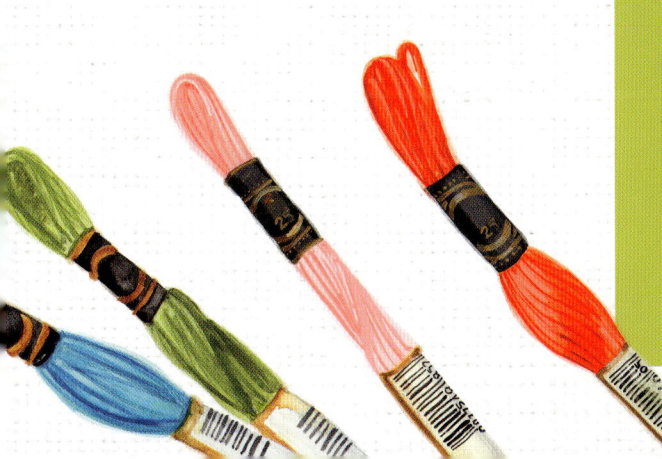

BACKSTITCH (BS)

Backstitch is a great stitch for outlining just about anything straight or curvy, including lettering. Backstitch also comes in handy when you just need a few stitches to fill or finish an area such as a short line on a leaf or petal.

HOW TO

Bring the needle up from the back of the fabric at 1. Insert the needle at 2. This length should generally be about ¼" (0.5 cm) or less. Bring the needle up at 3, which is one stitch length ahead of the last insertion. Insert the needle at 4 (same hole as 1). Continue making stitches. There should be no space between stitches.

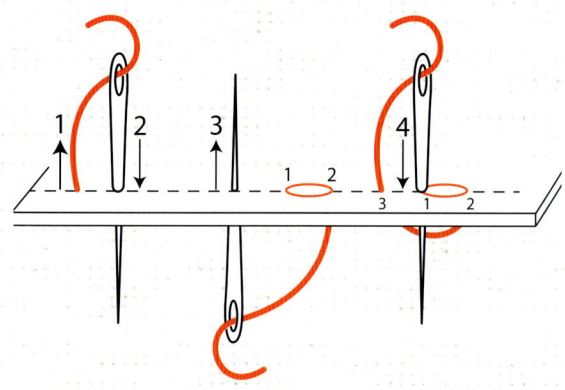

WHIPPED BACKSTITCH (WBS)

Like the threaded backstitch, the whipped backstitch is great for decorative borders or lettering.

HOW TO

Stitch a line of backstitch. With a second color bring the needle up at the starting point of the backstitched line. Tuck the thread under the first stitch and using a whipping motion wrap it around the first stitch, tucking it under the second stitch. Continue whipping around each backstitch until you reach the end. Insert the needle in the last backstitch and tie off on the backside. The needle does not pierce the fabric using the whipped stitch.

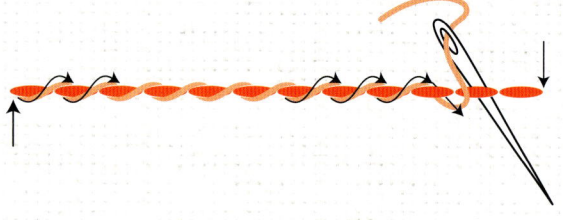

THREADED BACKSTITCH (TBS)

The threaded backstitch gives an added texture to a backstitched line and is great for decorative borders.

HOW TO

Stitch a line of backstitch. With a second color bring the needle up at the starting point of the backstitched line. Tuck the thread under the first stitch and weave it in and out between the backstitches. When you reach the end of the backstitched line, insert the needle in the last backstitch and tie off on the backside. The needle does not pierce the fabric using the threaded backstitch.

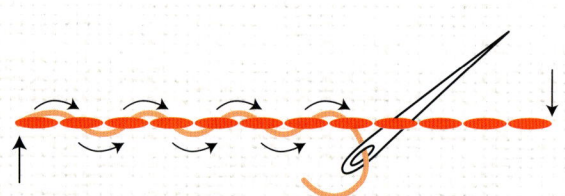

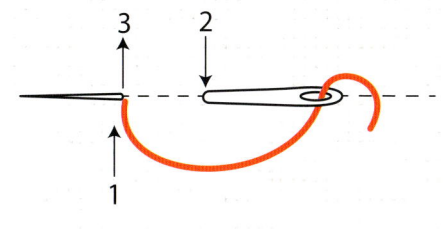

BULLION STITCH (BUL)

This stitch, also known as a bullion knot, is great for adding textures and for stitching the stamens and pistils in the center of flowers. The key to this stitch is keeping the tension correct and managing the wraps to keep them straight. This stitch takes some time and practice to master, but once you do, it is so much fun to add to your embroideries!

HOW TO

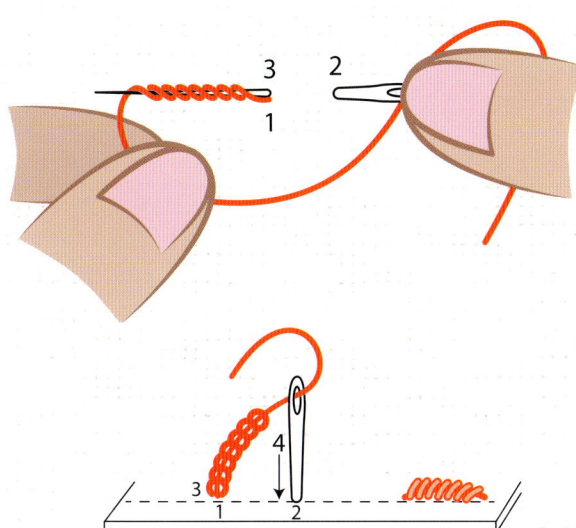

1. Bring the needle up through the front of the fabric at 1. Insert the needle at 2 but don't pull the thread all the way through. This length should generally be about ½" (1.25 cm). Bring the needle up at 3, the original point you brought the needle up at 1.

2. Holding the needle against the fabric with your dominant hand, wrap the thread around the needle about seven times. Holding the wraps against the needle, slide the needle through the wraps, pulling it up through the fabric.

3. Pull the wraps down the needle so the end of them is touching the fabric but is not smashed against it. Insert needle at point 4. Tie off the thread on the back of the fabric or continue stitching.

CHAIN STITCH (CS)

The chain stitch is such a versatile stitch, providing lots of texture to your embroidery. It can be used as an outline for stems or as a fill for leaves. Don't pull the thread too tight when stitching or you'll lose all that beautiful texture.

HOW TO

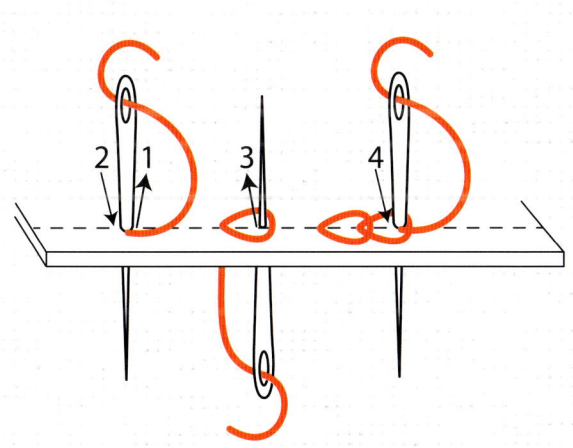

1. Bring the needle up through the back of the fabric at 1. Holding the thread in your nonstitching hand, create a loop. Insert the needle back into the same point (2) but don't pull the thread all the way through, keeping a loop about 1" (2.5 cm) in size.

2. Bring the needle back up about ¼" (0.5 cm) from the insertion point (3). You want to bring the needle up inside the loop, catching it and pulling the thread until the loop gently touches the thread coming out of the fabric.

3. Insert the needle back into the same point (4), forming another small loop and continue stitching your chain. To end the chain, add a small straight stitch to the last loop, tacking it down to the fabric. To fill an area such as a leaf, stitch rows of chains next to each other working back and forth or round and round.

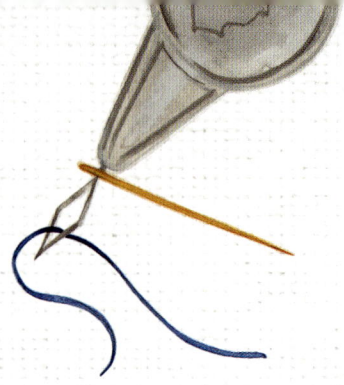

DETACHED CHAIN STITCH (DCS)

This variation of the chain stitch is perfect for making flowers and small leaves. It can be worked in singles or grouped together. Experiment with making long and short detached chain stitches to create different types of flowers.

HOW TO

Bring the needle up through the back of the fabric at 1. Holding the thread with your thumb against the fabric, create a loop. Insert the needle back into the same point (2) but don't pull the thread all the way through, keeping a loop about 1" (2.5 cm) in size. Bring the needle back up about ¼" (0.5 cm) from the insertion point (3). Forming a small stitch, insert needle at 4 outside the loop. This tiny stitch creates a single chain stitch and will hold the loop in place. Continue creating more detached chain stitches.

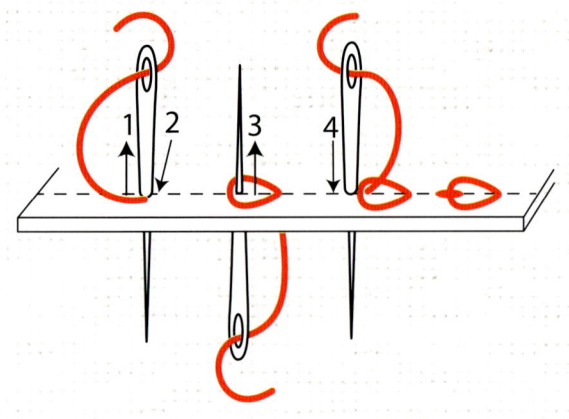

COUCHING STITCH (CH)

Couching stitch is embroidered using two threads. The first thread is laid on the surface of the fabric and stitched down using a second thread. The laid thread is usually thicker than the sewn thread, but not always, and can be contrasting in texture and color. Experiment with combining colors and shapes.

HOW TO

Bring your first thread up through the fabric from the back side. Lay this thread along the top of the fabric, following the design line, maneuvering it as you go. Using a second thread, stitch down the laid thread at evenly spaced intervals using small straight stitches. When finished, both threads pass through to the back of the fabric and are tied off.

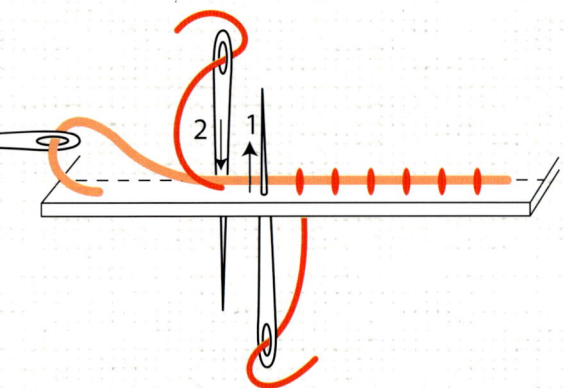

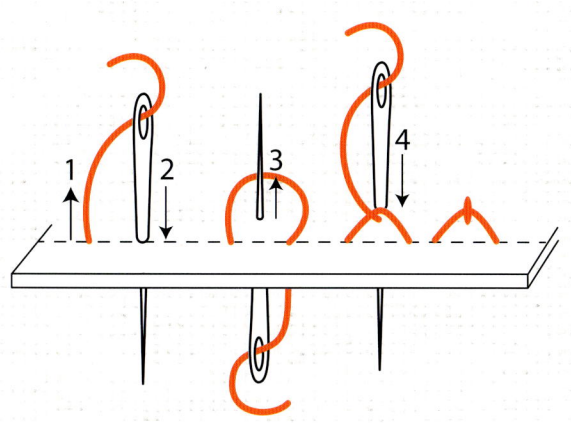

FLY STITCH (FLY)

The fly stitch is great for stitching stems and for texture when stitching groundcover. It can be stitched in a line or as single stitches like a detached chain stitch. Try combining fly stitches of different sizes, overlapping them using different colors of thread for an interesting effect.

HOW TO

Bring the needle up through the fabric from the back side at 1. Insert needle at 2, horizontally across from point 1, forming a small loop. Bring needle up at 3, inside the loop. Insert needle at 4 on the outside of the loop. This stitch will hold the loop in place.

FRENCH KNOT (FK)

French knots are great for stitch variety, from filling areas in the center of flowers to adding cute details. Making a French knot is all about managing the thread and its tension to avoid tangling. They can be time consuming to make, but the overall texture you can achieve is worth it.

HOW TO

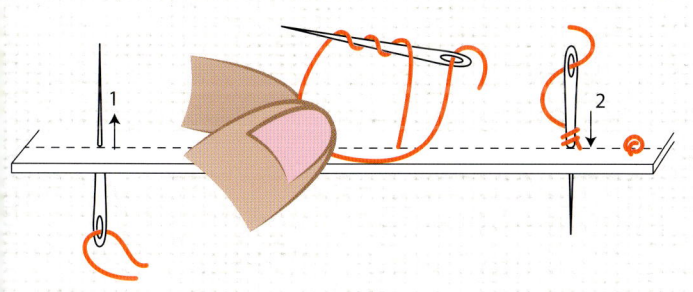

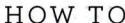

Bring the needle up through the fabric from the back side at 1. With your free hand hold the thread with your index finger and thumb to the side. Wrap the thread around the needle front to back three times and pull gently to tighten the wraps. Keeping the thread taut, insert the point of the needle into the fabric just next to point 1. As you push the needle through the fabric, slide the wraps down the needle against the fabric, keeping the thread held taut with your free hand. Push the needle into the fabric to form a knot. As you start to see the knot forming, watch to ensure the thread doesn't tangle. If the thread isn't tangling, let it go and keep pulling through.

Tip: Milliner's needles are great for working French knots, as they have the same shaft thickness throughout the length of the needle, making it easier to slide the knot off. The more wrap you make around the needle, the larger the French knot will be. Wrap fewer times for smaller knots.

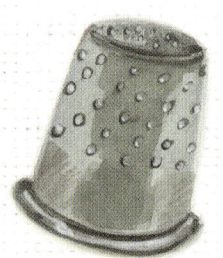

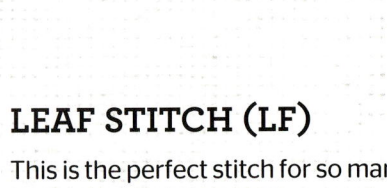

LEAF STITCH (LF)

This is the perfect stitch for so many different styles and shapes of leaves. The leaf stitch is essentially straight stitches (page 21) made at angles to fill a leaf shape.

HOW TO

Bring the needle up through the fabric from the back side at 1 at the top of the leaf shape. Stitch one straight stitch going down at 2. Continue stitching down the leaf making stitches at an angle next to each other as you would with satin stitch. Up at 3, down at 4; up at 5, down at 6; and so on. Adjust the angle of the stitches to match the leaf shape. Repeat for other side of the leaf. Add additional stitches if needed to fill in any empty spaces. To give the leaf a more finished look, backstitch or stem stitch down the center vein.

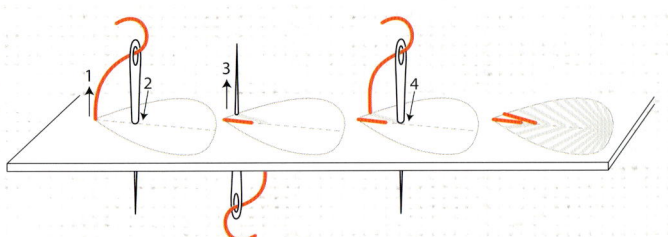

LONG AND SHORT STITCH (L+S)

Long and short stitch is a technique commonly used to fill an area, often while blending two colors. While filling leaves and petals with L+S, the stitches don't need to be perfectly aligned, and you can easily add extra filler stitches.

HOW TO

Beginning on the edge of the shape to be filled, bring the needle up through the back of the fabric at 1. Stitch across the shape, alternating between long and short stitches filling the area. Stitches should range in size from about ¼" to ½" (0.5 to 1.25 cm) depending on the size of the shape. Fill in the next row (above) the first row, stitching long and short straight stitches alternately to fill in the gaps of the first row. Continue this technique filling in the shape, adding extra stitches as needed to fill any remaining gaps.

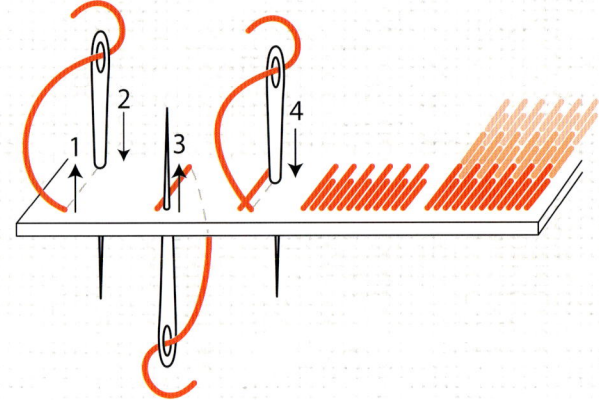

Tip: For the purposes of filling leaves and petals of flowers, L+S can also be used in place of Shaded Satin Stitch if desired and where indicated, as they are very similar.

SATIN STITCH (SAT)

The trick to keeping satin stitch looking neat is to outline it with a line stitch such as backstitch. By doing this, you can hide any imperfections or inconsistencies. Satin stitch is great for filling areas and adding a bit of dimension to shapes. Avoid making satin stitches over ½" to ¾" (1.25 to 2 cm) as this will create gaps in your stitches.

HOW TO

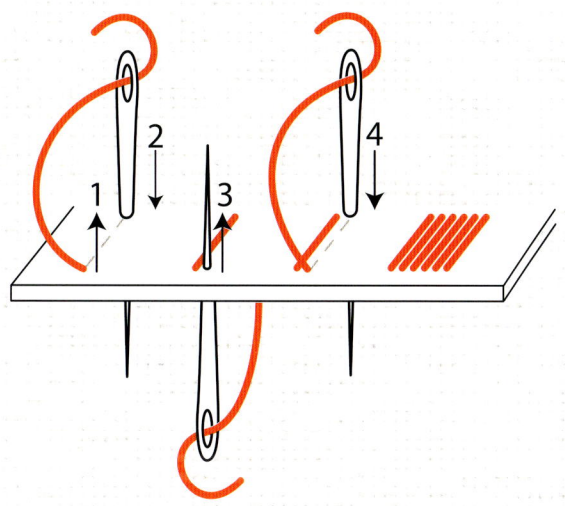

Define the shape to be filled. Bring the needle up through the fabric from the back side at 1. Make a stitch across the shape and insert the needle into fabric at 2. Cross back under the shape and bring the needle up at 3, next to 1. Keep crossing over and under until the shape is filled. The stitches should be laying side by side with consistent tension so they don't pucker. To add dimension to the shape, first stitch the outline of it with a backstitch or split stitch. Next, stitch around the outline stitch using the method above to fill the shape. To neaten up the outline of the satin stitches, stitch around the shape, close to the edge with backstitch or stem stitch.

SHADED SATIN STITCH (SHSAT)

Shaded satin stitches can be like long and short stitches, but with shaded satin stitch, the stitches line up next to each other to create a gradation of color versus L+S where each row fits into each other like bricks.

HOW TO

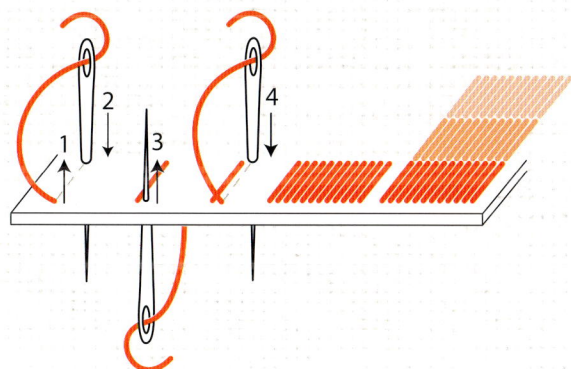

Define the shape to be filled. Bring the needle up through the fabric from the back side at 1. Begin stitching as satin stitch. When you are ready to blend the color, switch to a color that is close in value. Continue stitching to fill the shape, changing thread colors as you go. You can also alternate thread colors to create subtle shading, alternating stitches with colors. Try stitching with two or three different needles going at the same time. Be sure to keep them from getting tangled, especially on the backside.

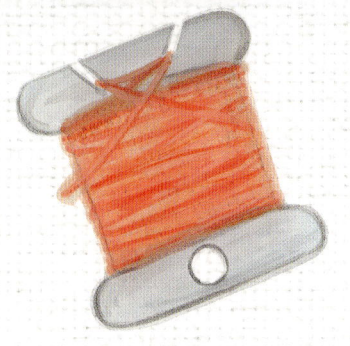
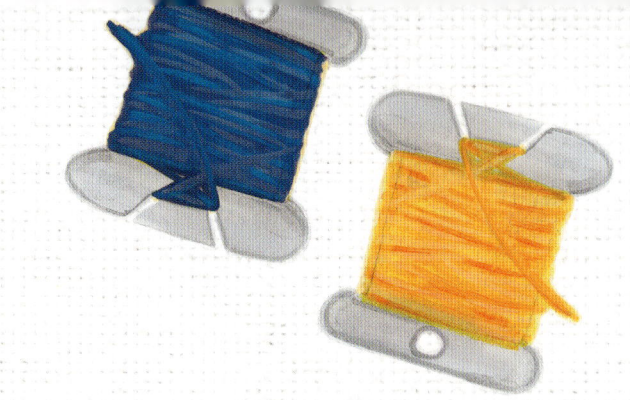

SPLIT BACKSTITCH (SPLBS)

This is a variation of split stitch and is easier to work than the main stitch. This method allows you to see where you split the stitch on top of the fabric instead of trying to find the center of the stitch to split from *under* the fabric. Try it and you won't go back to the ordinary split stitch!

HOW TO

Bring the needle up through the fabric from the back at the beginning of the line, at 1. Make one short ¼" (0.5 cm) stitch inserting needle at 2. Bring the needle up at 3, which is one stitch length ahead of the last insertion. Insert the needle at 4, splitting the stitch you made. Bring the needle up at 5 and continue stitching.

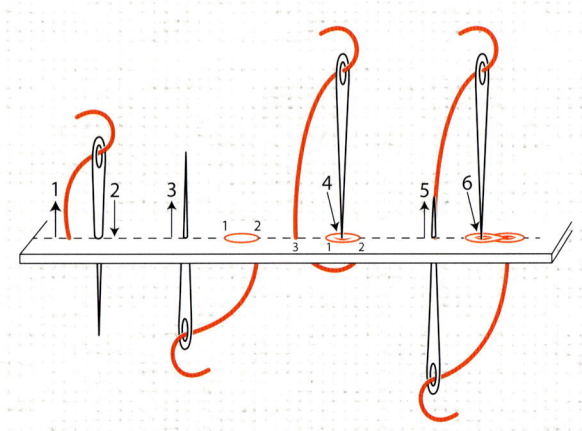

STAR STITCH (STR)

Star stitch is fun to use when making a decorative border, filling a large shape with pattern, and adding sparkly details. There are several variations on the star stitch, such as the Ermine and Smyrna stitches. An alternative to the star stitch is the Algerian Eye Stitch with a French knot in the center. Although these are technically different stitches, you can use these interchangeably in the floral embroideries.

HOW TO

Bring the needle up through the fabric from the back side at 1. Using straight stitches, make a cross going down at 2, up at 3, down at 4. Then work a diagonal cross, up at 5, down at 6, up at 7, down at 8. Make a small cross stitch in the center to hold the star stitches in place by going up at 9, down at 10.

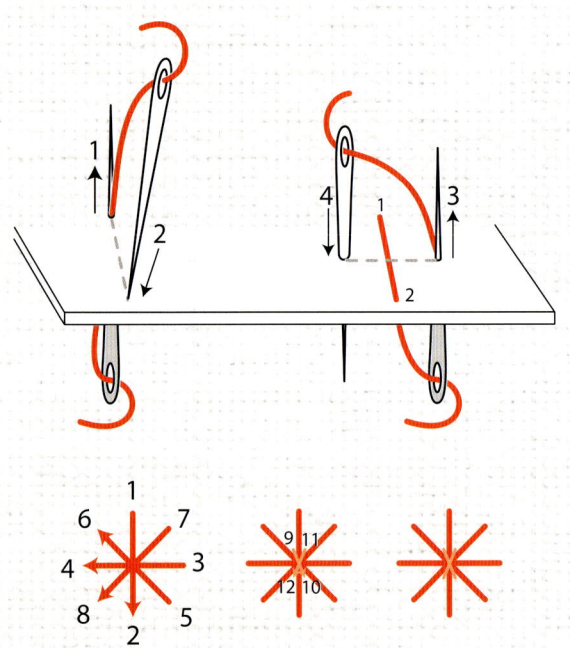

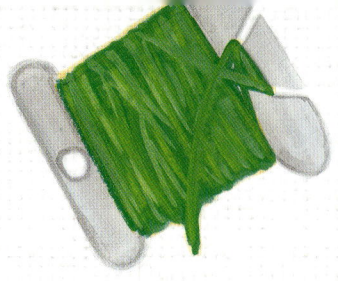

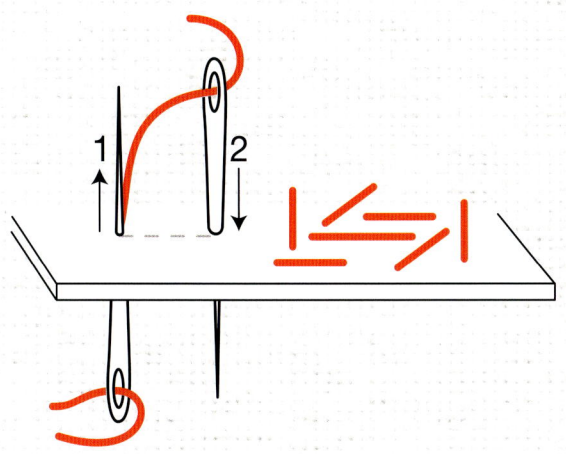

STRAIGHT STITCH (SS)

Arguably, this is the most versatile stitch on the planet. Straight stitches simply consist of up and down stitches. You can vary the length as needed. Straight stitches are ideal for building up texture and experimenting. A variation is seed stitches, which are small straight stitches used to fill an area.

HOW TO

Bring the needle up through the fabric from the back side at 1 and insert needle down at 2. Repeat, working in any direction and changing the length of the stitches as needed.

STEM STITCH (STM)

This is one of my favorite outline stitches. It is elegantly simple, has a bit of texture, and follows curves beautifully. To maneuver around tight curves, simply shorten the stitches. Experiment with stitch length and angles to create interesting lines and textures.

HOW TO

Working from left to right, follow the design line. Bring the needle up through the fabric from the back side at 1. Make a slightly diagonal stitch, inserting the needle at 2 to get started. Bring the needle back up halfway between the stitch points and slightly above the previous stitch at 3. Make another diagonal stitch, inserting needle at 4. Bring the needle back up just above the previous stitch point at 5. Continue making uniform stitches following the line.

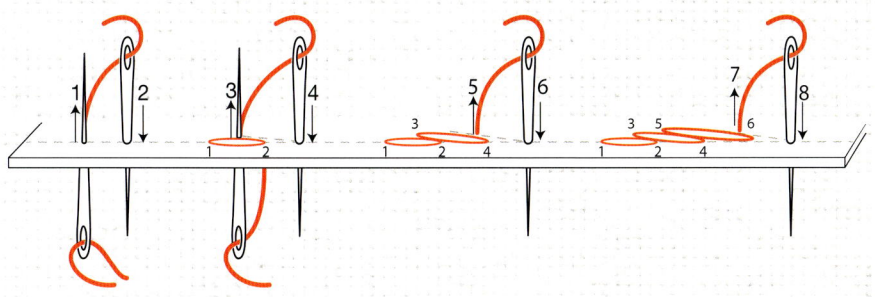

JANUARY

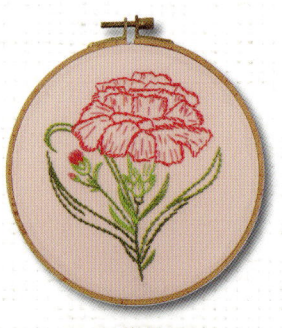

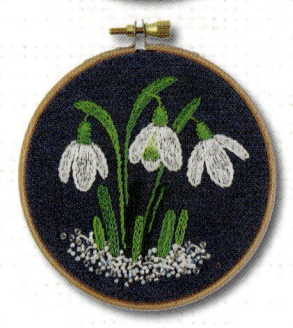

FEBRUARY

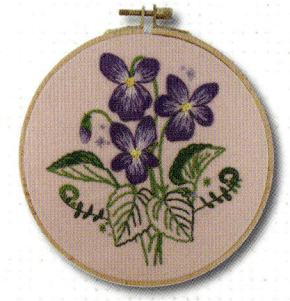

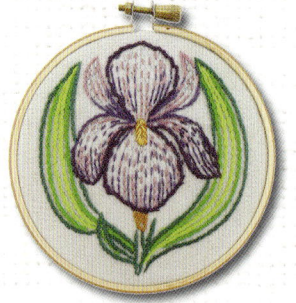

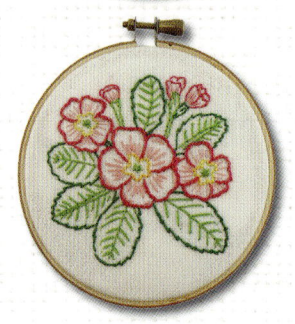

MARCH

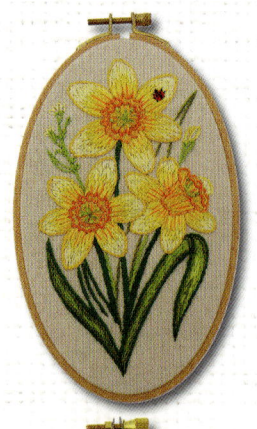

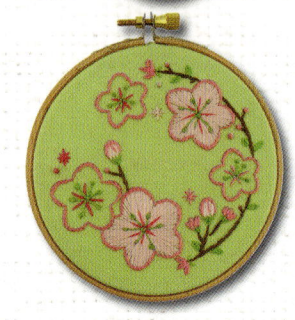

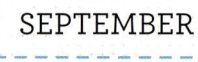

JULY

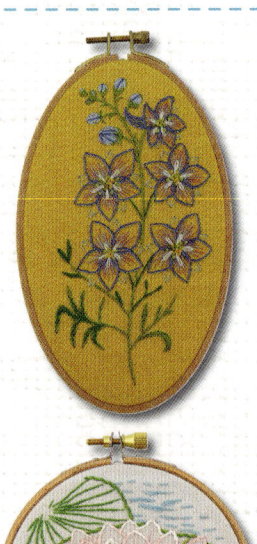

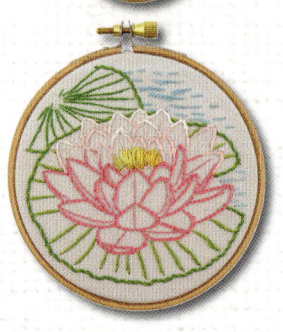

AUGUST

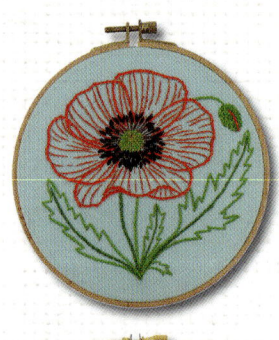

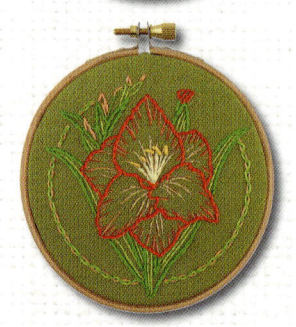

SEPTEMBER

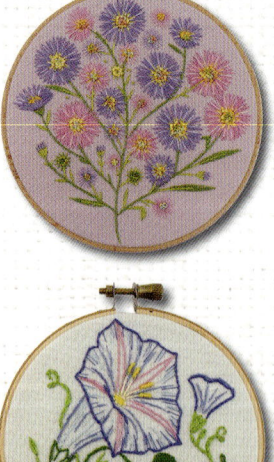

APRIL	MAY	JUNE

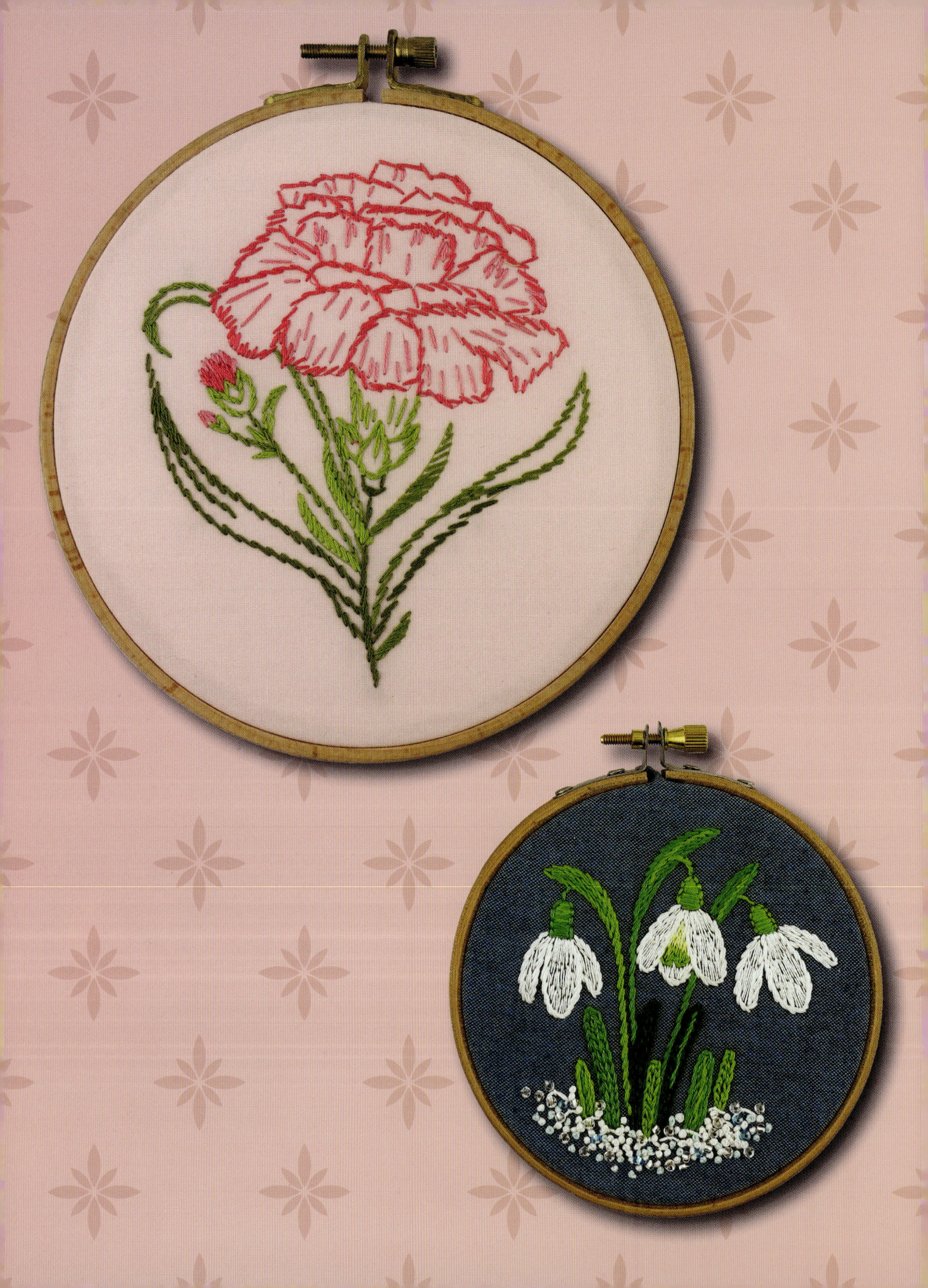

JANUARY

Carnation & Snowdrop

January brings with it a sense of renewal after the hectic holiday season at the end of the previous year. Its birth flowers, snowdrops and carnations, welcome new beginnings.

Cultivation of carnations goes back more than two thousand years, and they mean different things in different cultures, from Greek and Roman times to the Elizabethan era and beyond. In Greek culture, carnations are known as the "flower of the gods." They grew wild on the hillsides and were often used in art, garlands, and décor. Over the centuries, they've come to symbolize love, devotion, and fascination.

Snowdrops, a lesser-known January birth flower, are one of the earliest flowers to bloom in gardens experiencing winter conditions. They sometimes even grow when snow is still on the ground! They are adaptable and naturally hardy, requiring little attention to thrive. This led to their symbolism of hope, renewal, and resilience. The ancient Greeks recognized their medicinal properties and sweet fragrance, while Victorians warned against bringing them into homes, and considered snowdrops a bad omen or sometimes even a sign of death.

When stitching these early bloomers, keep in mind their meaning and significance. Your embroidery could be the perfect gift for a friend in need of a mid-winter pick me up!

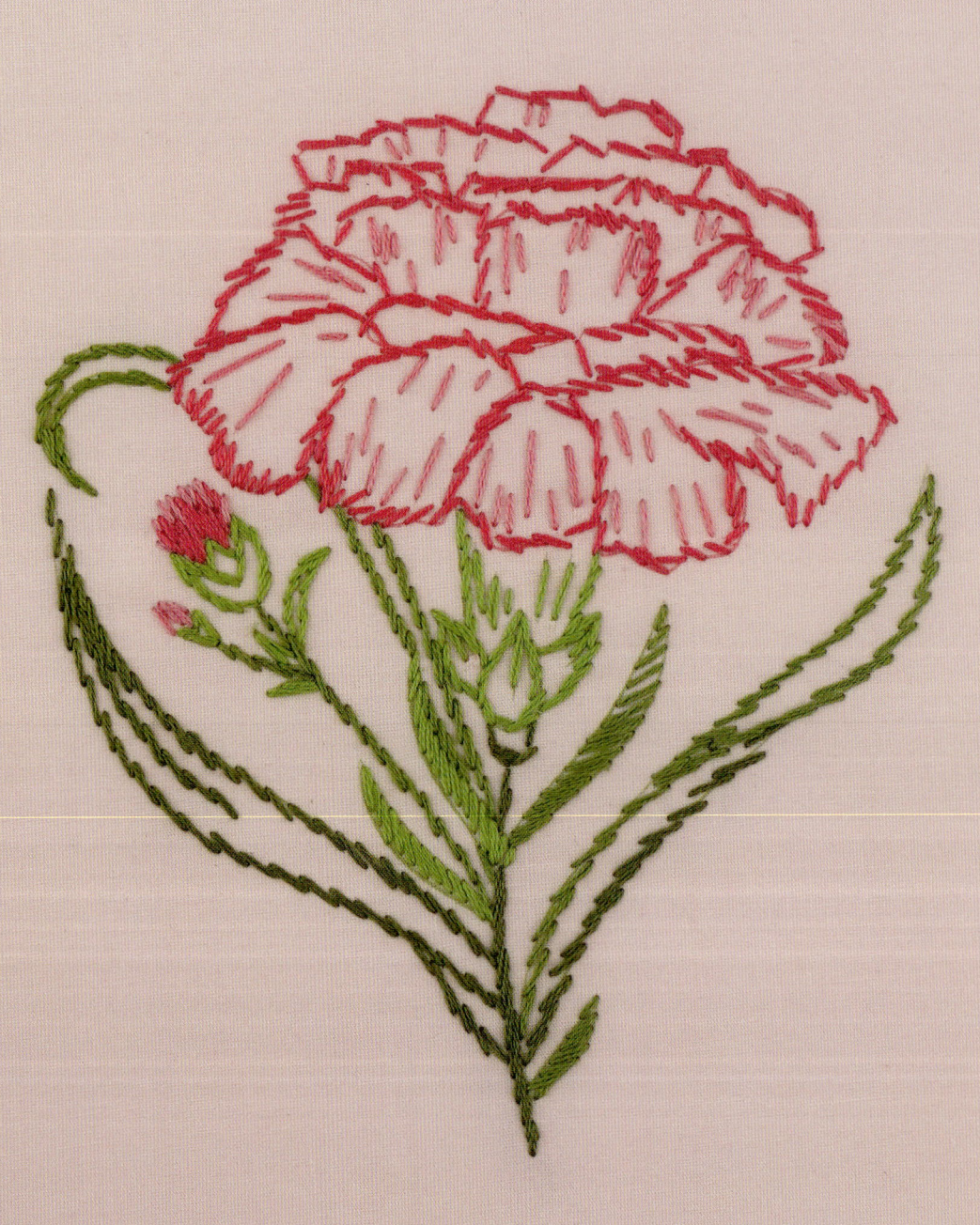

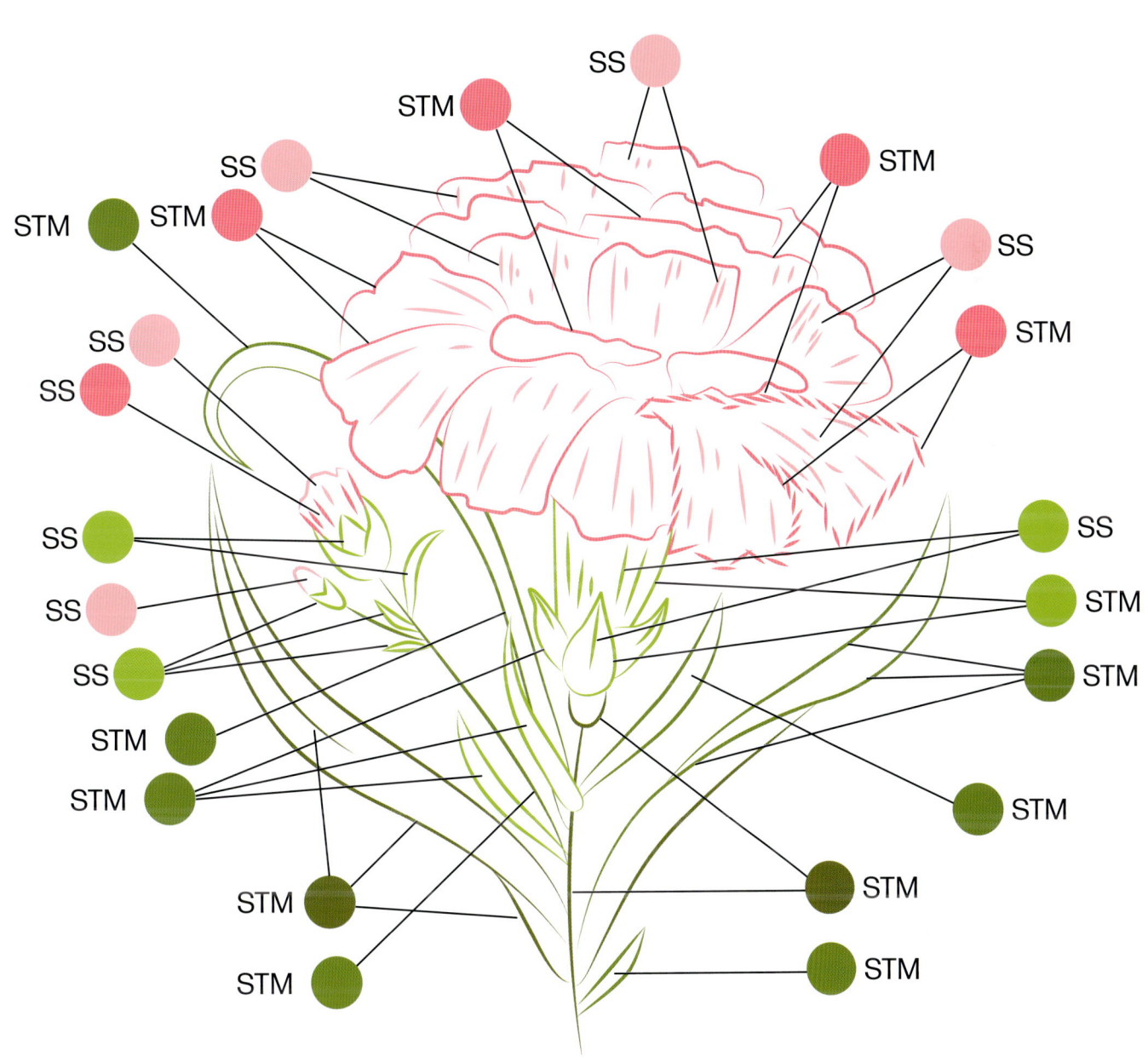

NOTE
Use three strands of floss throughout.

Thread Guide
DMC Thread Colors

704   470   937   3806   602

Stitches Used
Stitch Guide, pages 13-21

- Stem Stitch (STM)
- Straight Stitch (SS)

SS

STM

SS

STM   STM

STM   SS

STM

SS   SS

STM

SS

SS

SS

SS   STM

SS

SS   STM

STM

STM

STM   STM

STM

STM

STM

STM

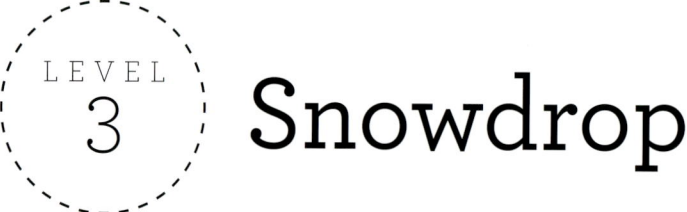

Snowdrop

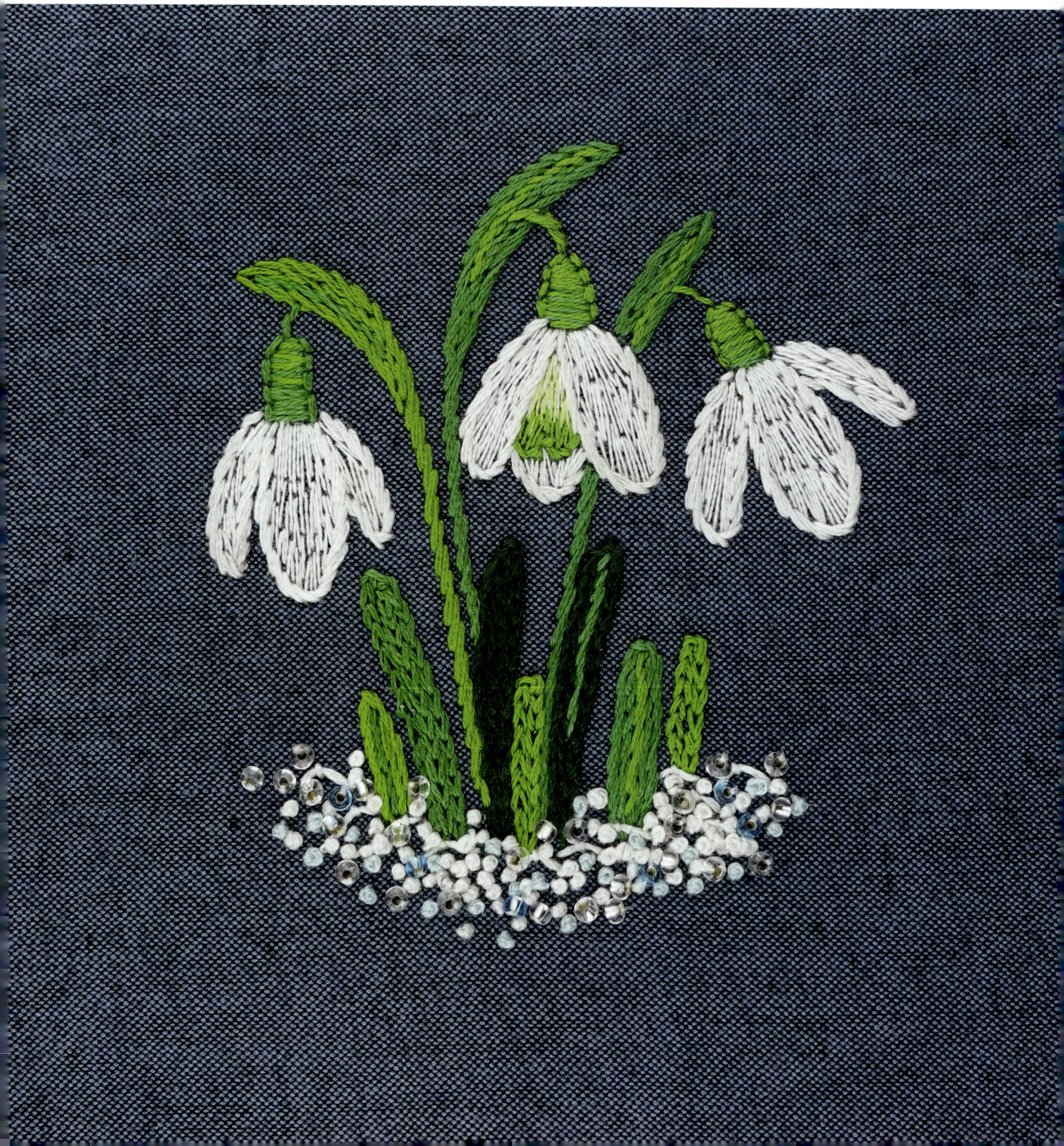

Thread Guide
DMC Thread Colors

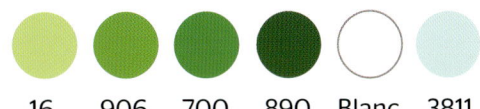

16   906   700   890   Blanc   3811

Stitches Used
Stitch Guide, pages 13–21

- Backstitch (BS)
- Chain Stitch (CS)
- Fly Stitch (FLY)
- French Knot (FK)
- Long and Short Stitch (L+S)
- Satin Stitch (SAT)
- Shaded Satin Stitch (SHSAT)
- Stem Stitch (STM)

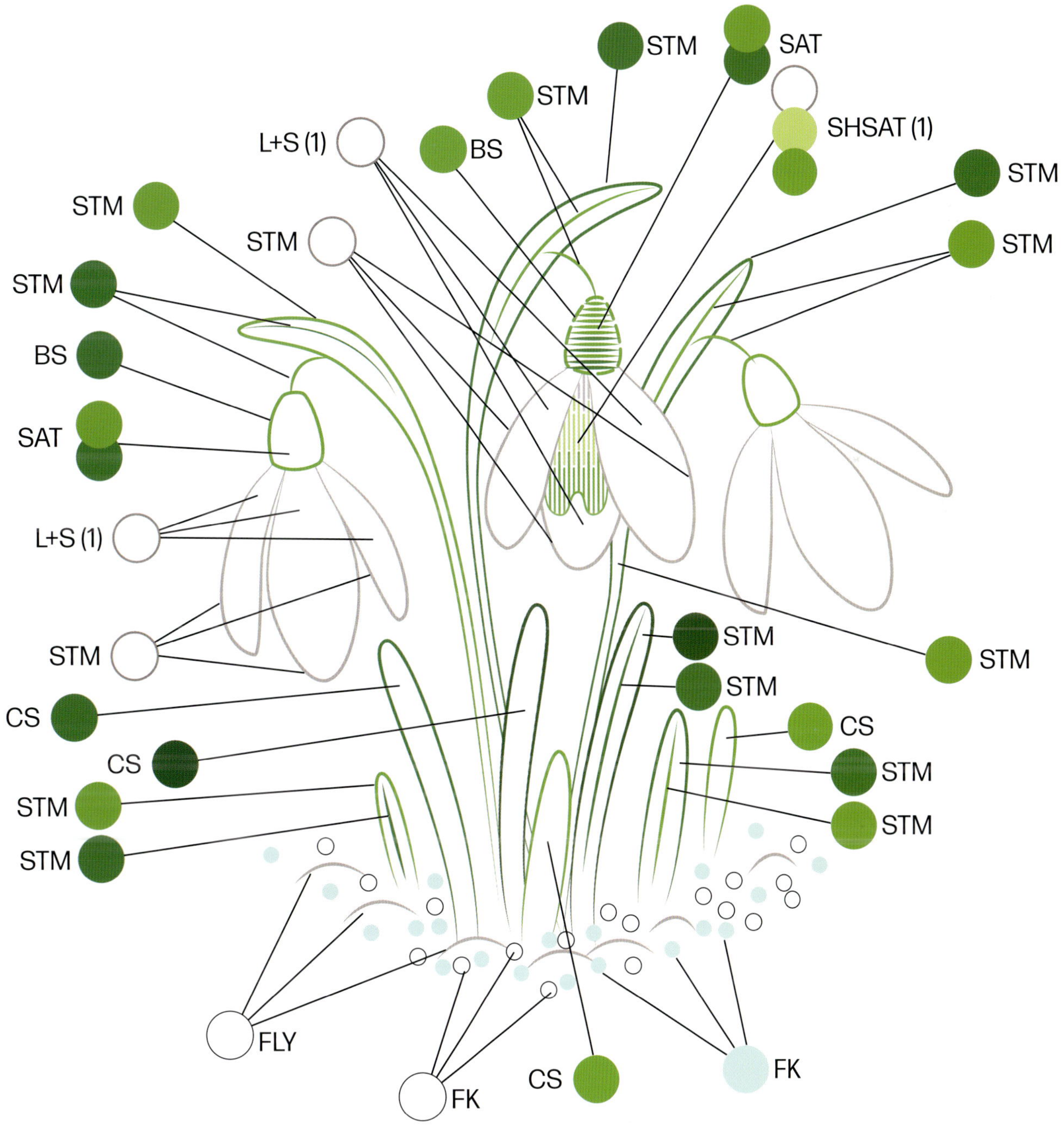

STM
SAT
STM
SHSAT (1)
BS
L+S (1)
STM
STM
STM
STM
STM
BS
SAT
L+S (1)
STM
STM
STM
CS
STM
CS
CS
STM
STM
STM
STM
FLY
FK
CS
FK

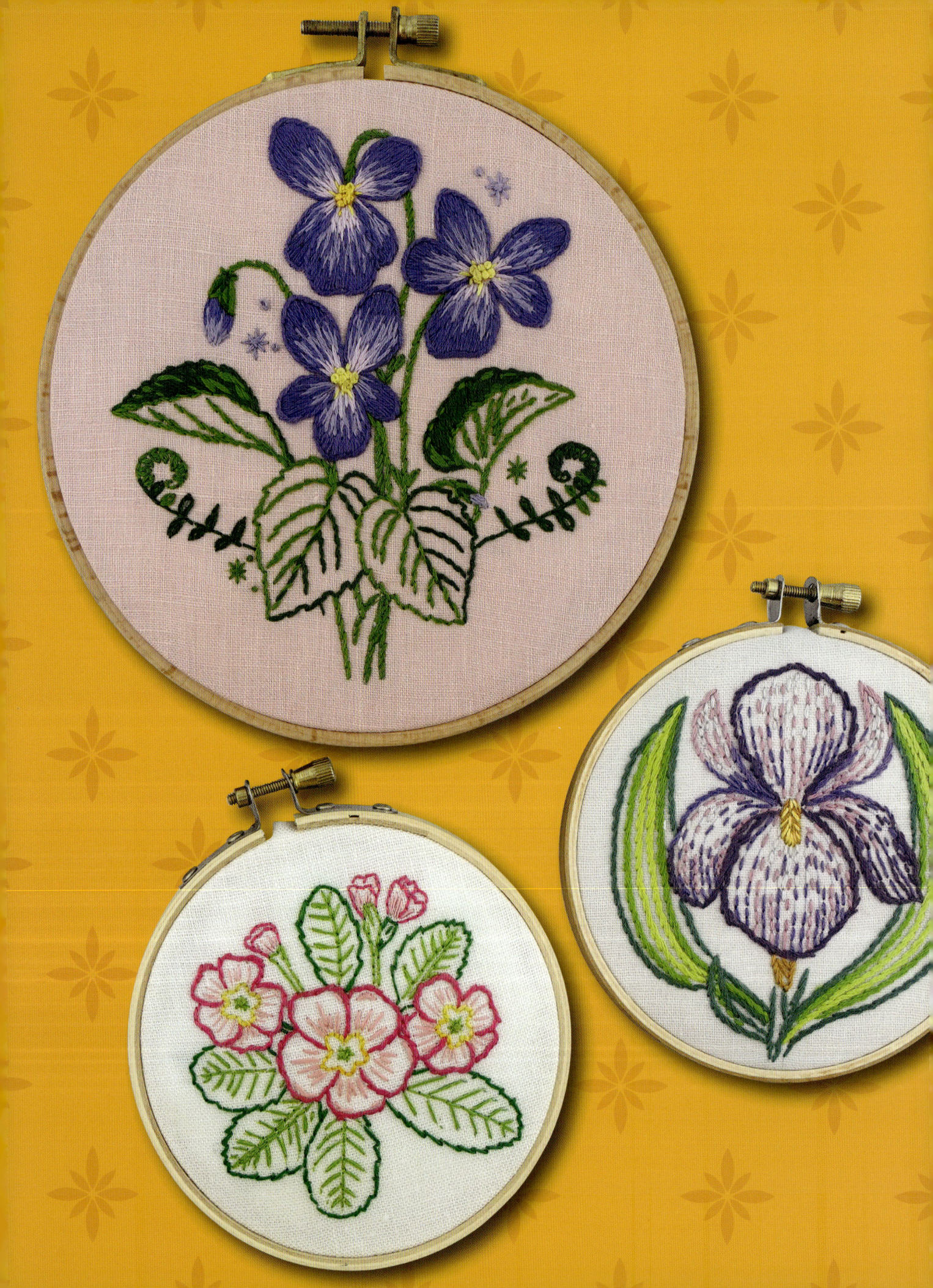

FEBRUARY

Iris, Primrose, and Violet

Irises are a meaningful choice when stitching a symbolic keepsake. They represent faith, wisdom, and admiration. Blue irises, in particular, denote courage, and purple irises are emblematic of friendship.

If you're interested in something brighter, the primrose is the perfect February birth month flower for you! These come in a variety of different colors, from pale yellow and pink, to bright blue and red. There are many myths surrounding primrose flowers. Most notably, they were believed to be Shakespeare's favorite flowers, adding literary charm to their significance. These amazing blooms symbolize youth, renewal, beauty, and optimism.

Violets are dainty flowers recognized for their bold purple tones and unique heart-shaped petals. Violets symbolize faithfulness, hope, spiritual wisdom, and loyalty. As their name implies, violets have bright purple flowers. They're also surprisingly a popular ingredient in love potions and herbal remedies! Whatever they mean to you, these purple beauties add a regal touch to February's floral representation.

No matter which flowers you choose for your February project, the recipient of your handstitched petals is sure to enjoy this special gift.

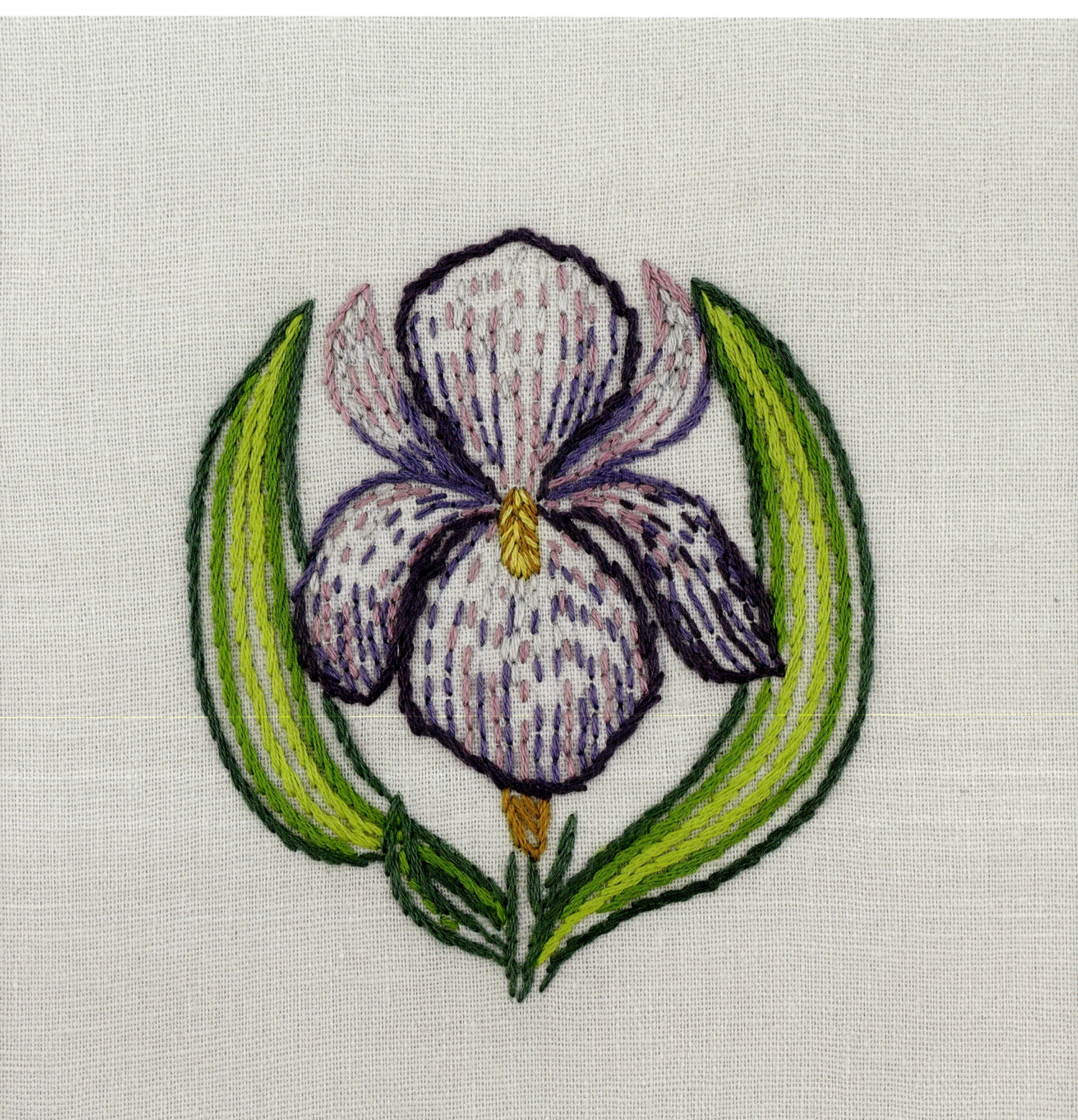

Thread Guide
DMC Thread Colors

Color	Number
29	32	316	415	561	906
907	782	4075			

Stitches Used
Stitch Guide, pages 13–21

- Backstitch (BS)
- Stem Stitch (STM)
- Straight Stitch (SS)

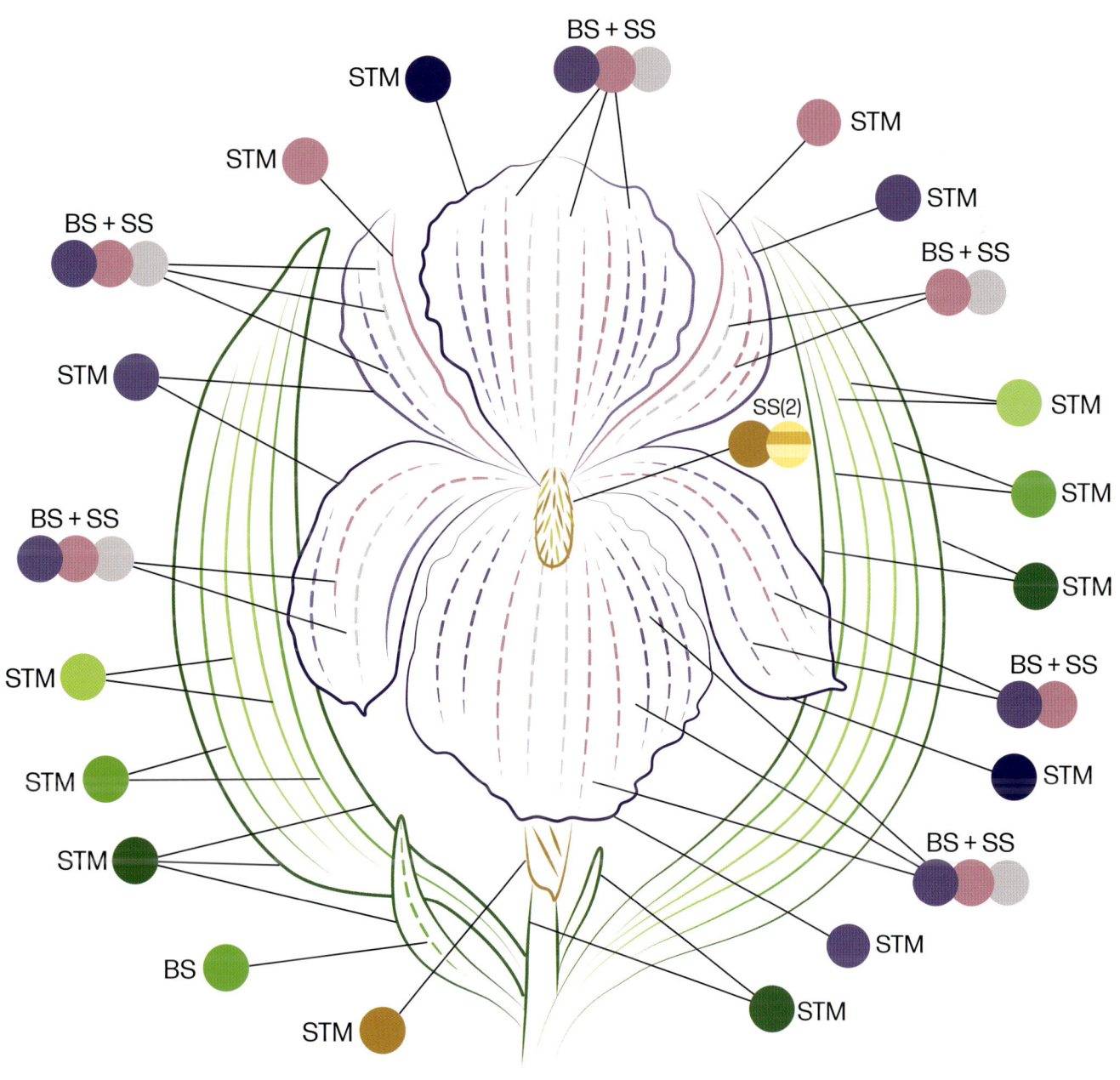

LEVEL 2 Primrose

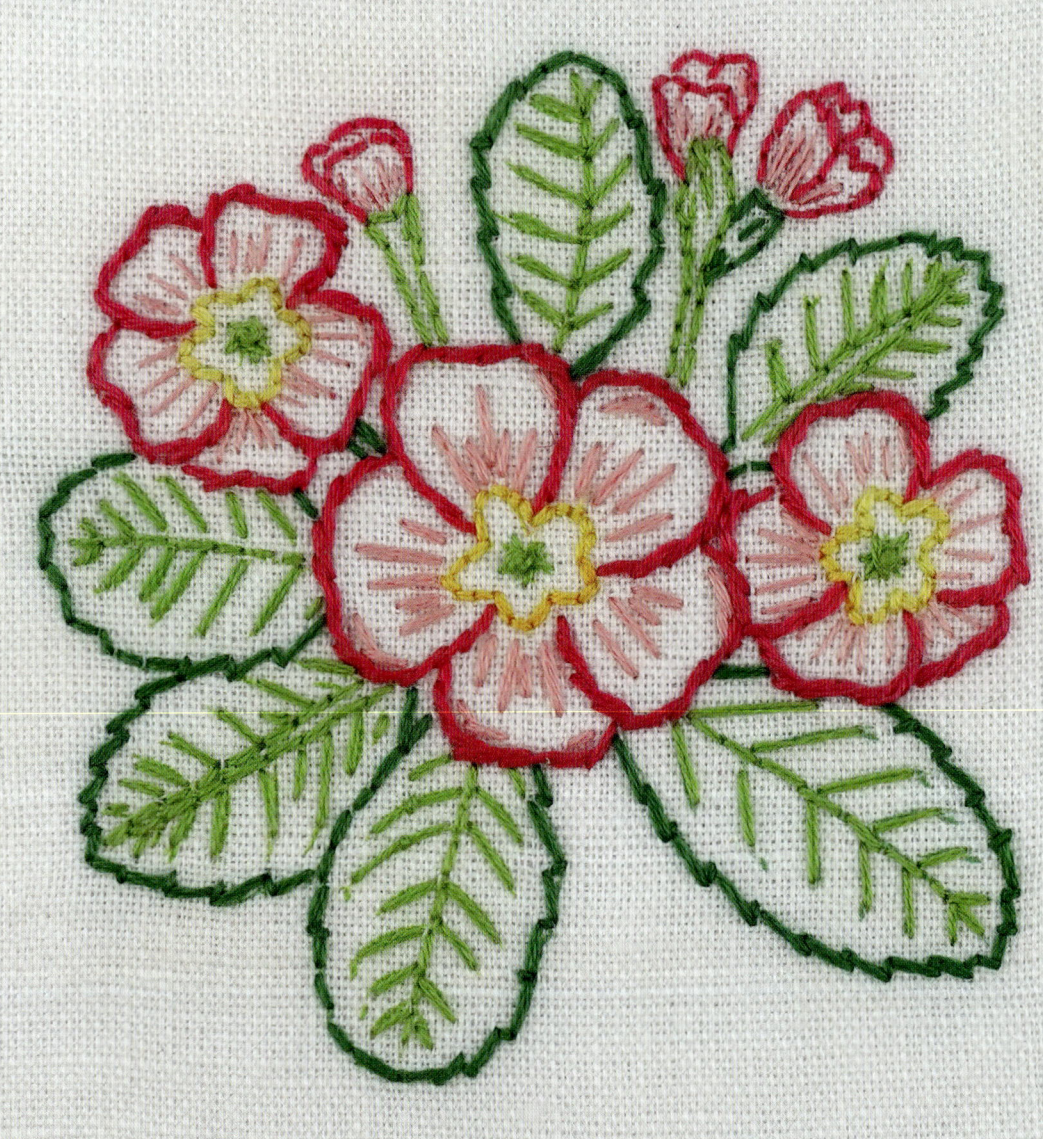

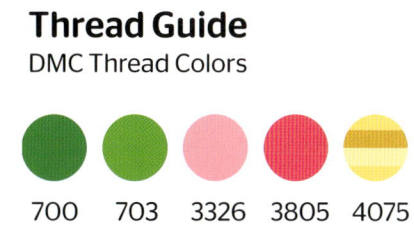

Thread Guide
DMC Thread Colors

700 703 3326 3805 4075

Stitches Used
Stitch Guide, pages 13-21

- Backstitch (BS)
- French Knot (FK)
- Star Stitch (STR)
- Stem Stitch (STM)
- Straight Stitch (SS)

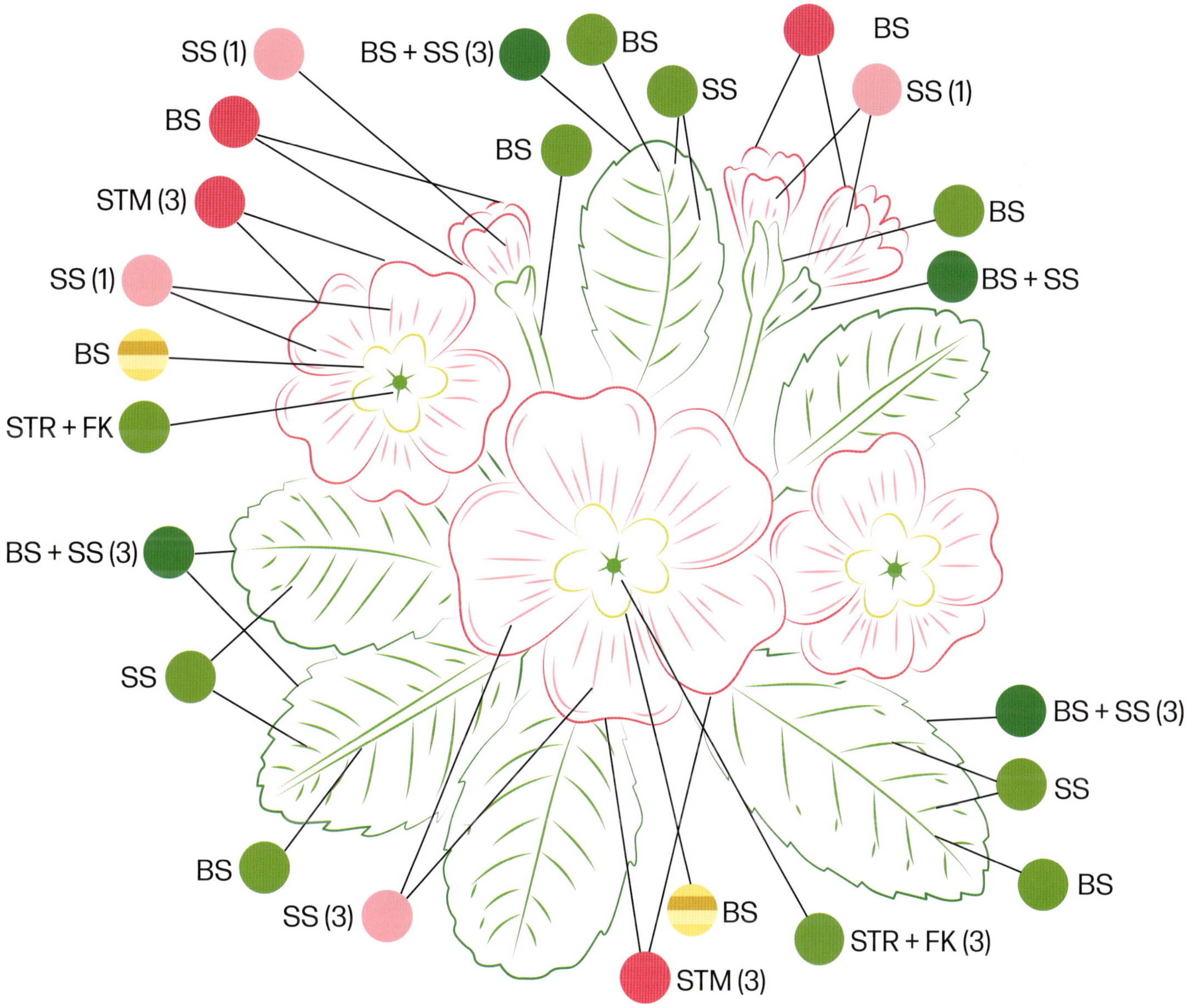

SS (1)

BS + SS (3)

BS

BS

SS

BS

BS

SS (1)

BS

STM (3)

BS

SS (1)

BS + SS

BS

STR + FK

BS + SS (3)

SS

BS + SS (3)

SS

BS

BS

SS (3)

BS

STR + FK (3)

STM (3)

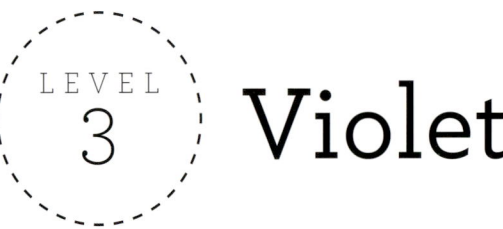

Violet

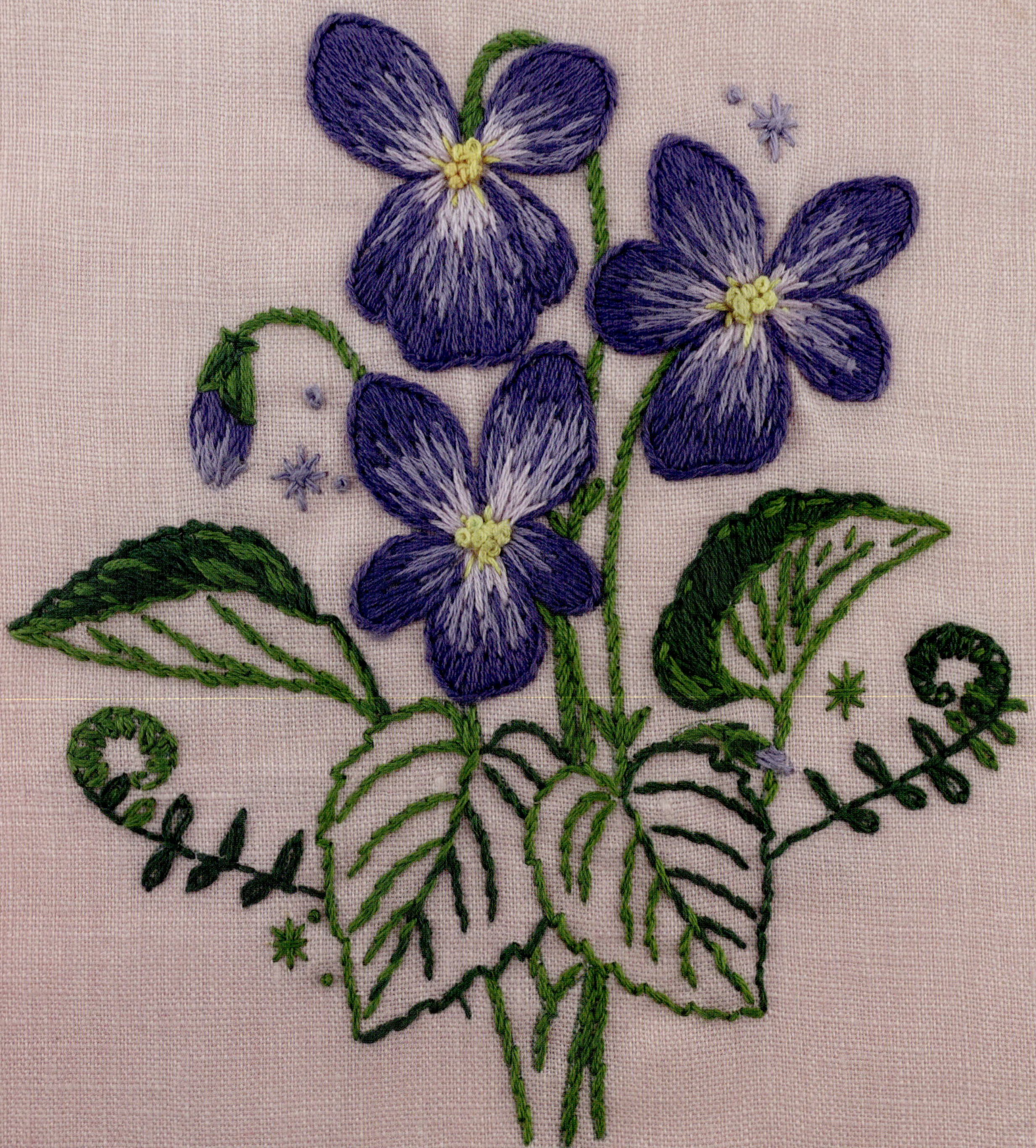

NOTE
Use three strands of floss throughout.

Thread Guide
DMC Thread Colors

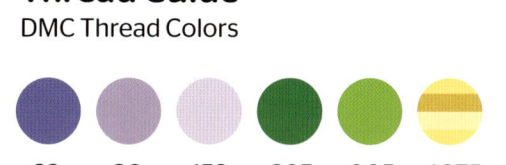

32 30 153 895 905 4075

Stitches Used
Stitch Guide, pages 13-21

- Backstitch (BS)
- Detached Chain Stitch (DCS)
- French Knot (FK)
- Long and Short Stitch (L+S)
- Satin Stitch (SAT)
- Star Stitch (STR)
- Stem Stitch (STM)
- Straight Stitch (SS)
- Whipped Backstitch (WBS)

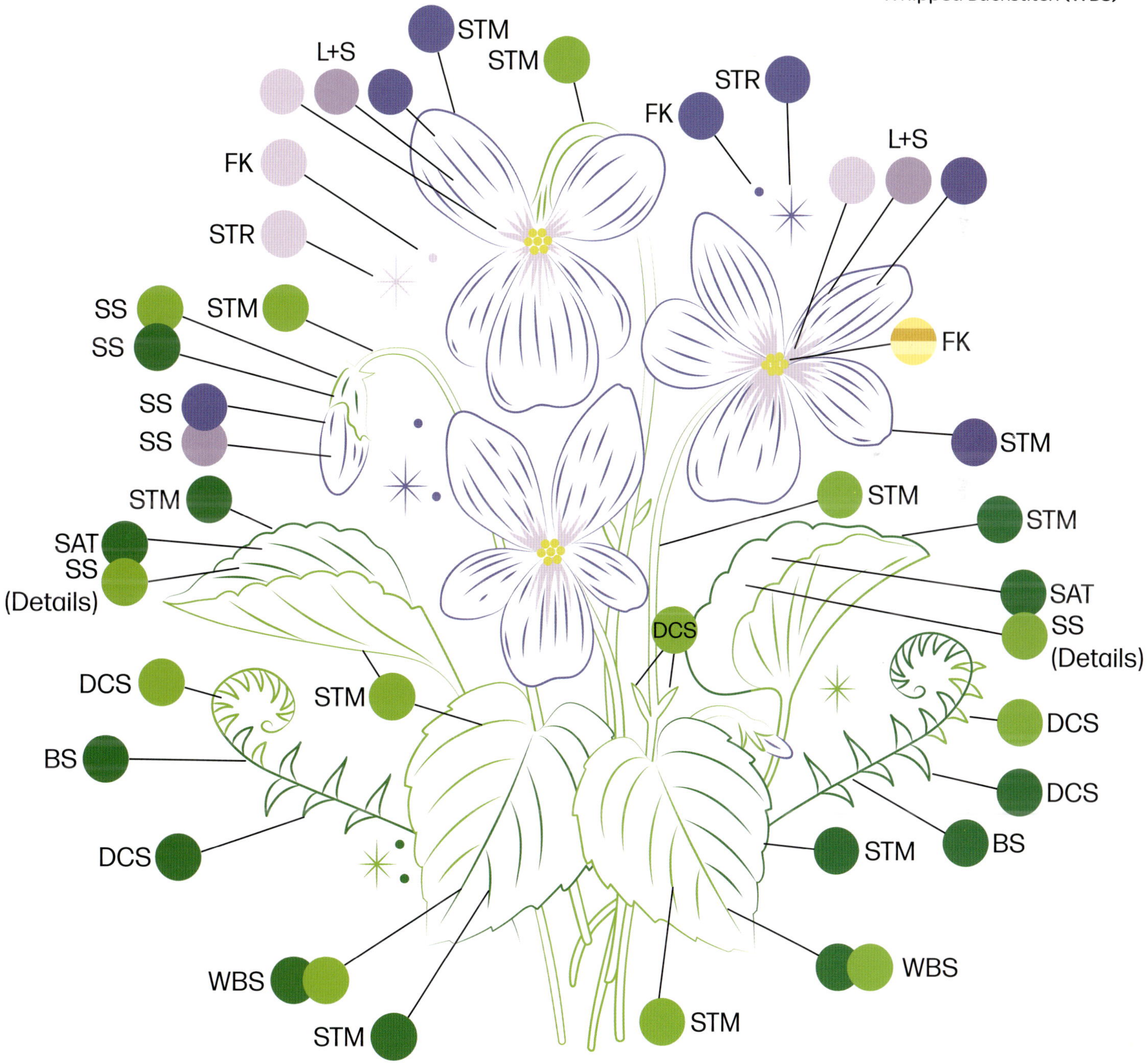

STM

STM

L+S

FK

STR

FK

STR

L+S

FK

SS

SS

STM

STM

SS

SS

STM

SAT
SS
(Details)

STM

SAT
SS
(Details)

DCS

DCS

DCS

BS

STM

BS

DCS

STM

WBS

WBS

STM

STM

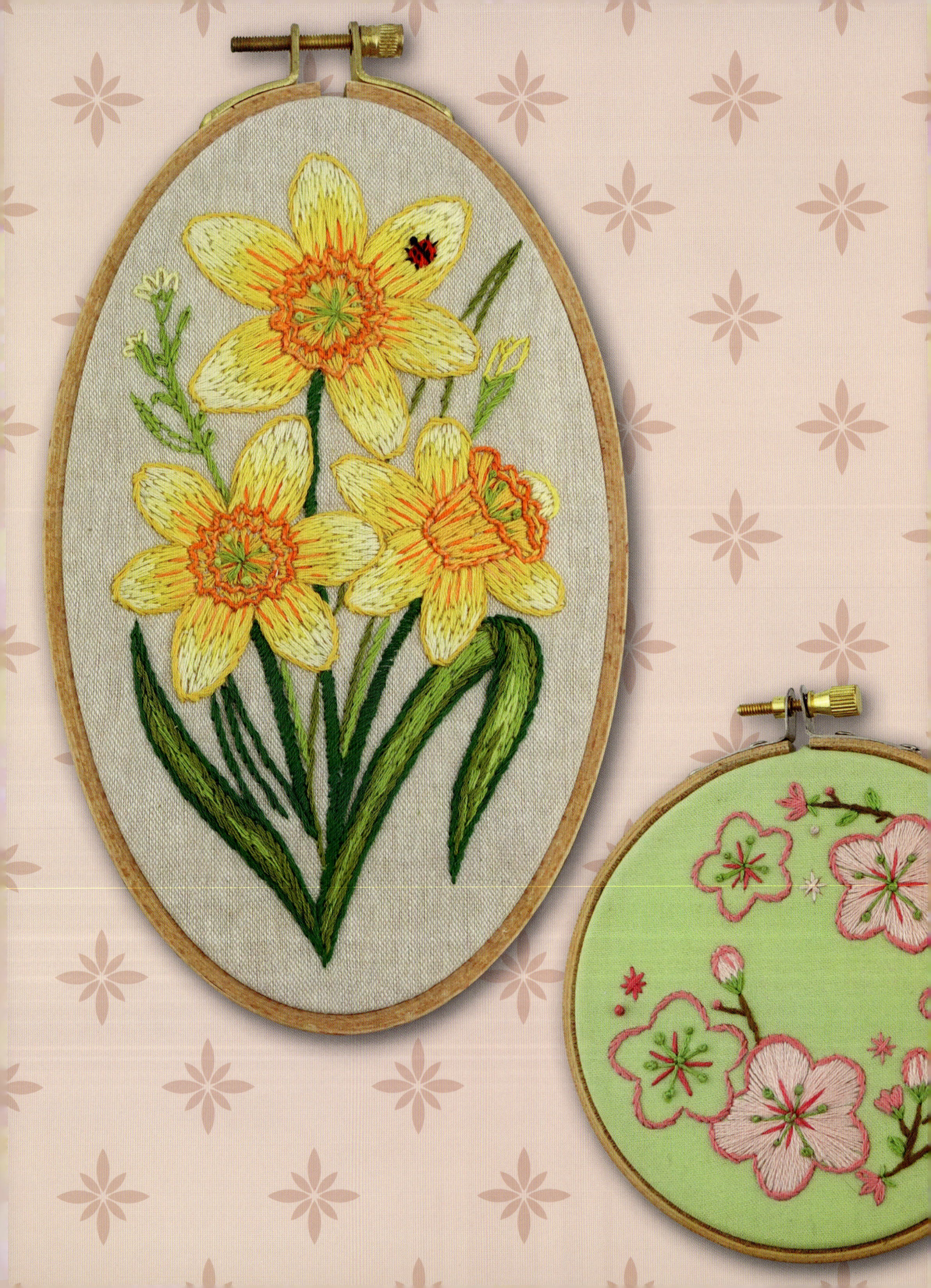

MARCH

Daffodil and Cherry Blossom

Daffodils and cherry blossoms take center stage this month, bringing their cheerful hues and fresh fragrance as the first signs of spring.

Daffodils are perhaps the most recognizable of March flowers, with their trumpetlike blooms and vibrant colors. These flowers are a favorite among embroiderers because of their striking shape and symbolism. Daffodils stand for new beginnings, joy, and hope, making them a meaningful choice for those looking to capture the promise of spring in their needlework. Their sunny yellow petals bring a sense of brightness and optimism, perfect for any project meant to uplift the spirit.

The secondary birth flower for March is the delicate pink and white cherry blossom. In Japanese culture, cherry blossoms, also known as sakura, are celebrated for their fleeting beauty, representing the impermanence of life and the delicate nature of existence. Their soft shapes and subtle hues can add a sophisticated and serene element to your embroidery, perfect for gifts meant to evoke calm and mindfulness.

Whether stitching daffodils or cherry blossoms, your March-themed embroidery will reflect the month's unique blend of energy and grace. So, gather your materials and start a piece that captures the beauty and promise of this month.

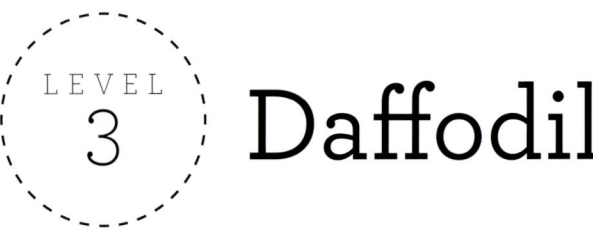

Daffodil

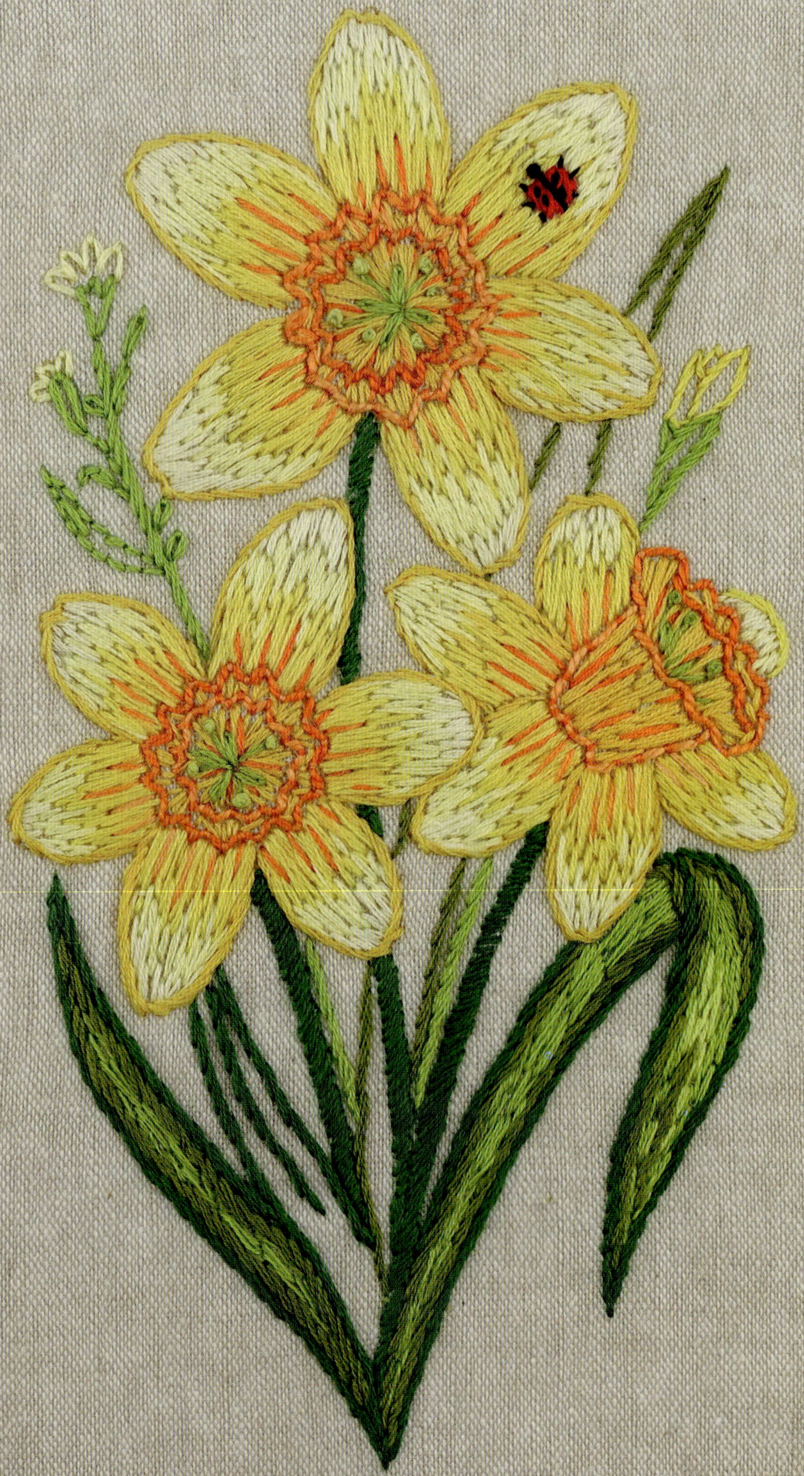

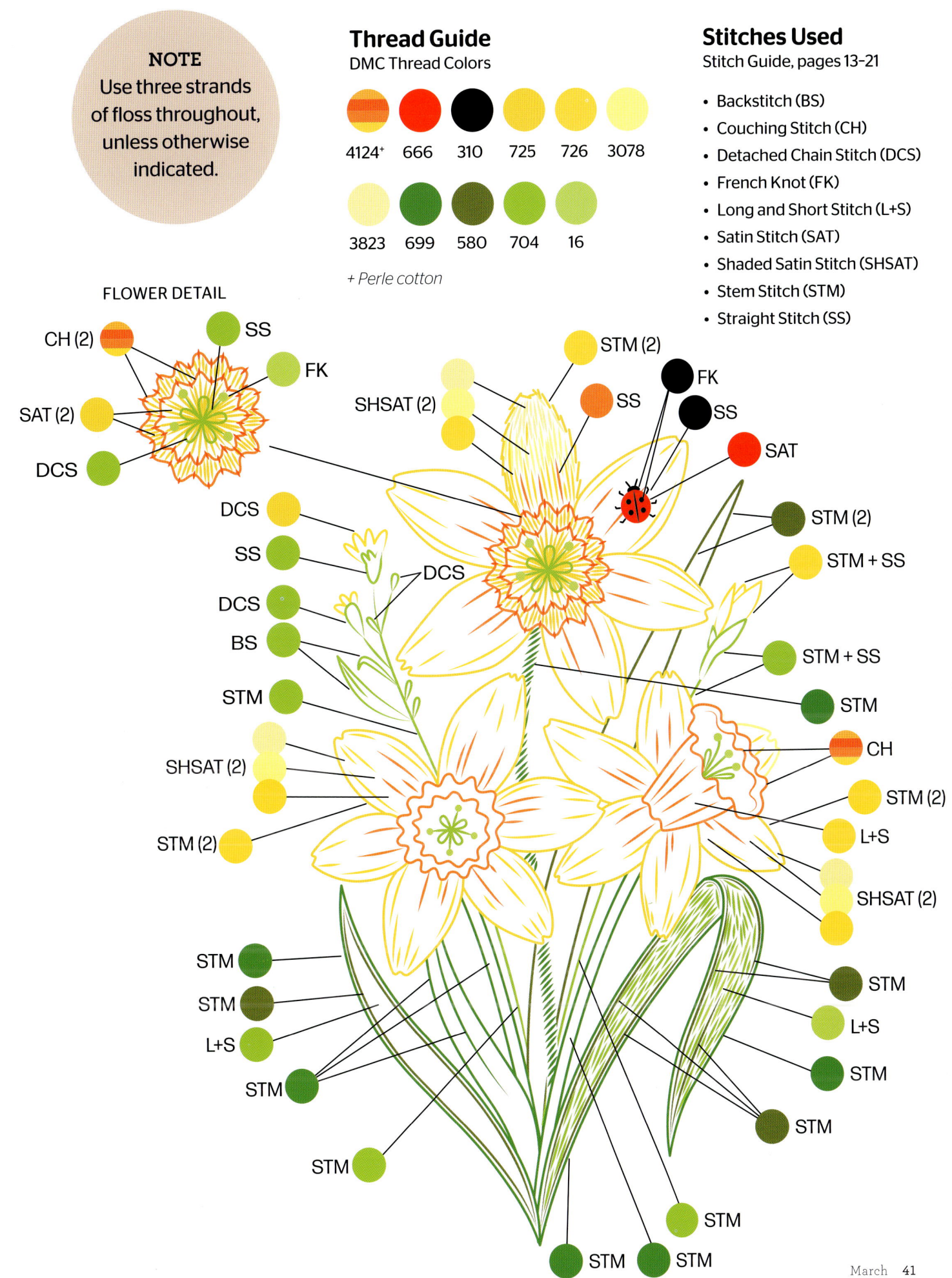

NOTE
Use three strands of floss throughout, unless otherwise indicated.

Thread Guide
DMC Thread Colors

4124+   666   310   725   726   3078
3823   699   580   704   16

+ Perle cotton

Stitches Used
Stitch Guide, pages 13–21

- Backstitch (BS)
- Couching Stitch (CH)
- Detached Chain Stitch (DCS)
- French Knot (FK)
- Long and Short Stitch (L+S)
- Satin Stitch (SAT)
- Shaded Satin Stitch (SHSAT)
- Stem Stitch (STM)
- Straight Stitch (SS)

FLOWER DETAIL

CH (2)   SS
          FK
SAT (2)
DCS

DCS
SS
DCS
BS
STM
SHSAT (2)
STM (2)

STM (2)   SHSAT (2)   SS   FK   SS   SAT
                                         STM (2)
                                         STM + SS
                                         STM + SS
DCS   STM
                                         CH
                                         STM (2)
                                         L+S
                                         SHSAT (2)

STM
STM
L+S
STM   STM
                         L+S
STM   STM
                         STM
STM   STM

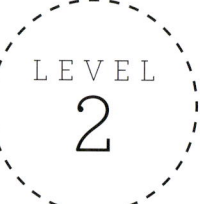

Cherry Blossom

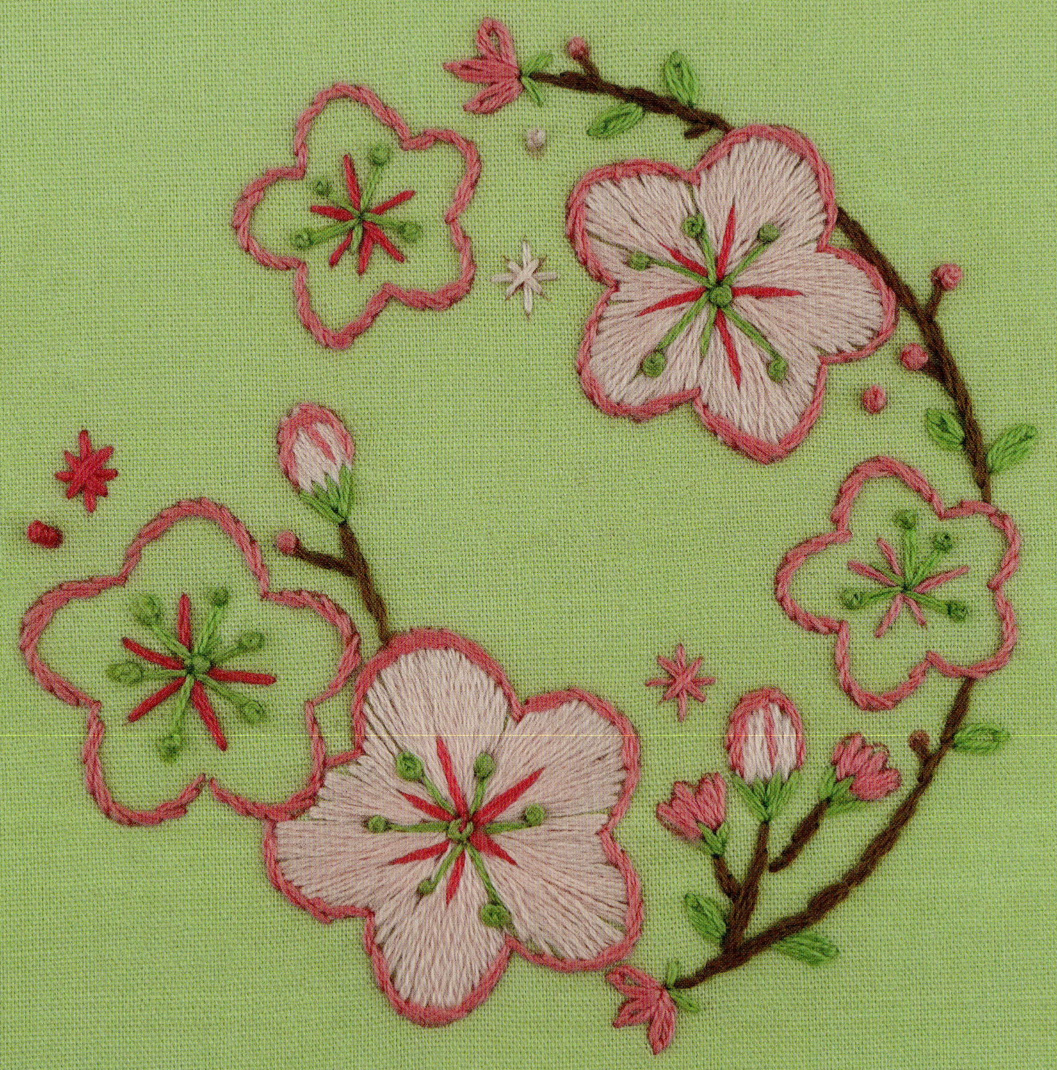

NOTE
Use three strands of floss throughout, unless otherwise indicated.

Thread Guide
DMC Thread Colors

703 869 963 603 602

Stitches Used
Stitch Guide, pages 13–21

- Detached Chain Stitch (DCS)
- French Knot (FK)
- Satin Stitch (SAT)
- Star Stitch (STR)
- Stem Stitch (STM)
- Straight Stitch (SS)

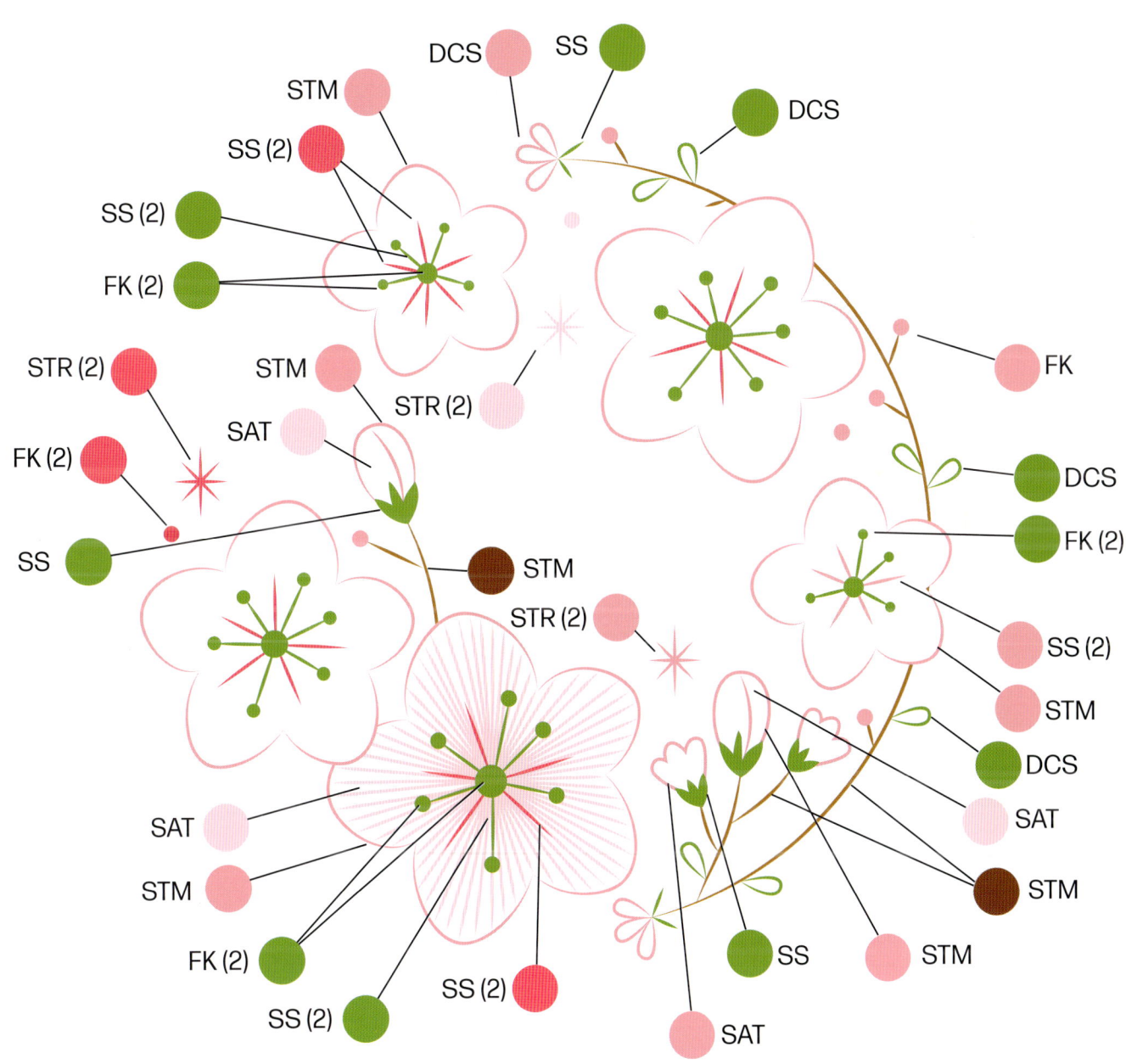

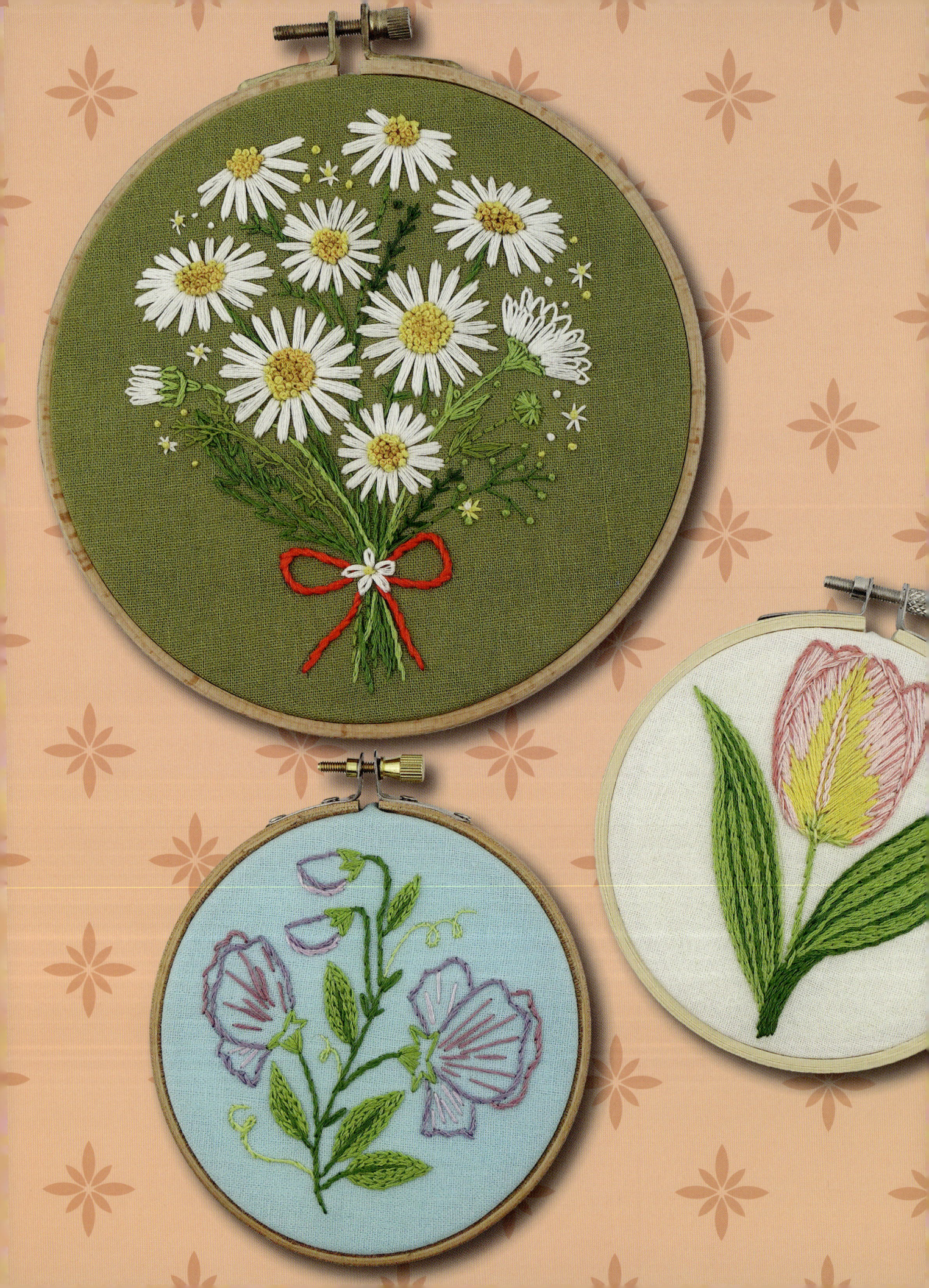

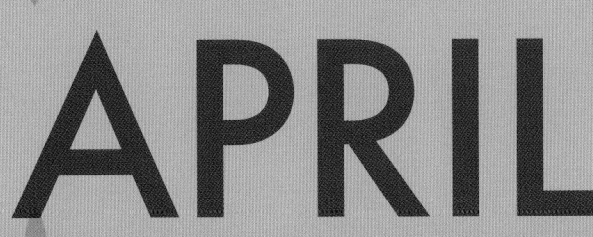

APRIL

Sweet Pea, Tulip, and Daisy

Three quintessential spring flowers, the daisy, tulip, and sweet pea, mark April birthdays. Each flower embodies the best of springtime with their simplicity and nostalgic charm.

Beautiful and edible sweet peas are often used in salads, teas, and flavored syrups. They come in a range of colors from pink and red, to purple, blue, and white, and symbolize gratitude and blissful pleasure. In Victorian England, they were given as a sign of departure or saying goodbye but also represented lasting friendship. Today they can be a sweet gift to a friend on their birthday.

Tulips were first discovered in Kazakhstan in the sixteenth century. The wealthy Turkish families who cultivated them treated the flowers like prized jewels. Their name is derived from the Persian word *tulipant*, which means "turban" and describes the distinct shape of the flowers. Today, their beauty has spread around the world. They can be found in gardens and farms across the globe.

Daisies are native to Europe and Asia and been around for more than 4,000 years! In Roman mythology, the daisy emerged to brighten and cheer up the earth after a long and dark winter. Now, as a symbol of friendship, daisies are often used to create charming accessories like bracelets, necklaces, and flower crowns by weaving the flowers and stems into daisy chains.

Whether you stitch these flowers individually or create a triumphant floral bouquet with all three, April birthdays are brighter with these lovely birth flowers.

Sweet Pea

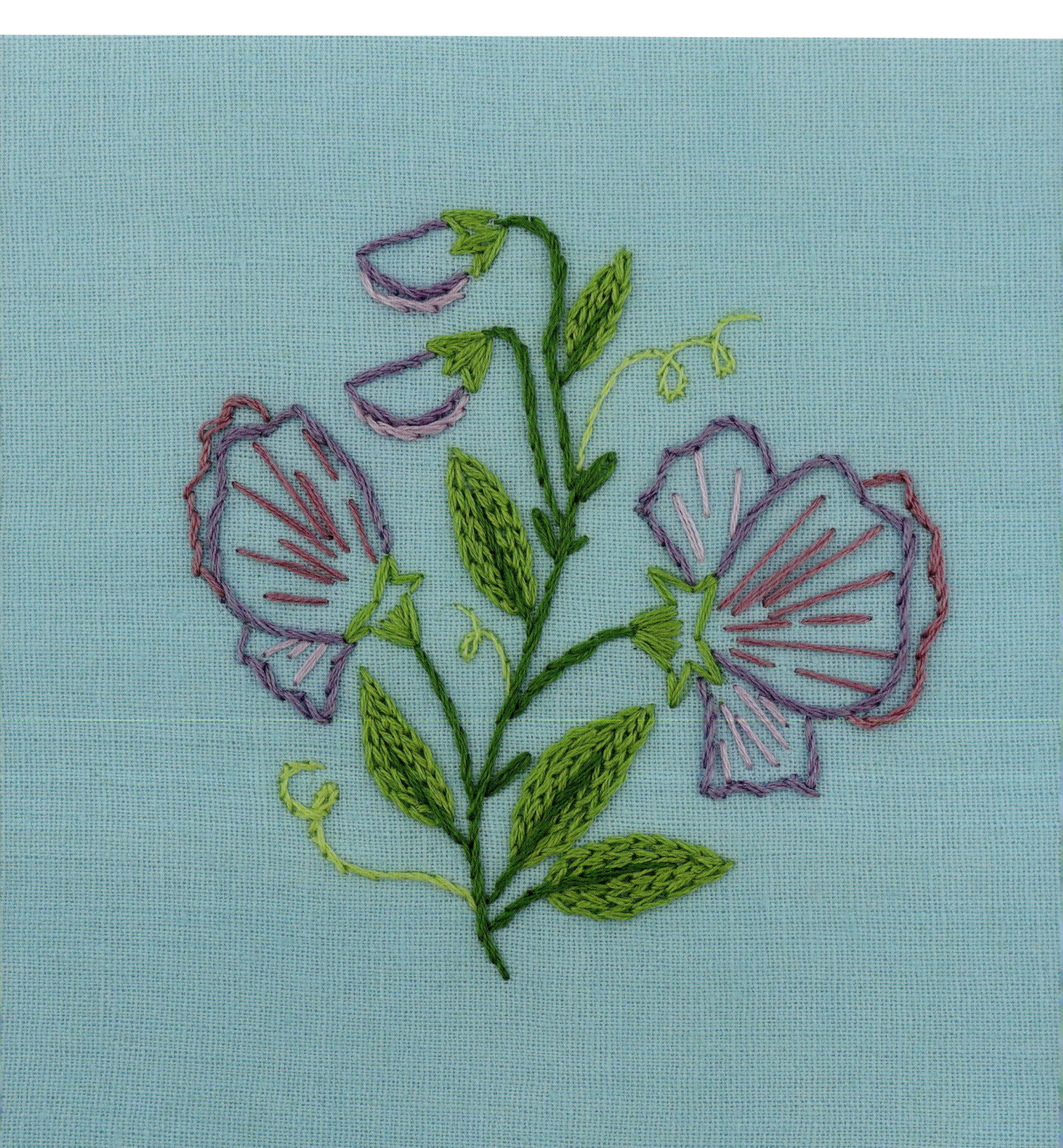

Thread Guide
DMC Thread Colors

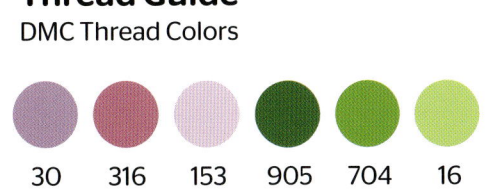

30   316   153   905   704   16

Stitches Used
Stitch Guide, pages 13–21

- Chain Stitch (CS)
- Detached Chain Stitch (DCS)
- Stem Stitch (STM)
- Straight Stitch (SS)

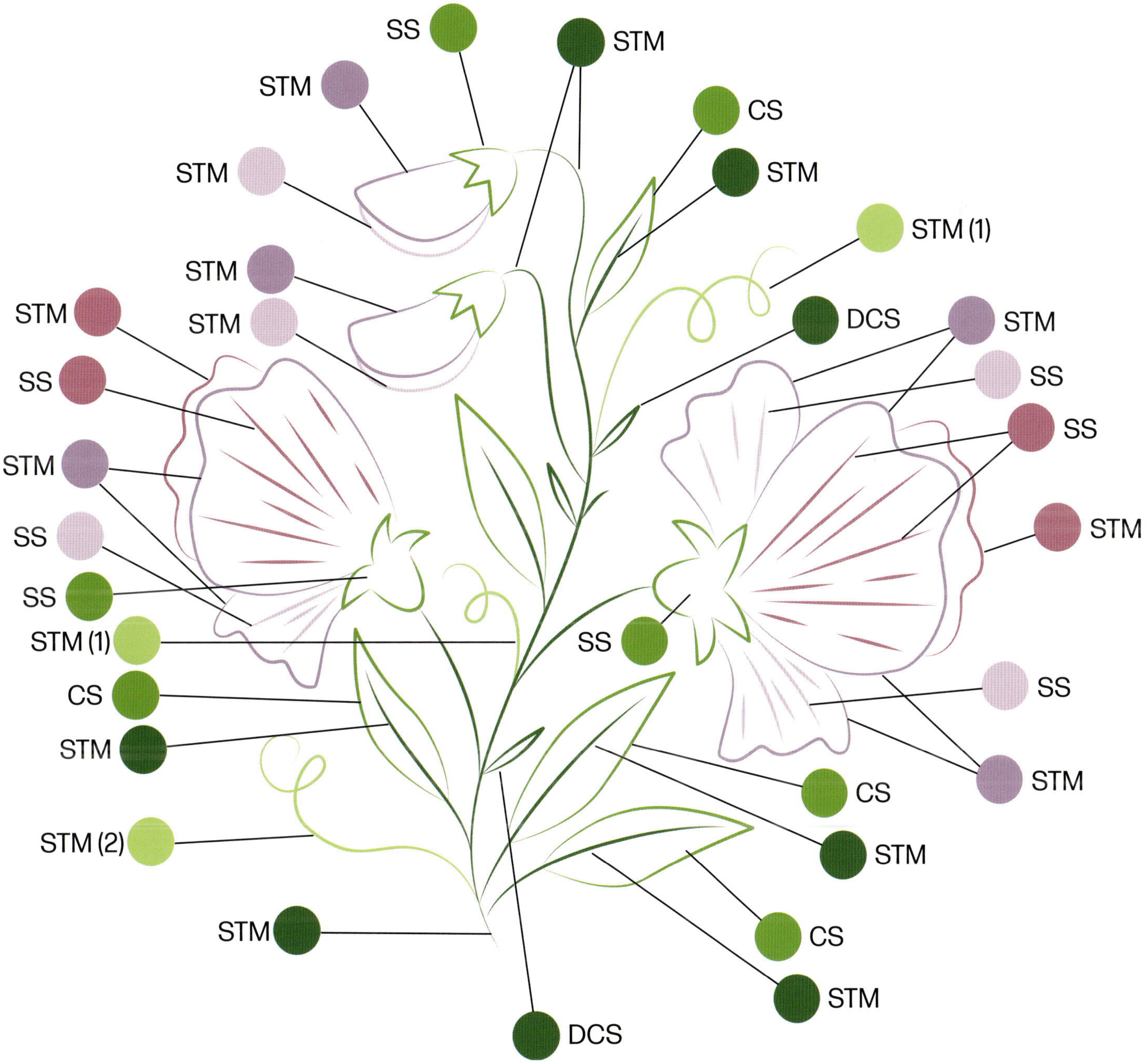

SS

STM

STM

CS

STM

STM

STM

STM (1)

STM

STM

STM

DCS

STM

STM

SS

SS

SS

SS

STM

STM

SS

SS

SS

SS

STM (1)

CS

STM

STM (2)

STM

SS

CS

STM

STM

CS

STM

DCS

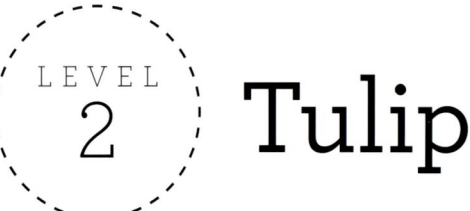

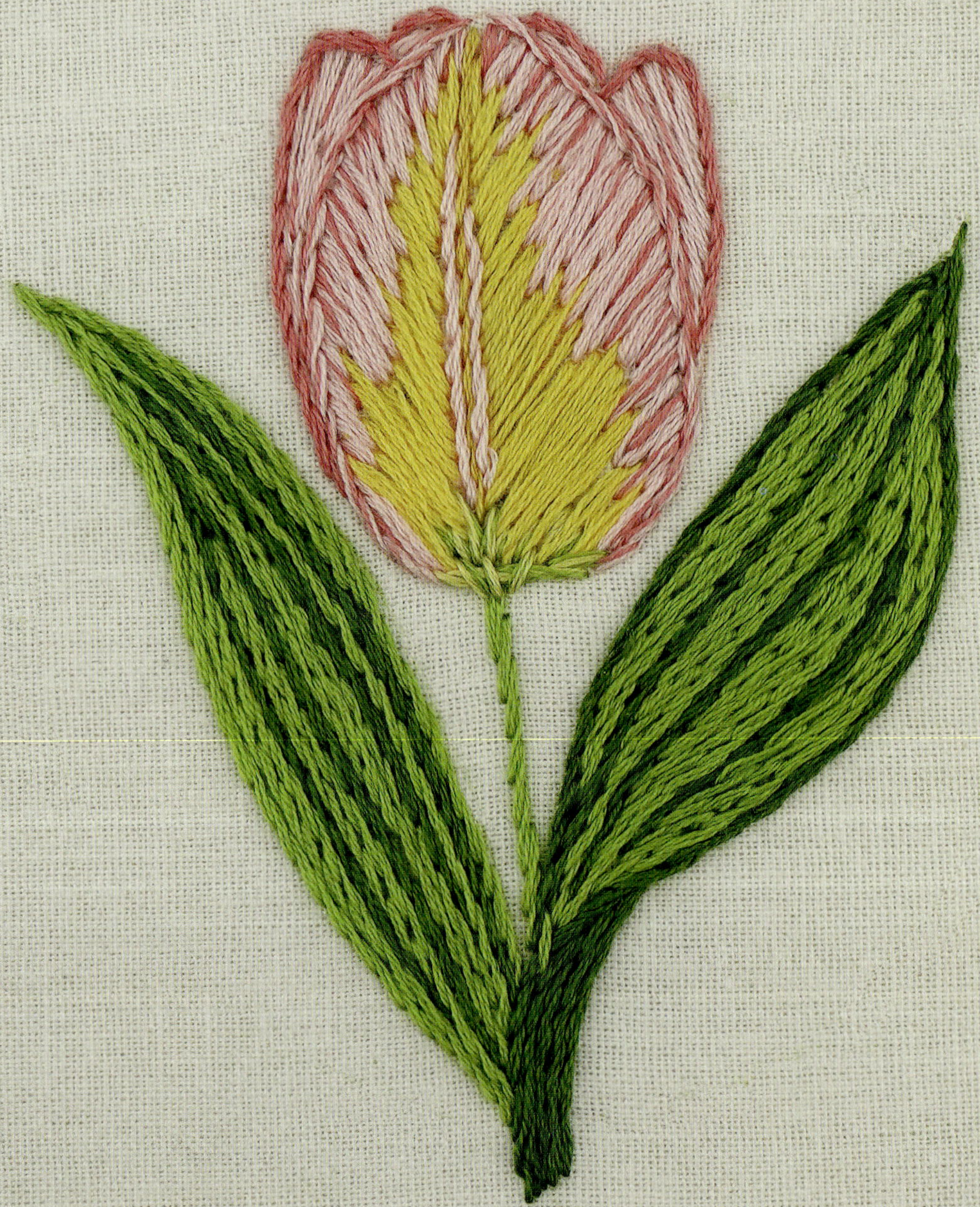

NOTES

Use three strands of floss throughout, unless otherwise indicated. To achieve the color effect, you'll be using a method of thread blending, which uses strands of two colors at once. Use the stitch diagram as a guide to the number of strands and colors to combine.

Thread Guide
DMC Thread Colors

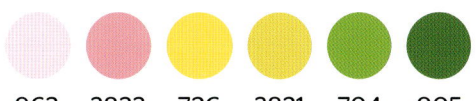

963   3833   726   3821   704   905

Stitches Used
Stitch Guide, pages 13–21

- Long and Short Stitch (L+S)
- Stem Stitch (STM)
- Straight Stitch (SS)

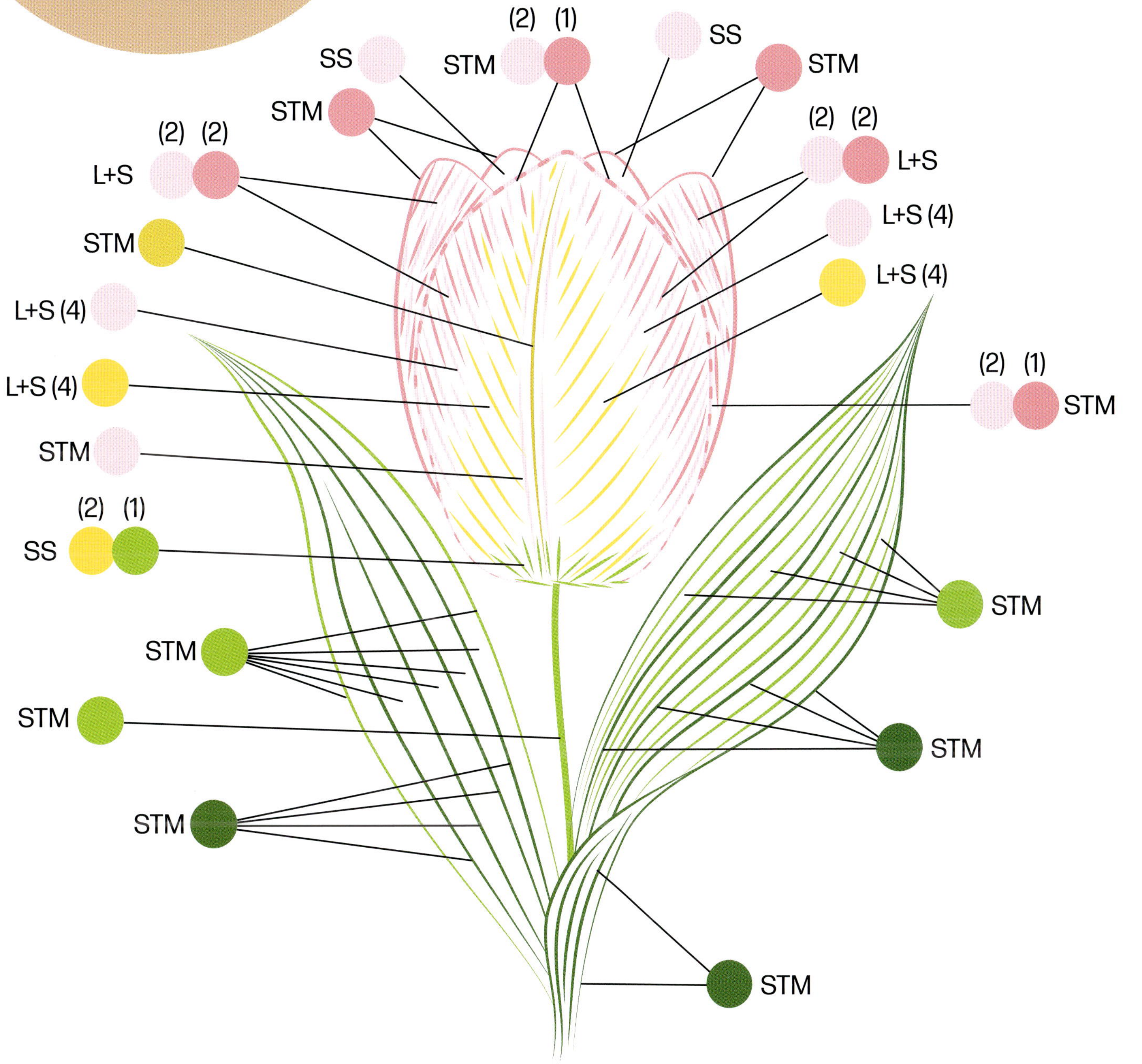

SS

(2) (1) STM

SS STM

STM

(2) (2) L+S

STM

L+S (4)

L+S (4)

STM

(2) (1) SS

STM

STM

STM

(2) (2) L+S

L+S (4)

L+S (4)

(2) (1) STM

STM

STM

STM

STM

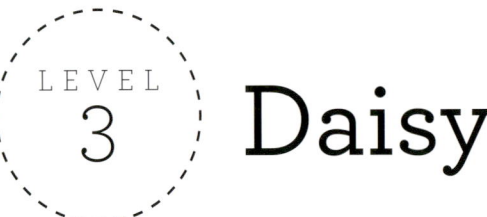

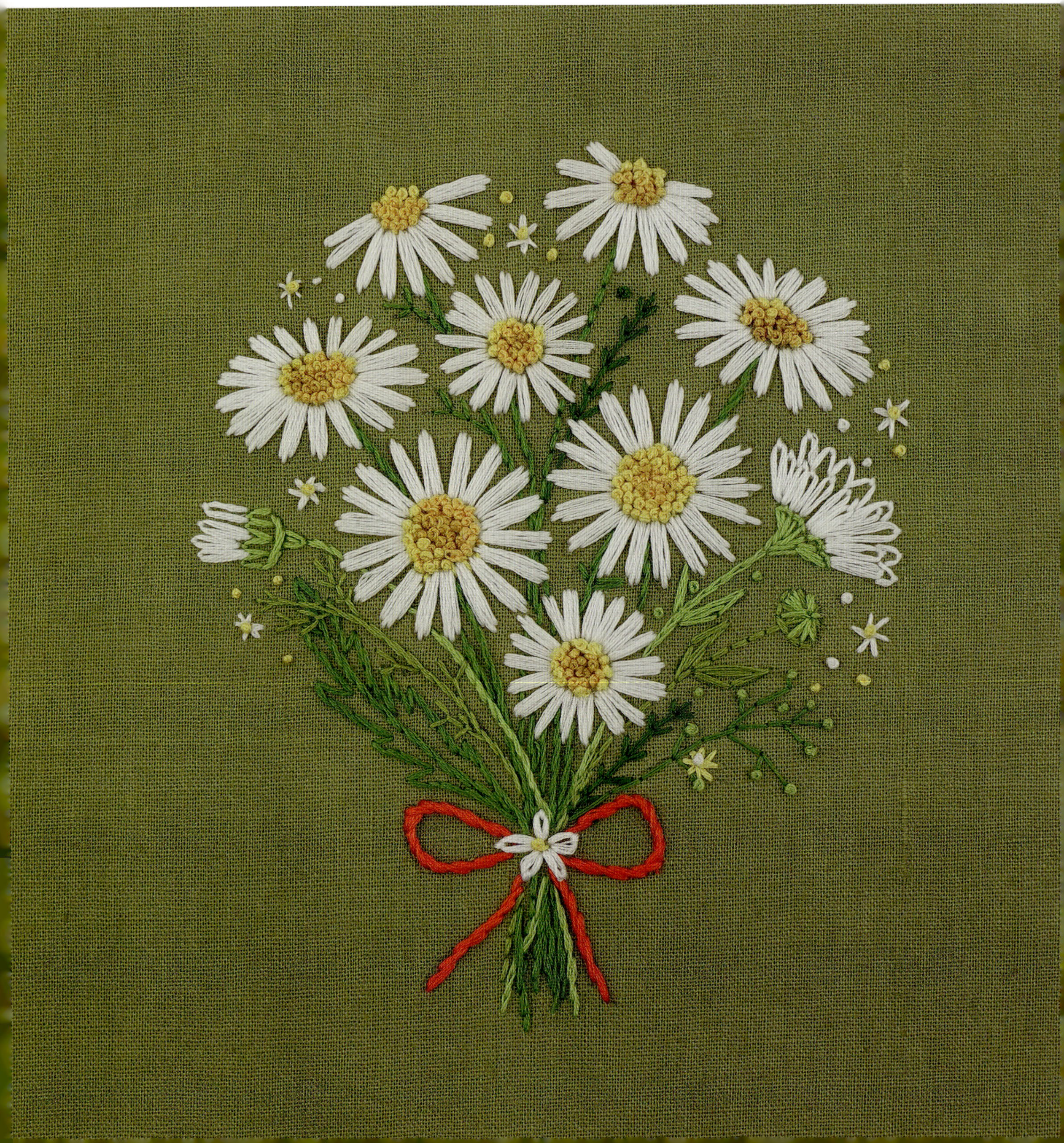

NOTE
Use three strands of floss throughout, unless otherwise indicated.

Thread Guide
DMC Thread Colors

Blanc 3820 725 726 3801 704

581 905 986

Stitches Used
Stitch Guide, pages 13-21

- Backstitch (BS)
- Detached Chain Stitch (DCS)
- Fly Stitch (FLY)
- French Knot (FK)
- Split Backstitch (SPLBS)
- Star Stitch (STR)
- Stem Stitch (STM)
- Straight Stitch (SS)

FLOWER DETAIL

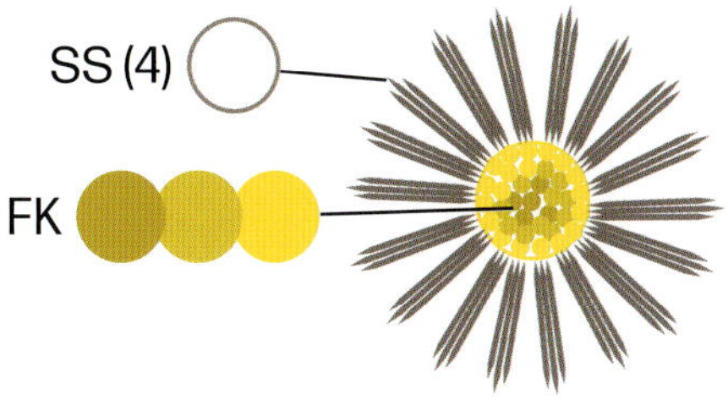

SS (4)

FK

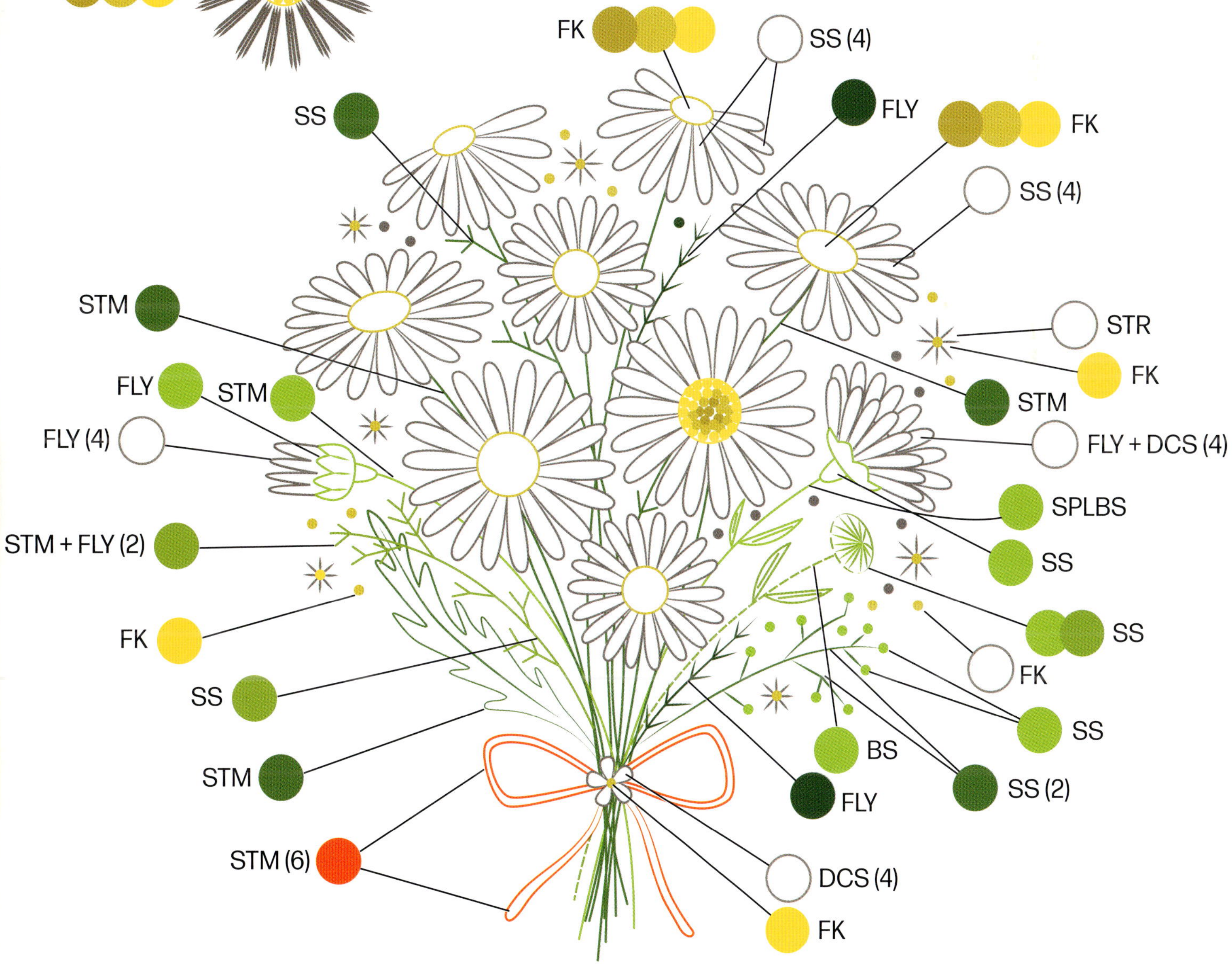

SS

FK

SS (4)

FLY

FK

SS (4)

STM

STR

FLY

STM

FK

FLY (4)

STM

FLY + DCS (4)

STM + FLY (2)

SPLBS

SS

FK

SS

SS

FK

SS

SS (2)

BS

STM

FLY

DCS (4)

STM (6)

FK

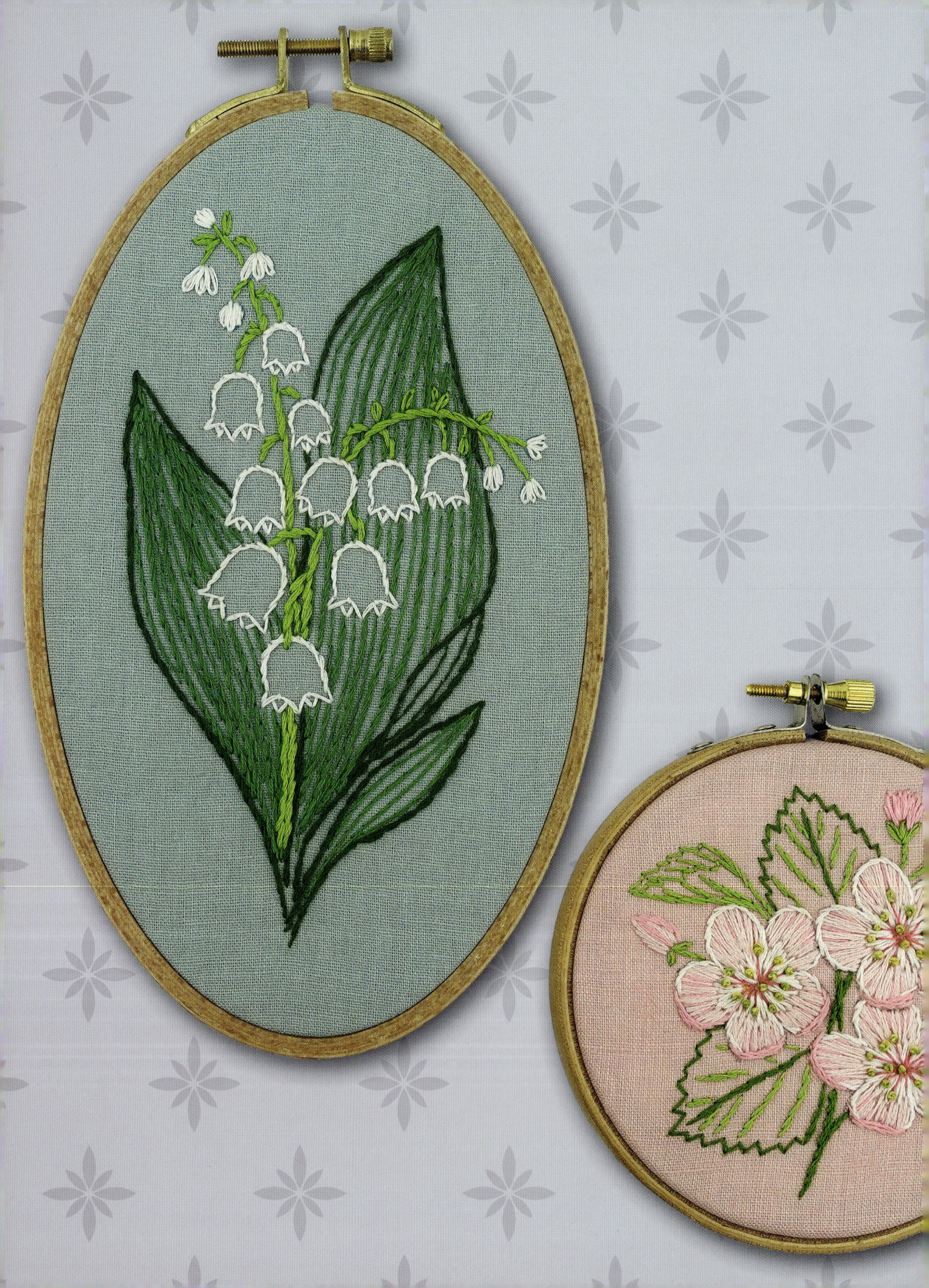

MAY

Lily of the Valley and Hawthorn

May's birth flowers continue to celebrate the spring season's "return to happiness" and the anticipation of summer.

Lily of the valley is tied to a beautiful legend that says this flower fell so deeply in love with the nightingale that it refused grow until the bird returned to the woods in May. Beyond this, it's most closely associated with May Day. People in England, France, and Serbia have historically given lily of the valley as a token of good luck.

Hawthorn's cultural influences are also entwined with folklore. While it has been long considered a symbol of hope, it is also said to mark the entrance to other worlds and that it could slay vampires. Today, this flowering shrub is a symbol of hope and fertility. It is also a staple for May Day celebrations and most often used in garlands.

May flowers have a limited color range, from white to pink, but they're a sweet celebration of the shift from spring to summer nonetheless. While these two spring flowers bloom, it is also a great time to dig into stitching sweet flowers for yourself or a loved one.

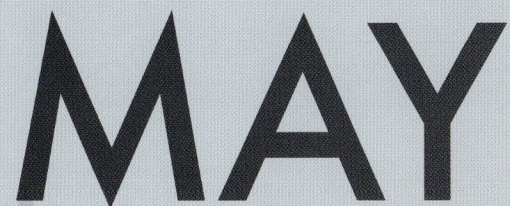

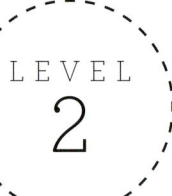

LEVEL
2

Lily of the Valley

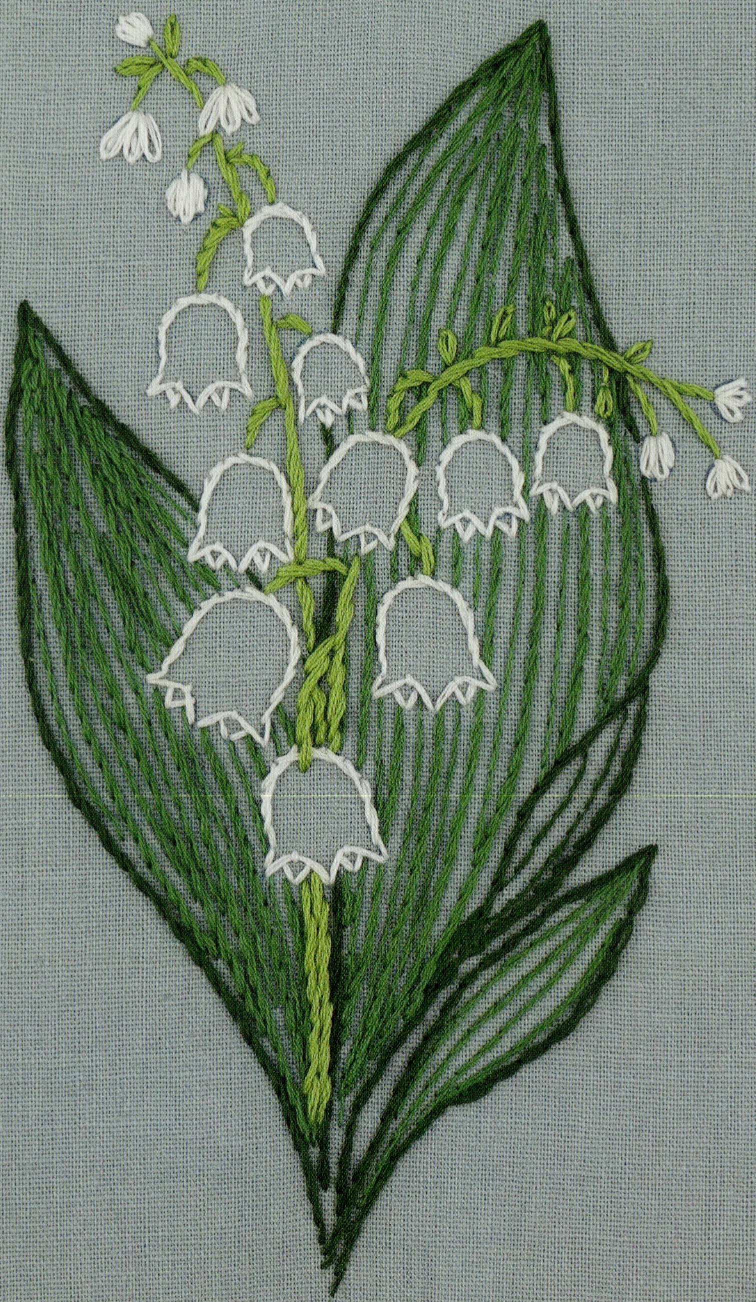

Thread Guide
DMC Thread Colors

Blanc   986   700   704

Stitches Used
Stitch Guide, pages 13–21

- Detached Chain Stitch (DCS)
- Fly Stitch (FLY)
- Stem Stitch (STM)
- Straight Stitch (SS)

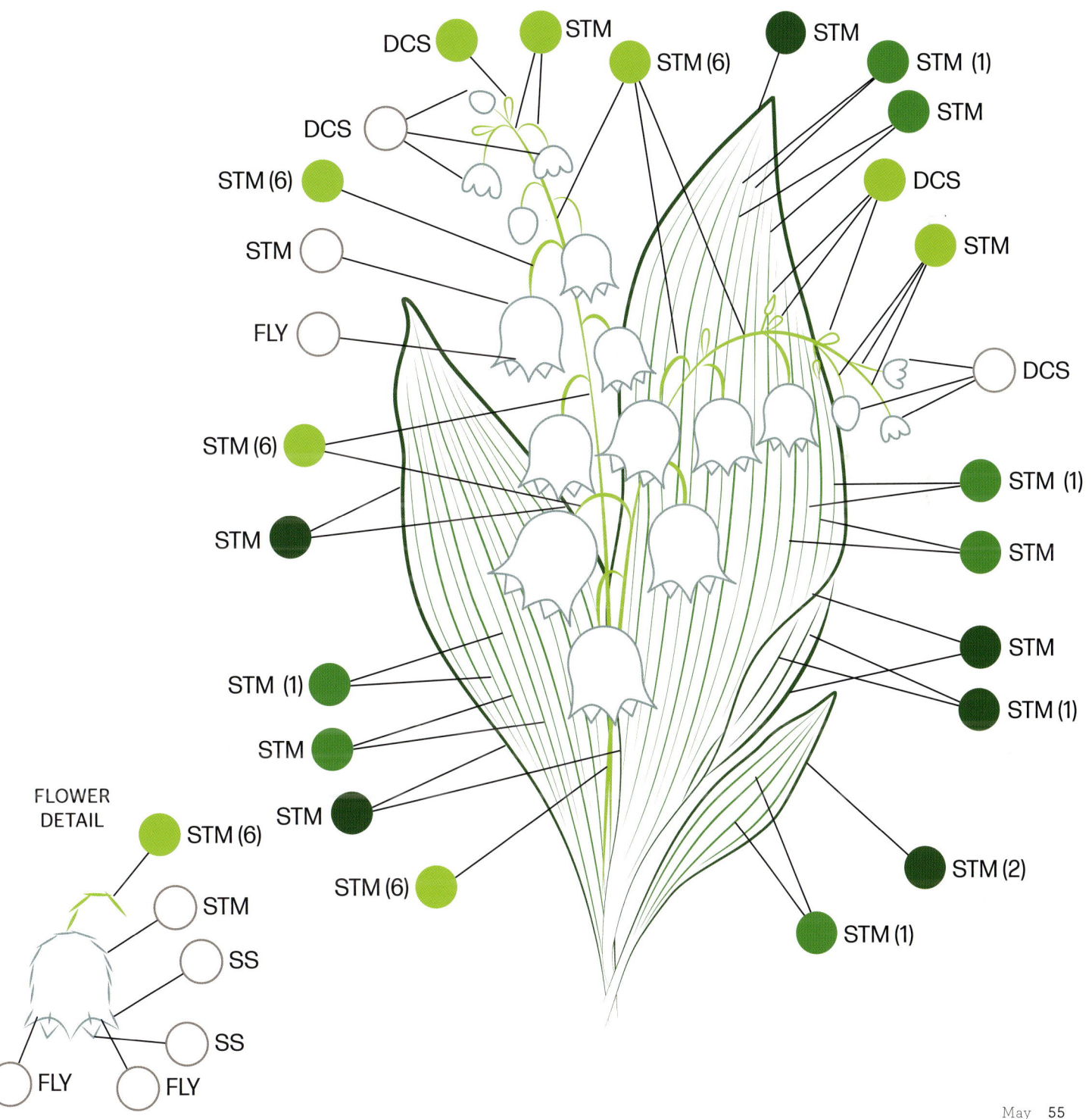

DCS · STM · STM (6) · STM · STM (1) · STM · DCS · STM · DCS

DCS · STM (6) · STM · FLY · STM (6) · STM

STM (1) · STM · STM · STM (1)

FLOWER DETAIL
STM (6) · STM · SS · SS · FLY · FLY

STM (1) · STM · STM · STM (6)

STM (2) · STM (1)

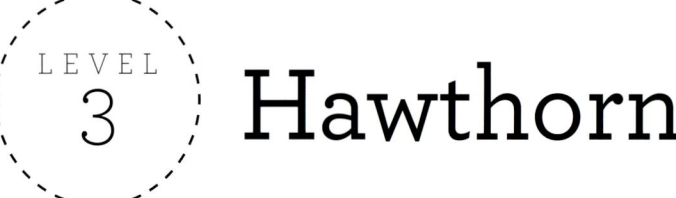

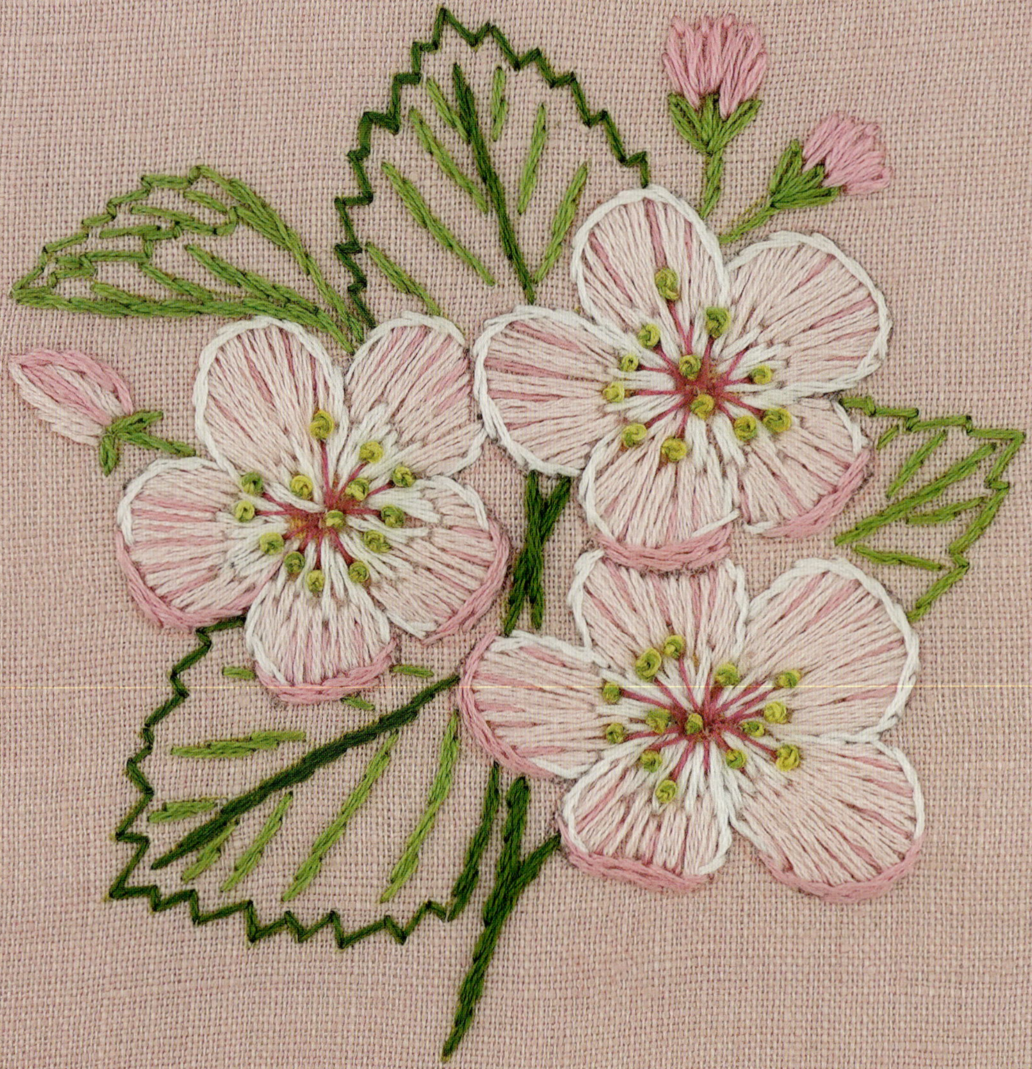

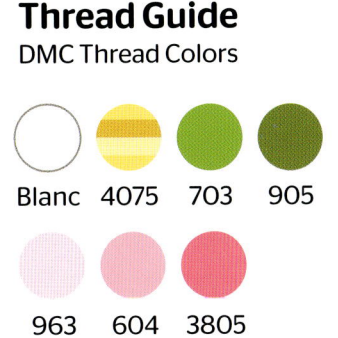

NOTE
Use three strands of floss throughout, unless otherwise indicated.

Thread Guide
DMC Thread Colors

Blanc 4075 703 905

963 604 3805

Stitches Used
Stitch Guide, pages 13–21

- Detached Chain Stitch (DCS)
- French Knot (FK)
- Long and Short Stitch (L+S)
- Satin Stitch (SAT)
- Stem Stitch (STM)
- Straight Stitch (SS)

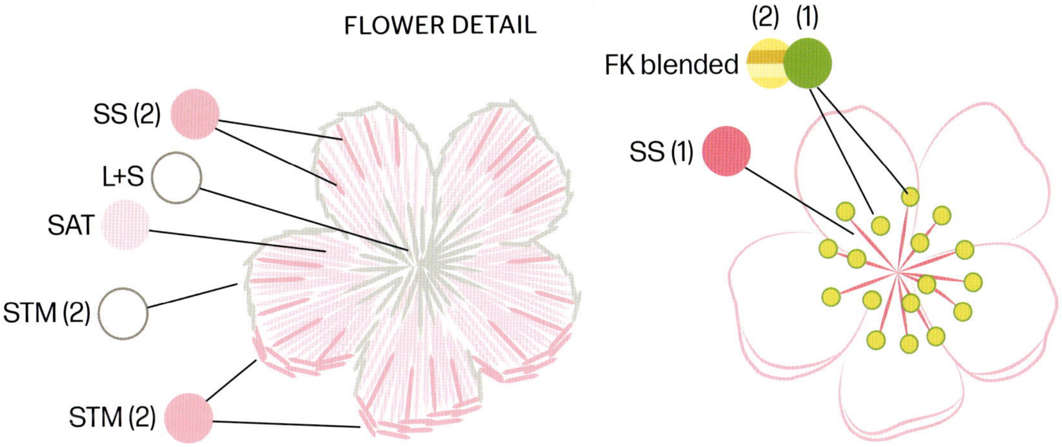

FLOWER DETAIL

SS (2)
L+S
SAT
STM (2)
STM (2)

(2) (1)
FK blended
SS (1)

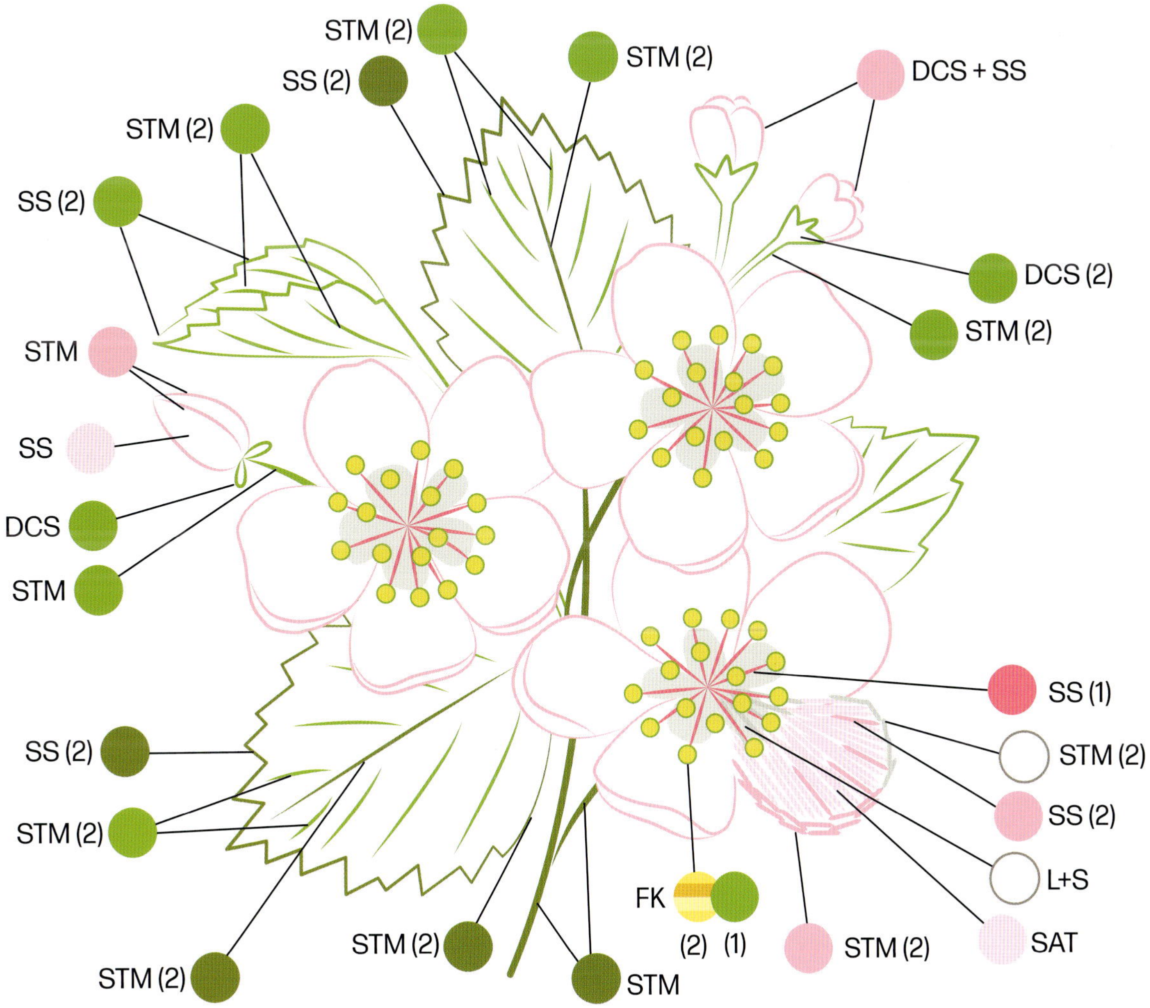

STM (2)
SS (2)
STM (2)
STM (2)
SS (2)
STM
SS
DCS
STM

STM (2)
DCS + SS
DCS (2)
STM (2)

SS (1)
STM (2)
SS (2)
L+S
SAT

SS (2)
STM (2)

STM (2)
STM (2)
FK
(2) (1)
STM
STM (2)

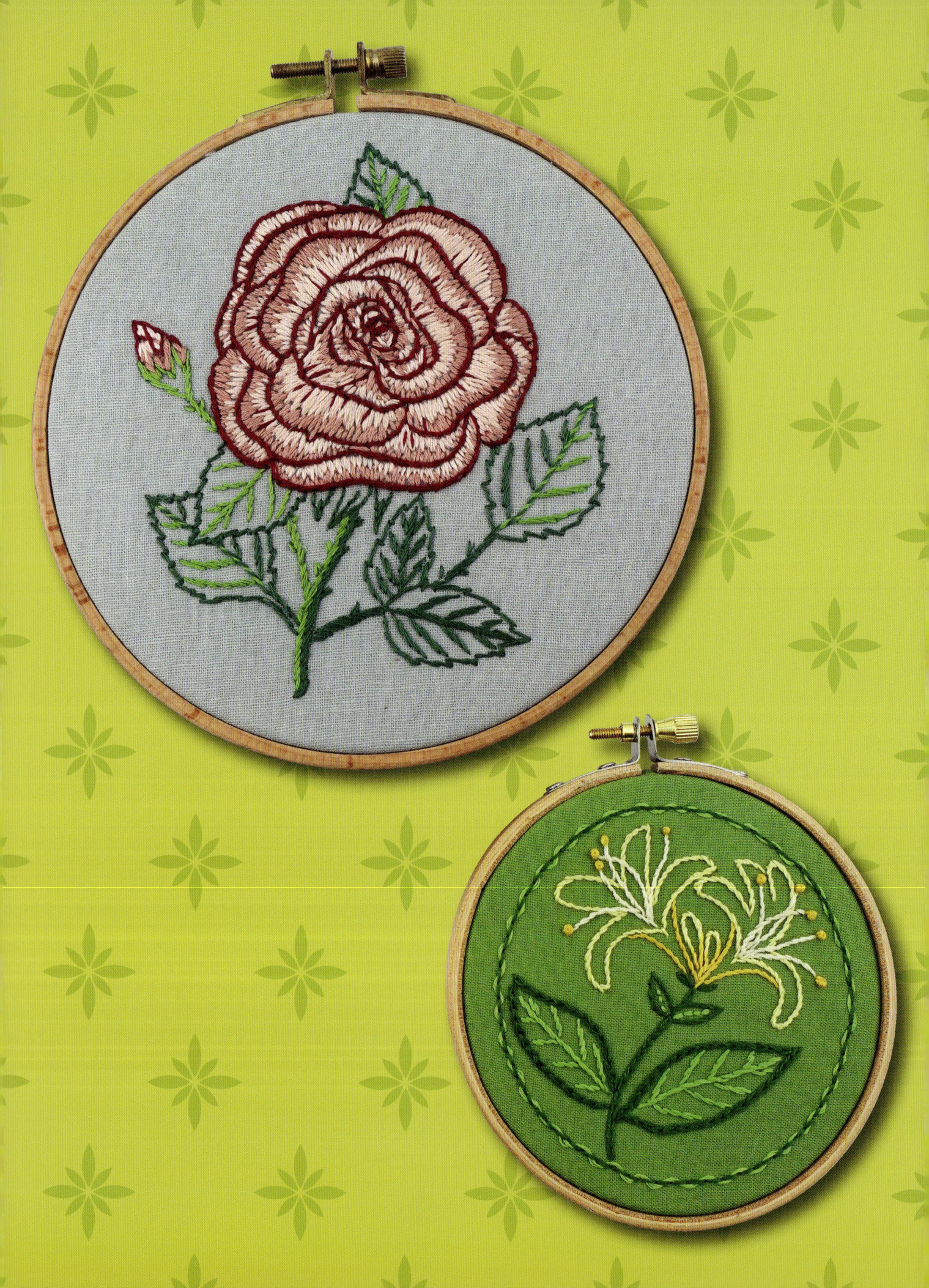

JUNE

Rose and Honeysuckle

As the warmth of the summer season sets in, one of the most iconic flowers of all time takes center stage for June birthdays—the rose. Its co-star is the cheerful and fragrant honeysuckle.

You may be surprised to learn that roses have been cultivated for over 5,000 years, but they're actually much older than that. There is fossil evidence that roses have been around for 35 million years! According to the Greek writer Pausanias, the rose obtained its red color from the blood of Aphrodite, who cut her feet on the thorns of a rosebush while rushing to her dying lover, Adonis. Today, each color of rose has a specific meaning from the classic red signifying deep love and passion, to yellow for joy and friendship.

Like the rose, honeysuckle has come to symbolize romantic love as well. Known for its sugary scent, it also represents sweetness and affection, along with happiness and good fortune. According to Greek mythology, the long-distance lovers Chloe and Daphnis were only allowed to see each other when the honeysuckle was in bloom. So, this blooming vine is also said to strengthen bonds between loved ones.

Whether you stitch a rose or honeysuckle for a romantic partner or a dear friend, know that these flowers herald joy and happiness to those who receive them! They're also a special way to say "Happy Birthday!" to people born in June.

Rose

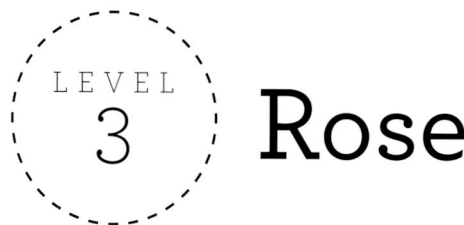

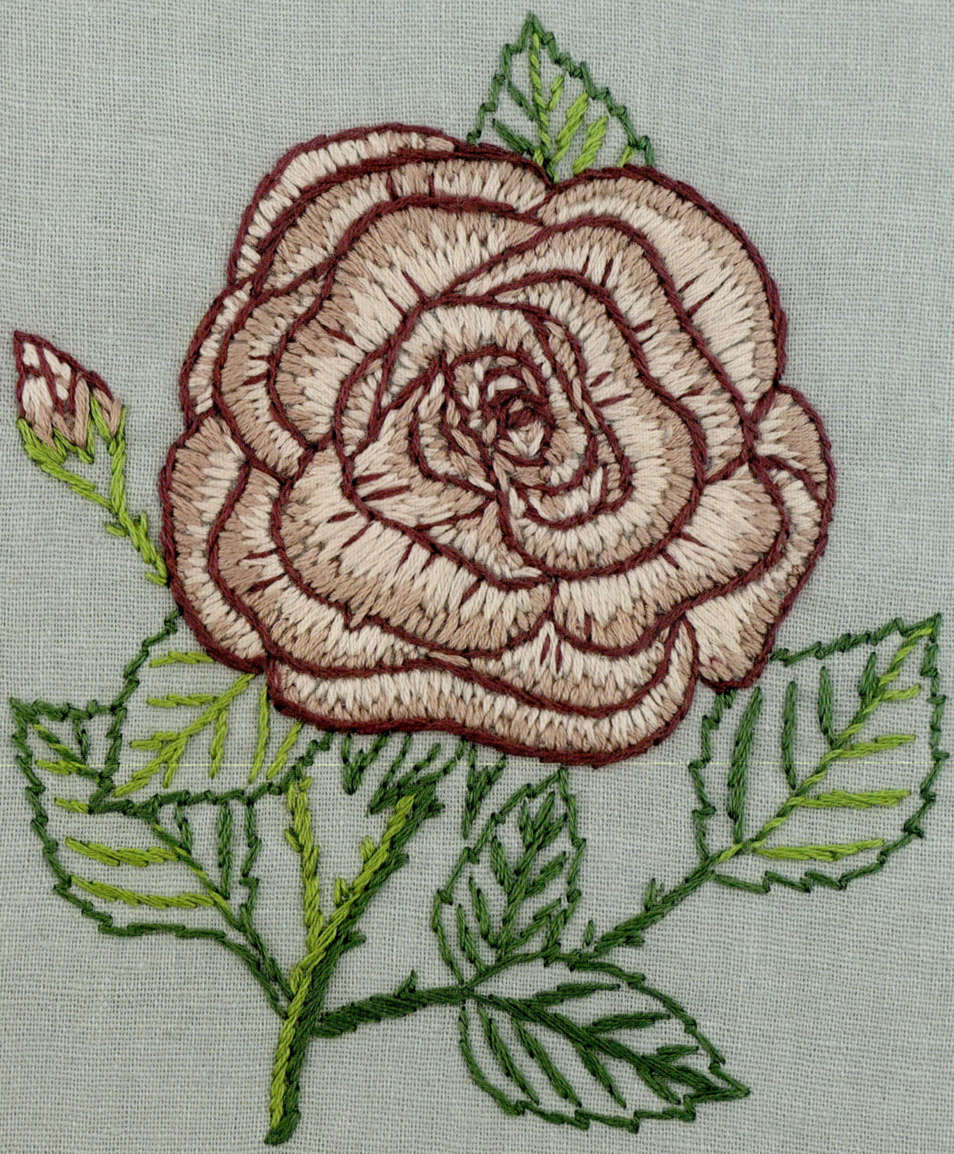

Thread Guide
DMC Thread Colors

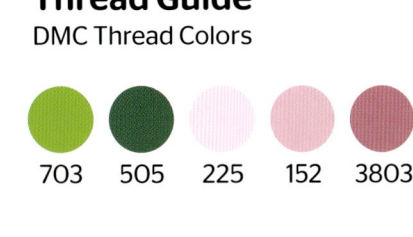

703 505 225 152 3803

Stitches Used
Stitch Guide, pages 13–21

- Backstitch (BS)
- Detached Chain Stitch (DCS)
- Long and Short Stitch (L+S)
- Stem Stitch (STM)
- Straight Stitch (SS)
- Whipped Backstitch (WBS)

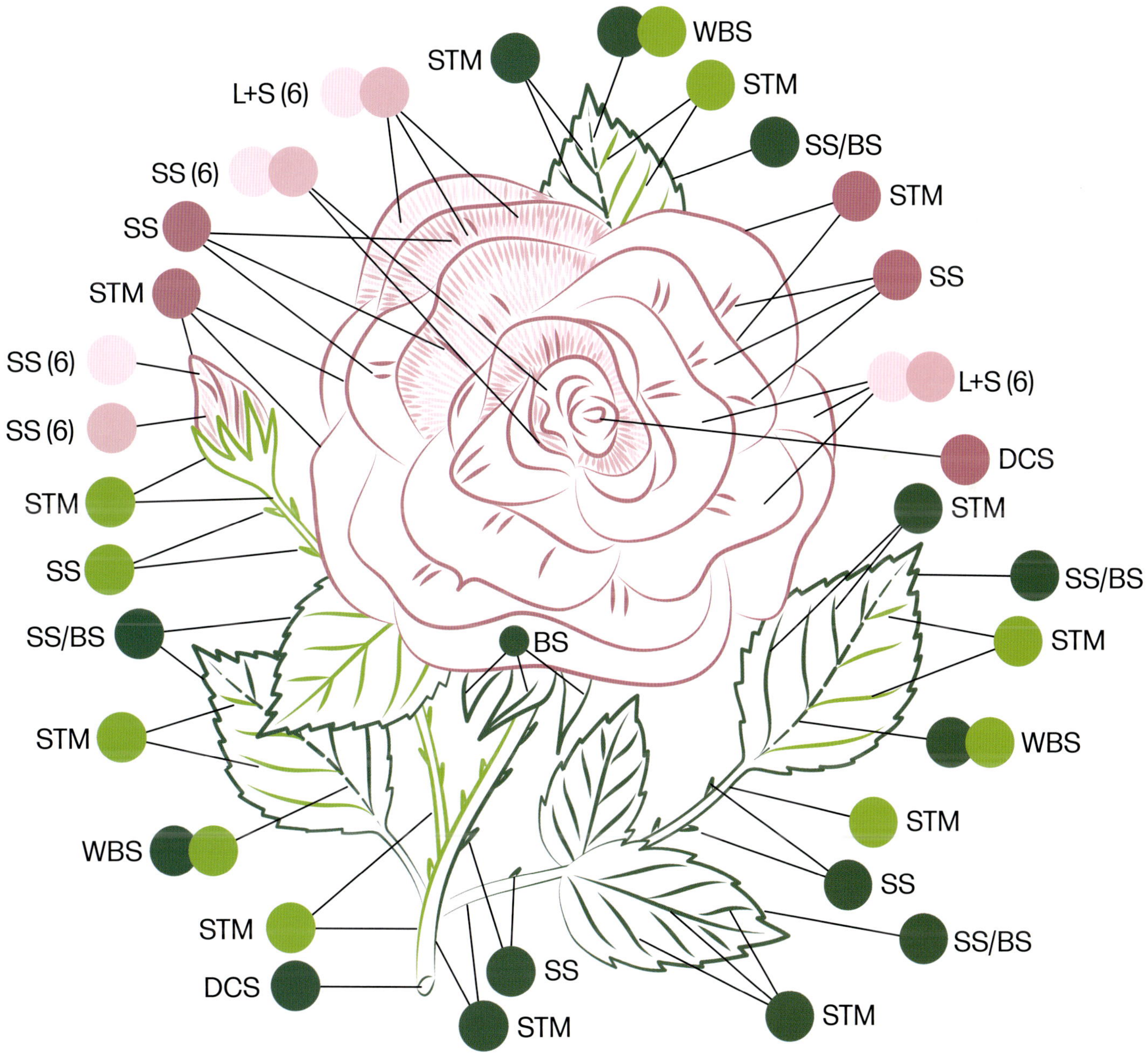

STM
WBS
STM
SS/BS
STM
SS
L+S (6)
DCS
STM
SS/BS
STM
WBS
STM
SS
SS/BS
STM
SS
STM
L+S (6)
SS (6)
SS
STM
SS (6)
SS (6)
STM
SS
SS/BS
STM
WBS
STM
DCS
SS
STM
BS

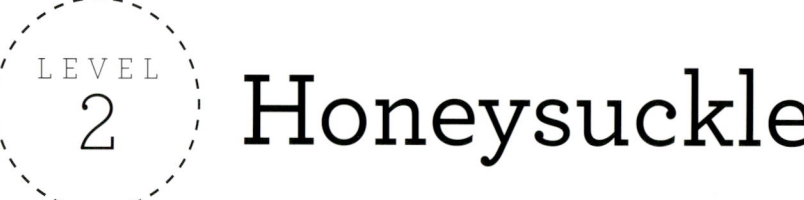

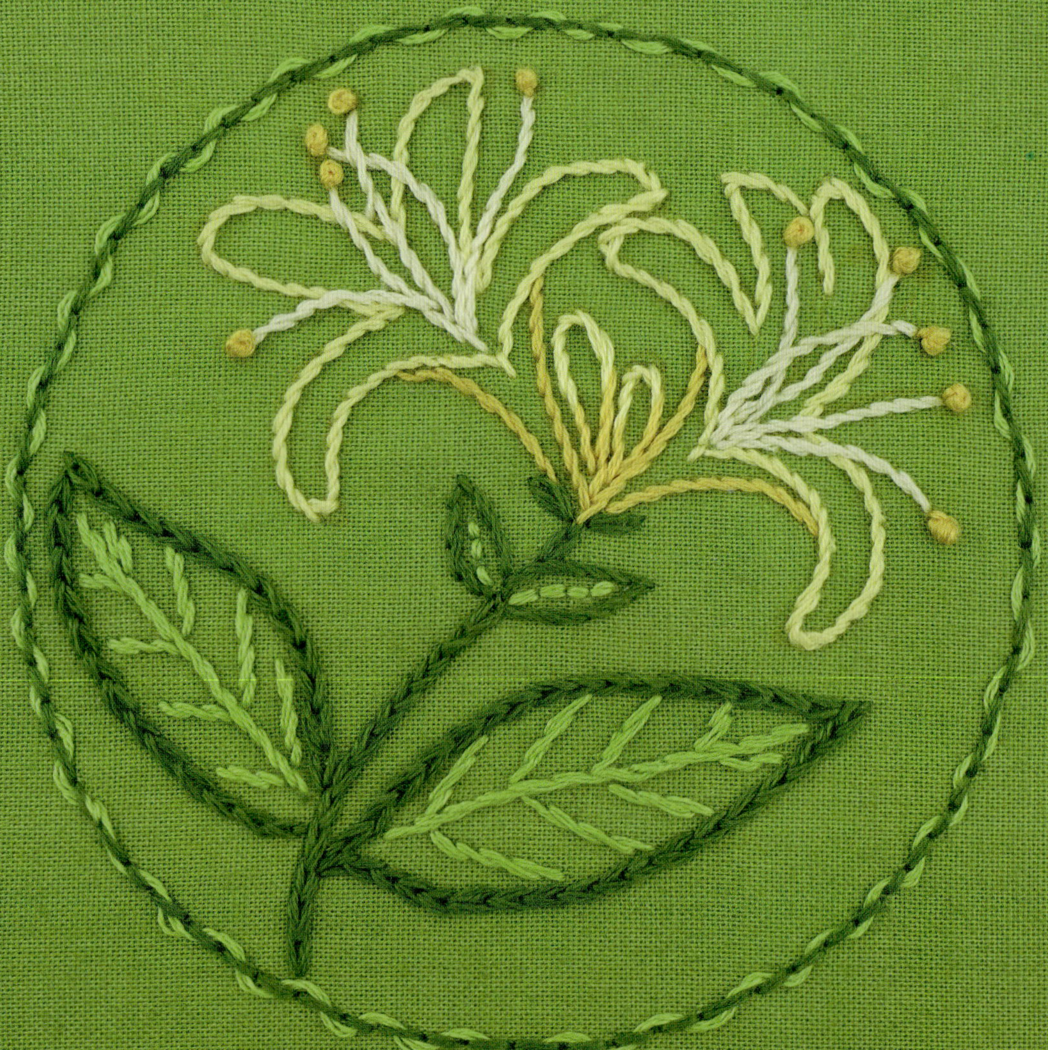

NOTE
Use three strands of floss throughout.

Thread Guide
DMC Thread Colors

703   986   725   727   3823

Stitches Used
Stitch Guide, pages 13–21

- Backstitch (BS)
- Chain Stitch (CS)
- Detached Chain Stitch (DCS)
- French Knot (FK)
- Stem Stitch (STM)
- Threaded Backstitch (TBS)

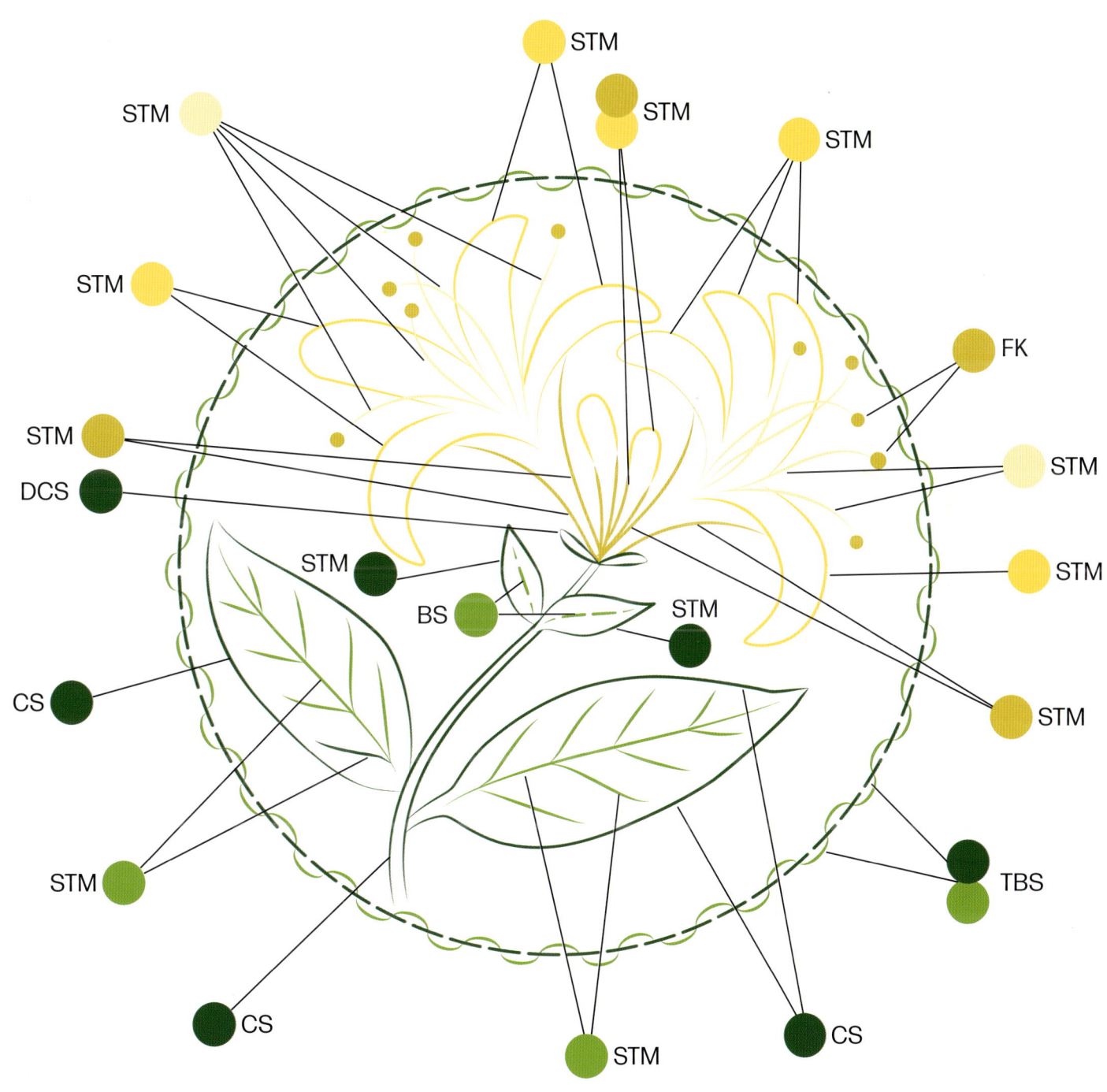

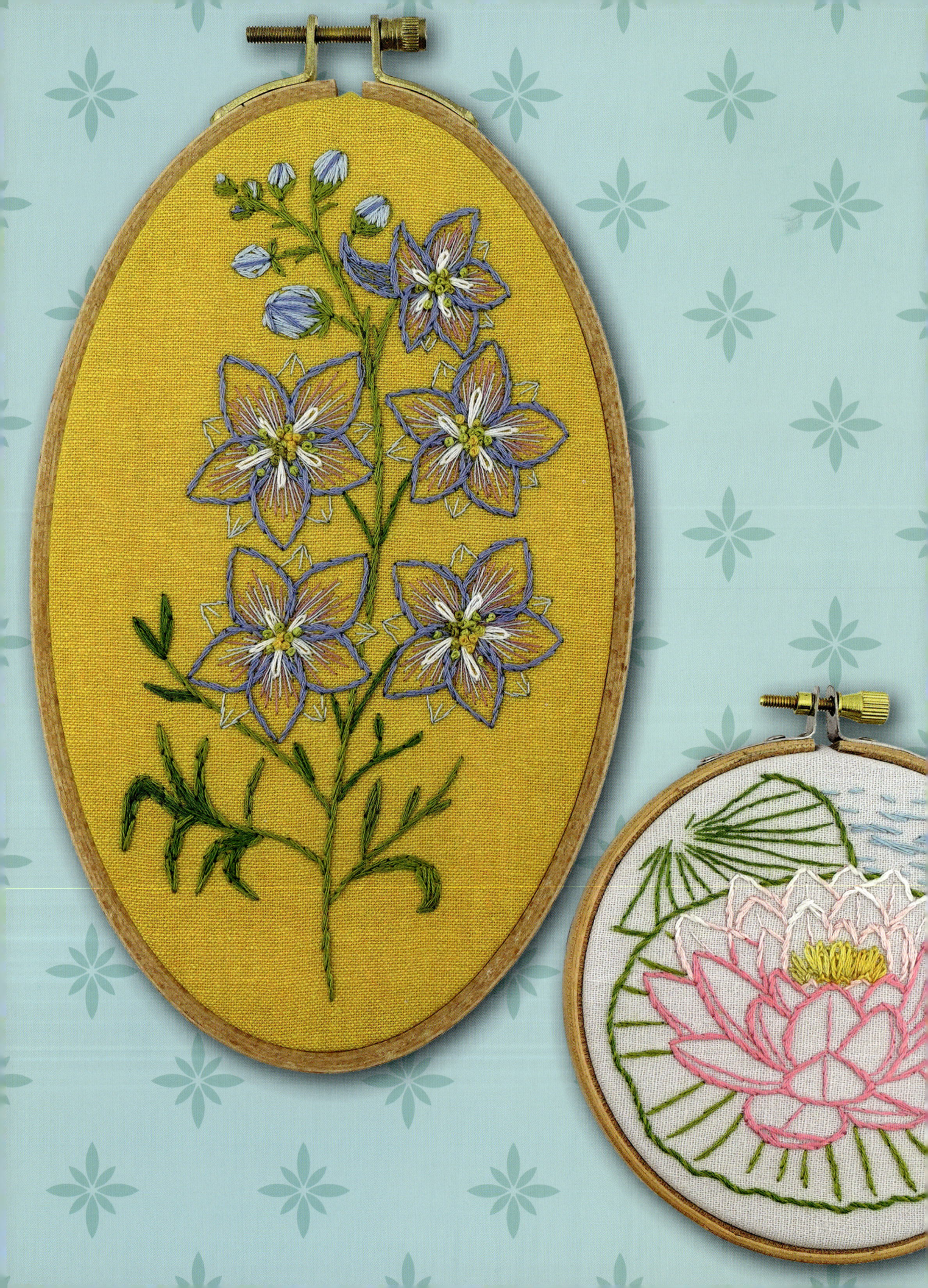

JULY

Larkspur and Water Lily

July's birth flowers, larkspur and water lily, are as distinct in meaning and charm as the flowers themselves.

The tall and elegant larkspur is tied to the legend of the Battle of Troy in Greek mythology. For the Victorians, larkspur was a way to ward off evil. Across cultures, the flower also symbolizes positivity and dedication, while each color holds an additional meaning. The rarest color these small buttercuplike blooms grow is blue, which stands for gracefulness and dignity. Purple represents first love, while white conveys happiness.

Water lilies, flowers that famously captivated French artist Claude Monet and appeared in many of his great works, have also been a part of myth and legend for centuries. Their botanical name, *Nymphaeaceae*, is fitting, as in Greek mythology nymphs were water protectors. In the Victorian era's *The Language and Poetry of Flowers* (1854), water lilies took on the meaning of purity, and its ability to bloom from mud suggested resilience and rising above difficulty.

As you stitch and embroider these unique flowers for yourself, or someone else born in July, know you're spreading a powerful message steeped in rich history.

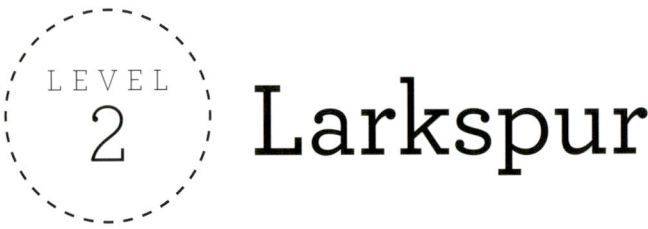

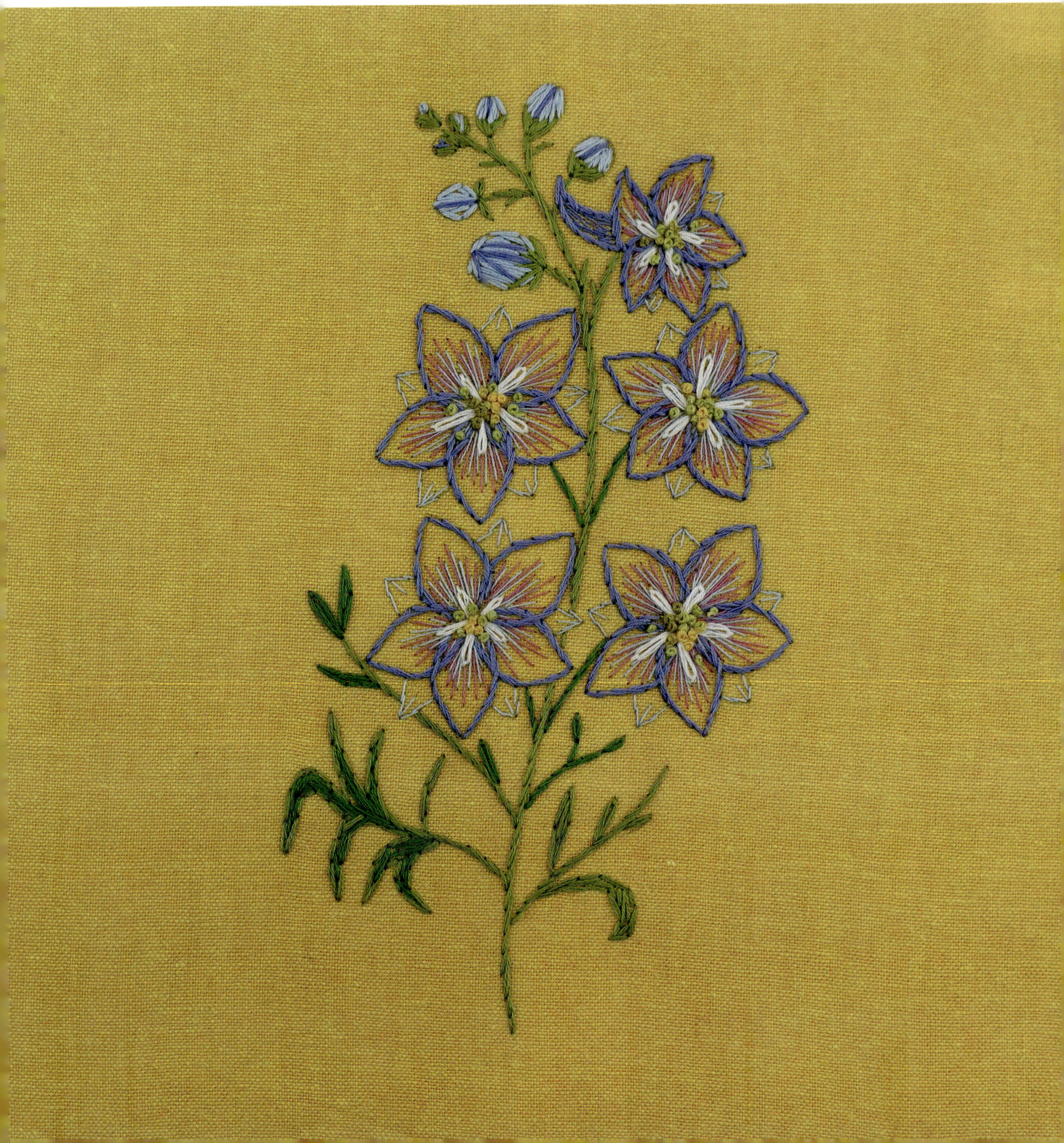

Thread Guide
DMC Thread Colors

Blanc · 316 · 827 · 799 · 4070

581 · 905

Stitches Used
Stitch Guide, pages 13–21

- Backstitch (BS)
- Detached Chain Stitch (DCS)
- French Knot (FK)
- Stem Stitch (STM)
- Straight Stitch (SS)

FLOWER DETAIL

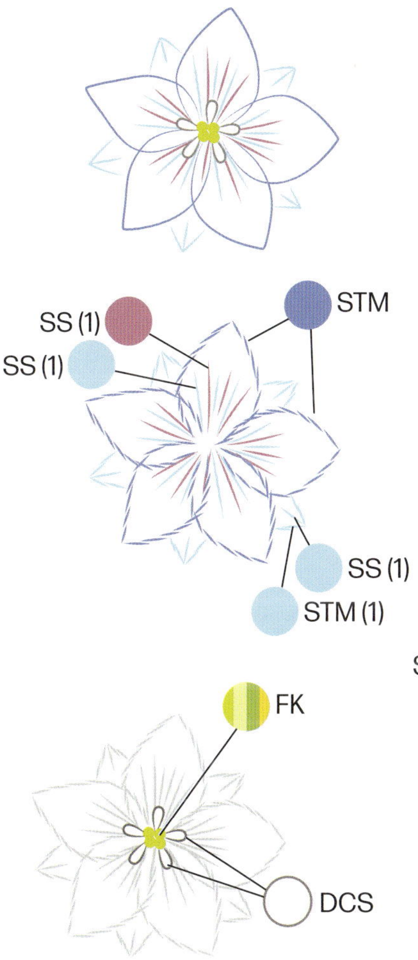

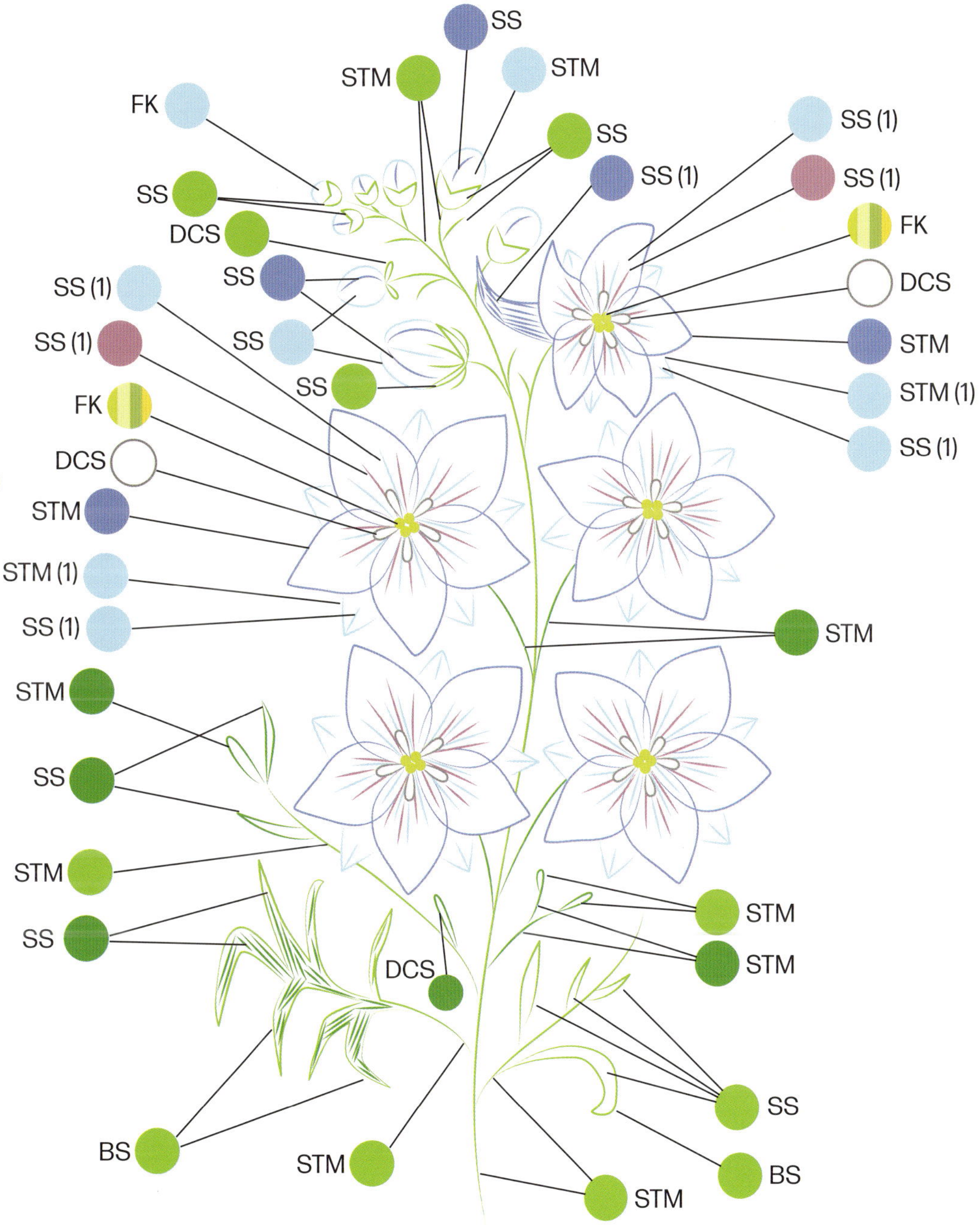

SS (1)
SS (1)
STM

SS (1)
STM (1)

FK
DCS

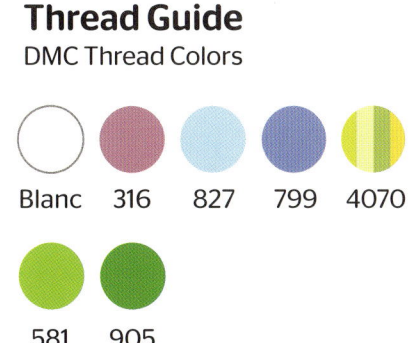

SS
STM
SS
STM
FK
SS
SS (1)
DCS
SS
SS (1)
FK
SS
DCS
STM
STM (1)
SS (1)
STM
SS
STM
SS

SS
STM
SS (1)
SS (1)
FK
DCS
STM
STM (1)
SS (1)

STM

STM
STM
DCS
SS
BS

BS
STM
STM

Water Lily

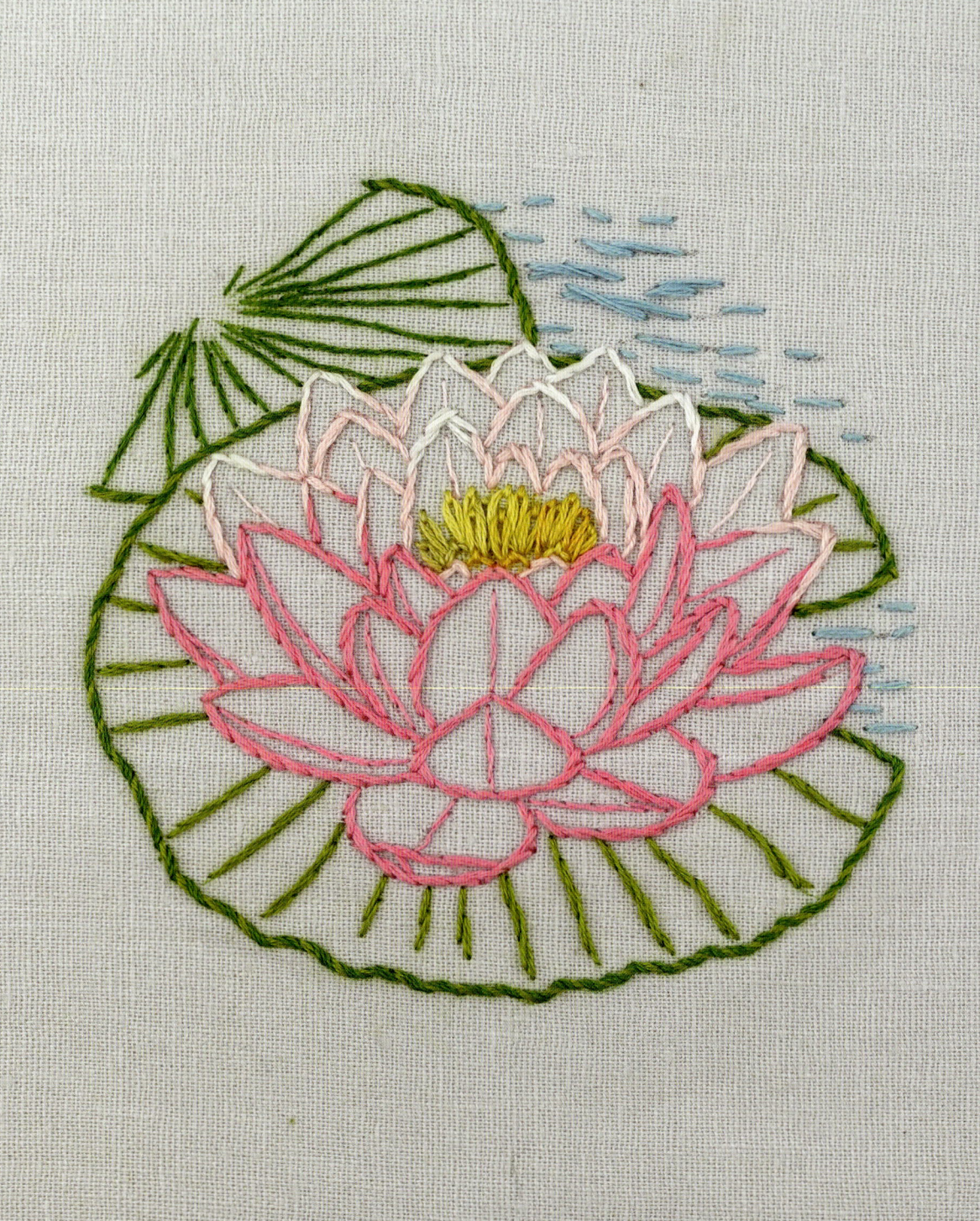

NOTE
Use three strands of floss throughout, unless otherwise indicated.

Thread Guide
DMC Thread Colors

Blanc 4075 905 581 963

603 3766

Stitches Used
Stitch Guide, pages 13-21

- Detached Chain Stitch (DCS)
- Fly Stitch (FLY)
- Stem Stitch (STM)
- Straight Stitch (SS)
- Whipped Backstitch (WBS)

FLOWER DETAIL

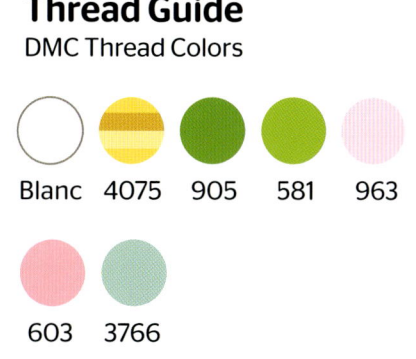

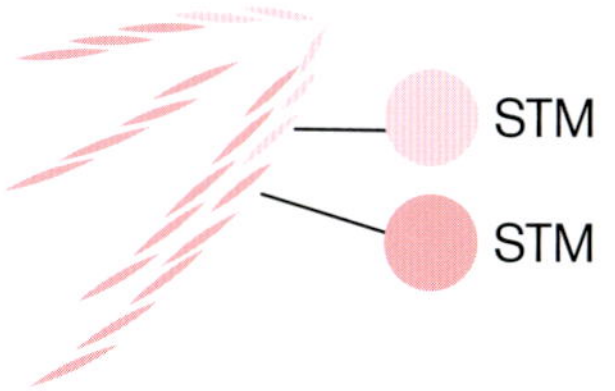

STM

STM

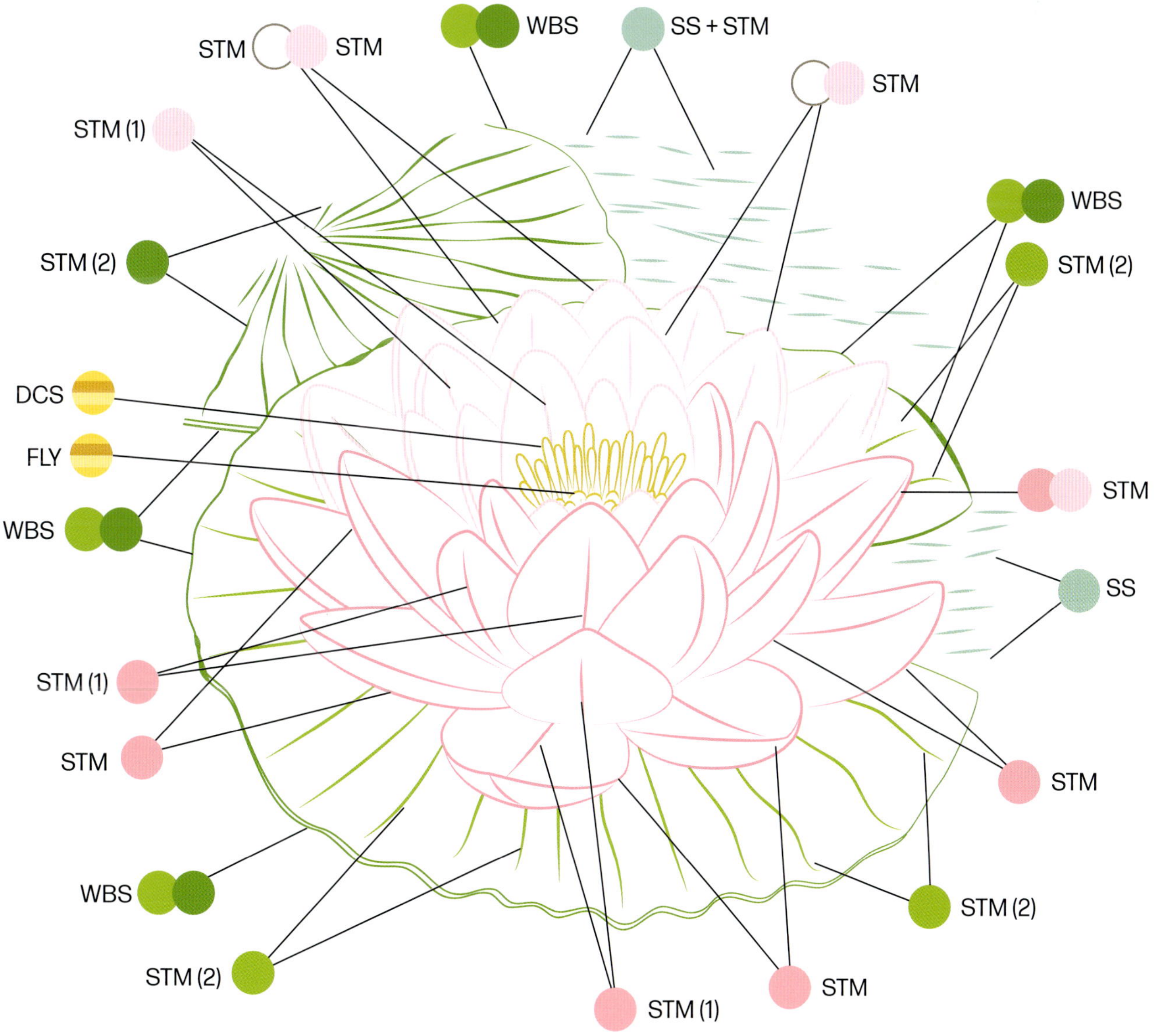

STM — STM   WBS   SS + STM   STM

STM (1)

STM (2)   WBS   STM (2)

DCS

FLY   STM

WBS   SS

STM (1)

STM

STM

WBS   STM (2)

STM (2)   STM (1)   STM

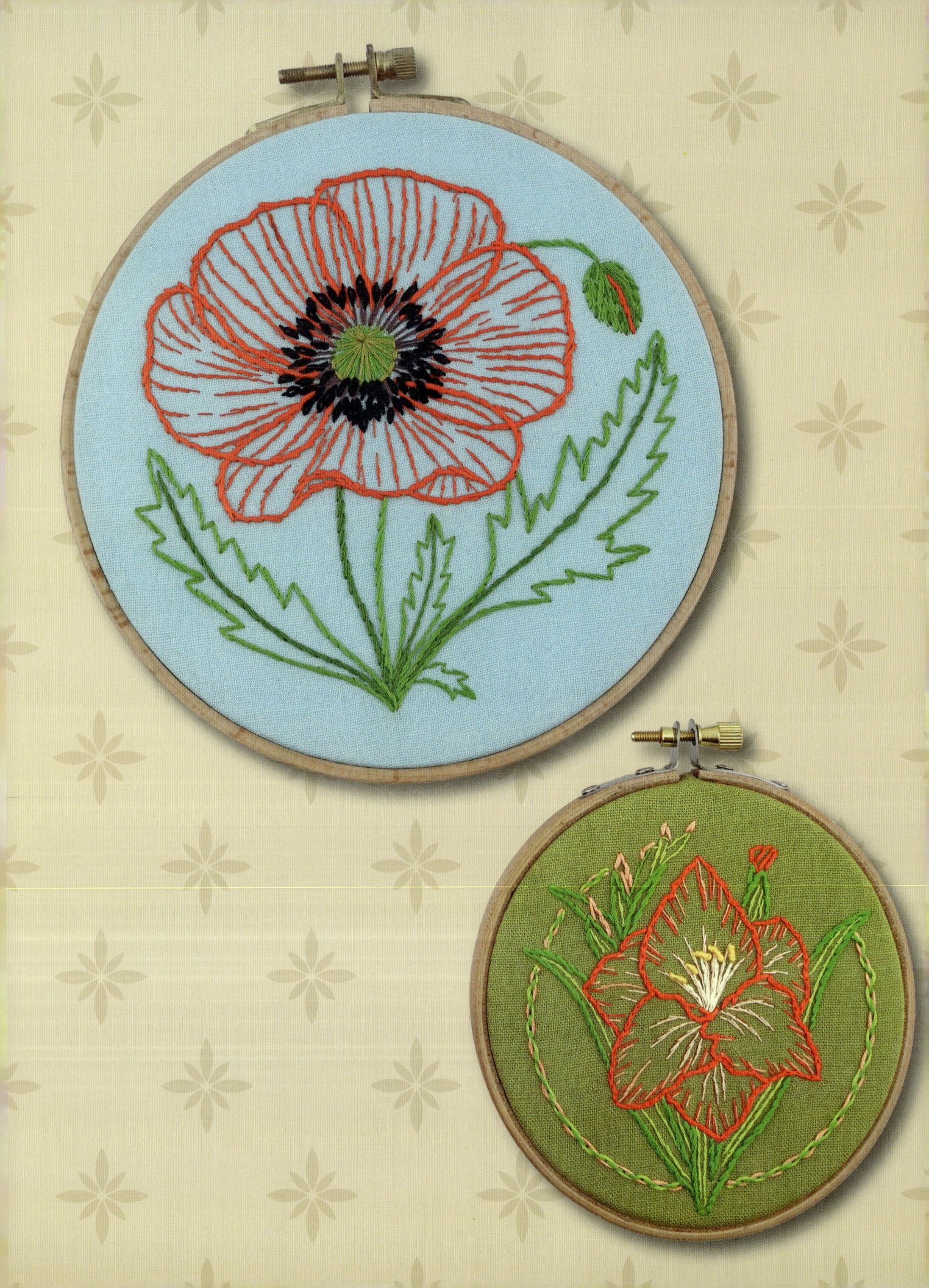

AUGUST

Poppy and Gladiolus

Poppies and gladioluses are both popular flowers in the late summer months and spectacular representatives of August birthdays.

Poppies, widely known for their bright red petals and black centers, also come in a range of colors including pink, salmon, yellow, orange, purple, and white. There are hundreds of varieties of poppies. The earliest known reference to them was in 3400 BCE when the opium poppy was cultivated in Mesopotamia or Southwest Asia, where it was referred to as the "joy plant." Their showy petals will surely bring you joy as you stitch them.

Colorful, long, and thin, the gladiolus flower is known as the "sword lily," with the Latin word *gladius* translating to "sword." They've come to symbolize love and strength. One popular legend says the giver of a gladiolus is piercing the recipient's heart with love. Step aside, Cupid! Traditionally, they were used for medicinal needs, while in the modern day these colorful blooms make a bold statement in flower arrangements and bouquets.

Both of August's birth flowers are bold expressions of love and honor. No matter what color you choose to stitch them in, or who you gift them to, they will be long cherished as an heirloom for generations.

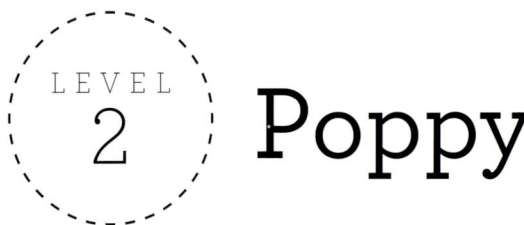

Poppy

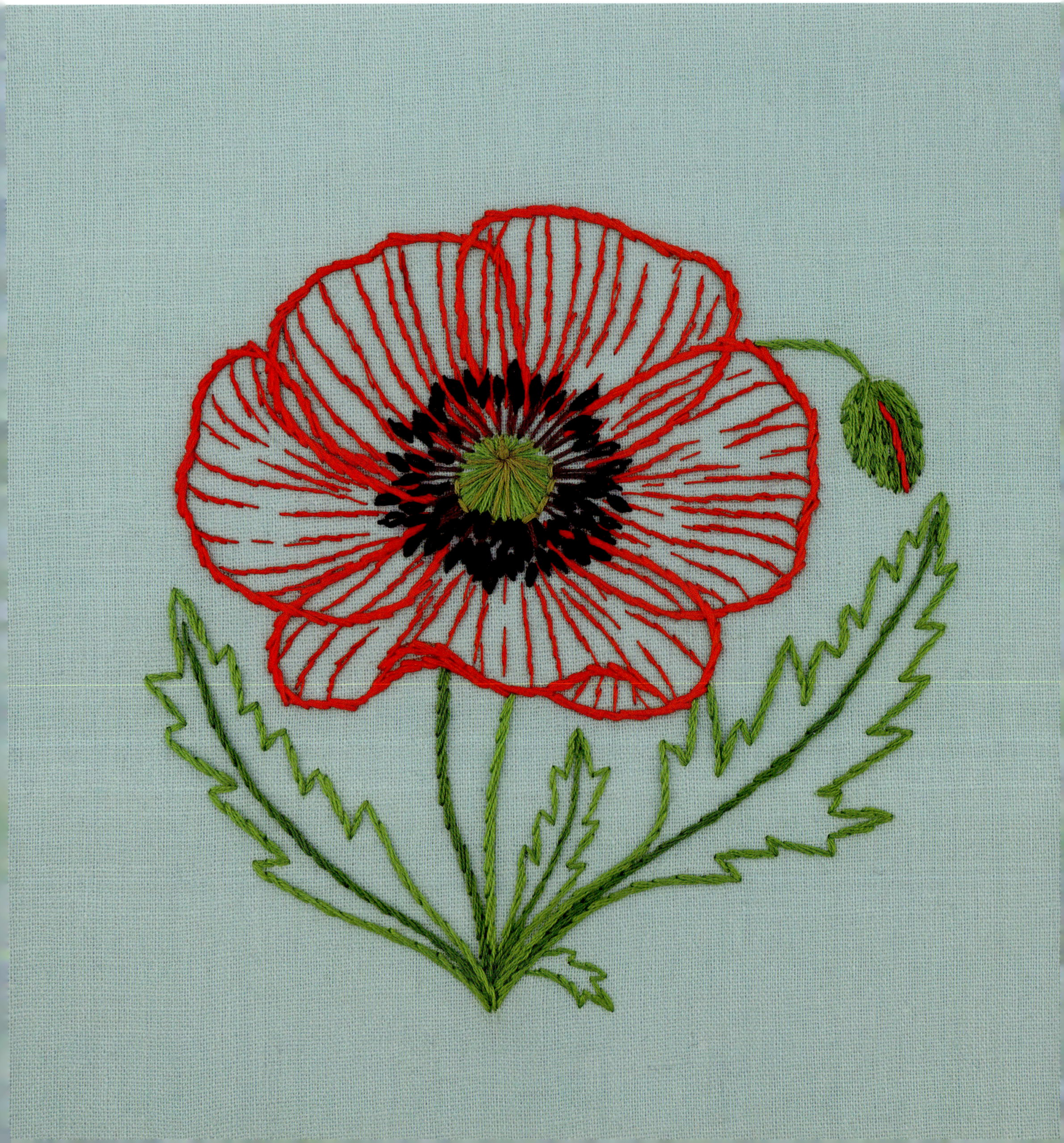

NOTE
Use three strands of floss throughout, unless otherwise indicated.

Thread Guide
DMC Thread Colors

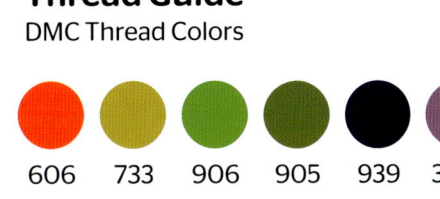

606 733 906 905 939 3740

Stitches Used
Stitch Guide, pages 13–21

- Detached Chain Stitch (DCS)
- French Knot (FK)
- Long and Short Stitch (L+S)
- Satin Stitch (SAT)
- Stem Stitch (STM)
- Straight Stitch (SS)

FLOWER DETAIL

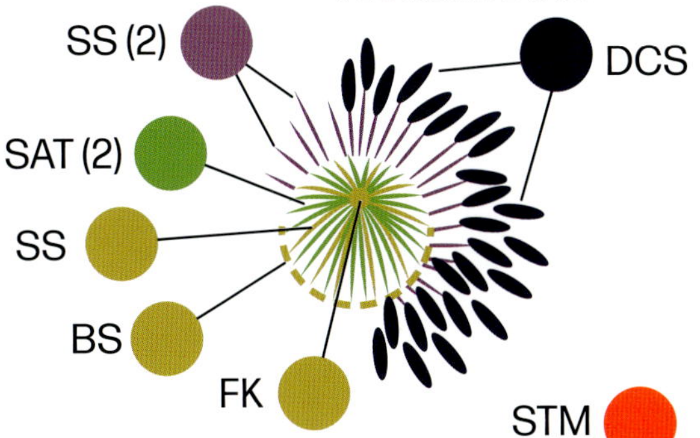

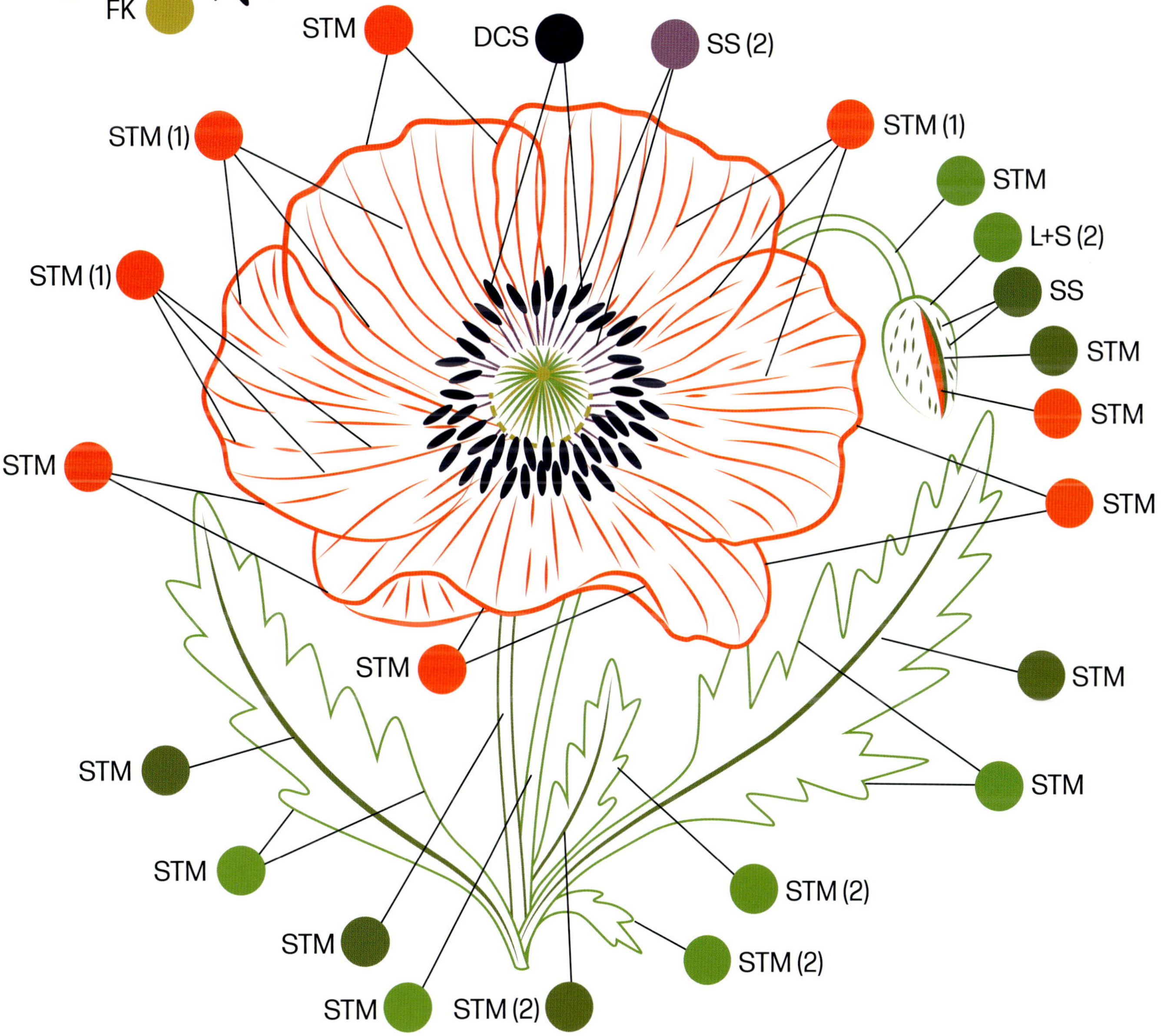

SS (2)

SAT (2)

SS

BS

FK

DCS

STM DCS SS (2)

STM (1) STM (1)

STM (1)

STM

STM

L+S (2)

SS

STM

STM

STM

STM STM

STM

STM

STM

STM

STM

STM

STM (2)

STM

STM

STM (2)

STM (2)

Gladiolus

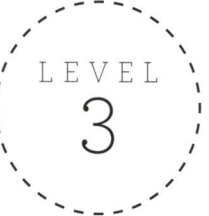

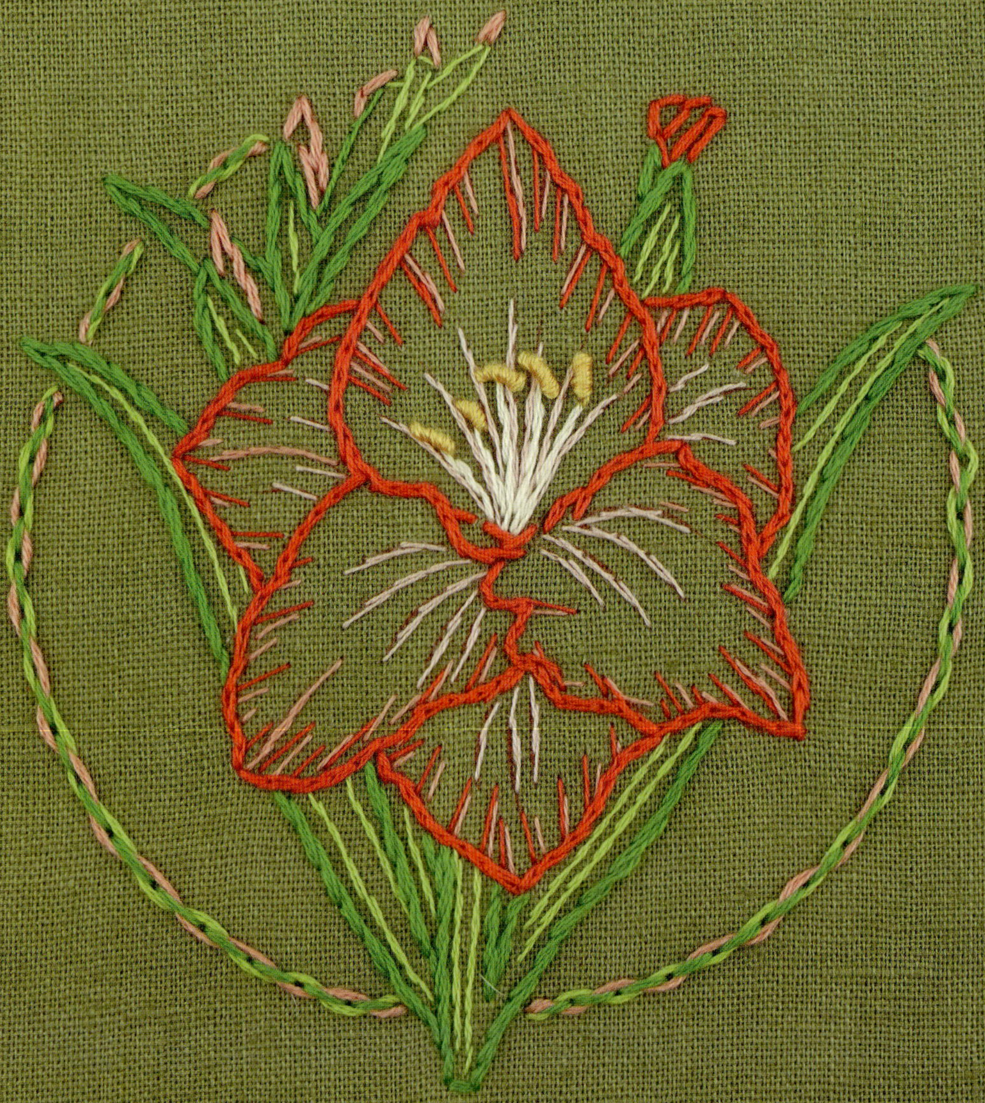

NOTE
Use three strands of floss throughout, unless otherwise indicated.

Thread Guide
DMC Thread Colors

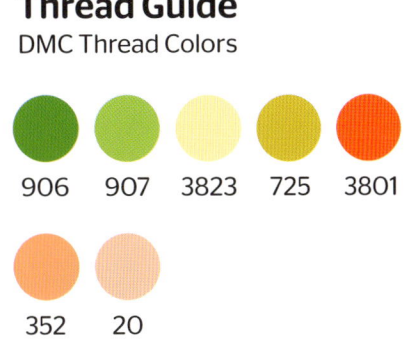

906 · 907 · 3823 · 725 · 3801

352 · 20

Stitches Used
Stitch Guide, pages 13–21

- Bullion Stitch (BUL)
- Split Backstitch (SPLBS)
- Stem Stitch (STM)
- Straight Stitch (SS)
- Threaded Backstitch (TBS)

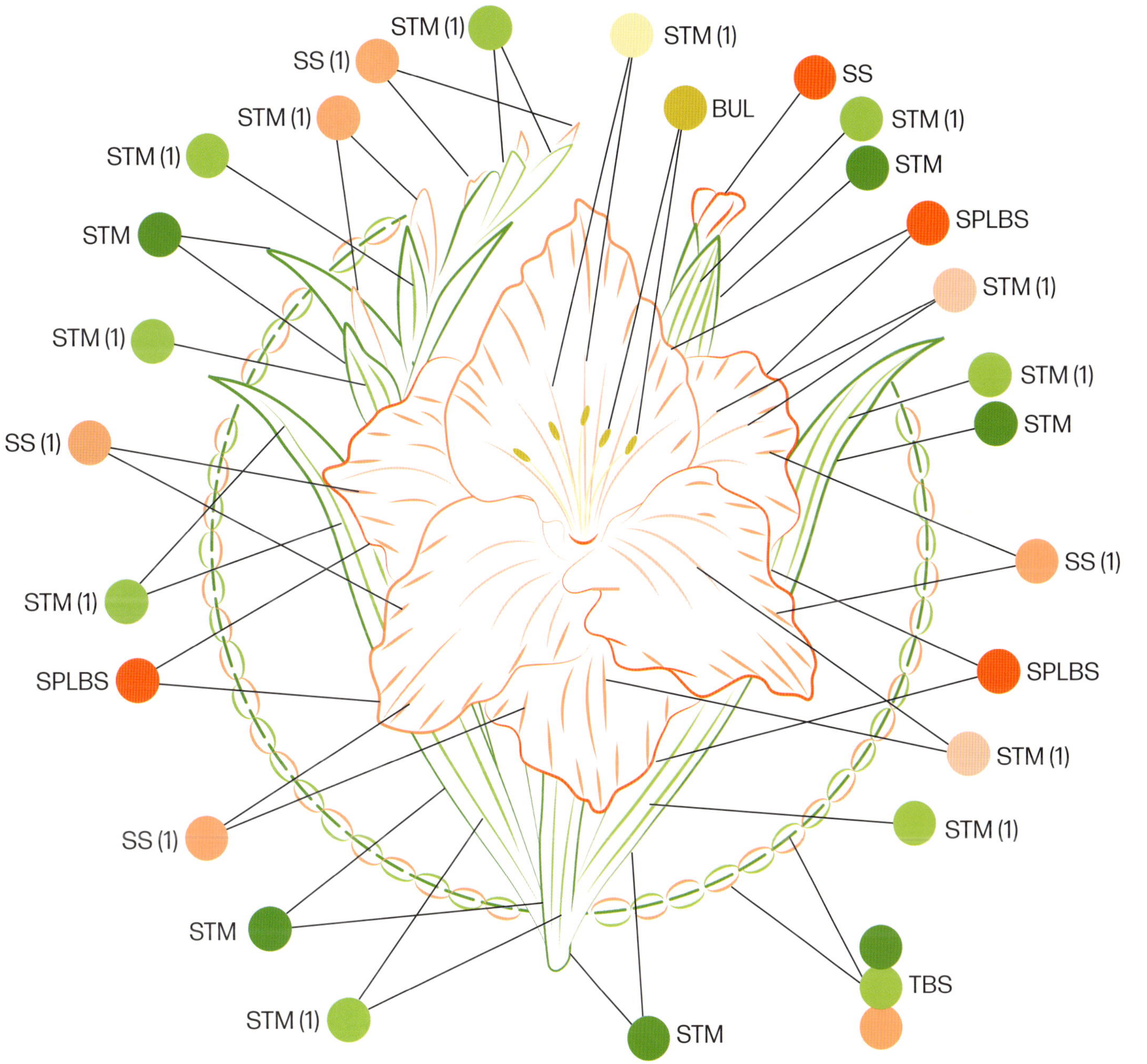

STM (1)
SS (1)
STM (1)
STM (1)
STM
STM (1)
SS (1)
STM (1)
SPLBS
SS (1)
STM
STM (1)

STM (1)
BUL
SS
STM (1)
STM
SPLBS
STM (1)
STM (1)
STM
SS (1)
SPLBS
STM (1)
STM (1)
TBS
STM

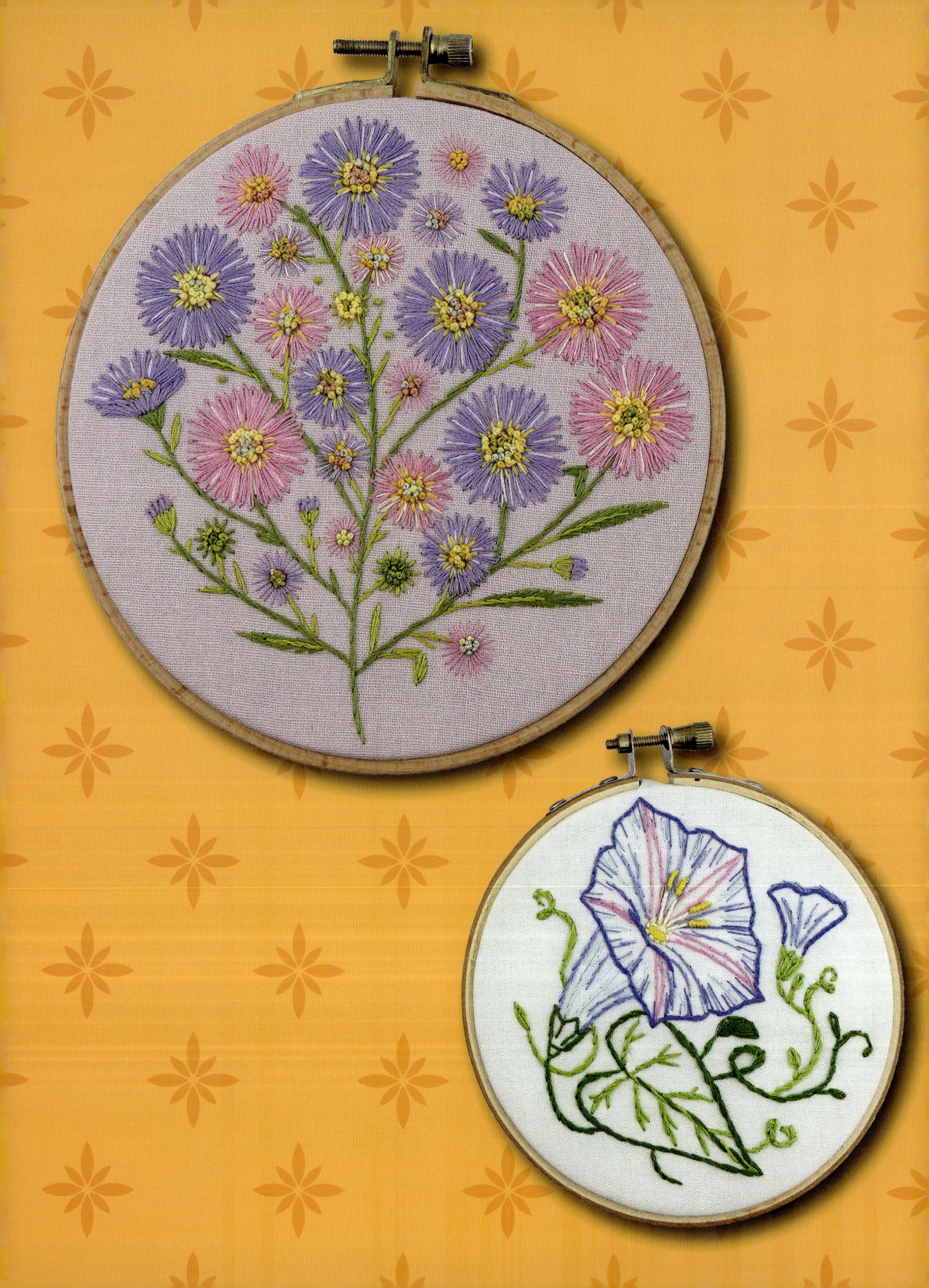

SEPTEMBER

Aster and Morning Glory

As we enter the transitional month of September, its birth flowers—aster and morning glory—bring a charming touch to the early autumn season.

Asters get their name from the Greek word for "star." Ancient Greeks thought asters came from the tears of the goddess Astraea, which explains their celestial backstory. In Victorian times, asters symbolized patience, love, and daintiness, making them a favorite flower for sweet, heartfelt messages.

Morning glories greet each day with a fresh bloom before closing by evening. This daily routine makes them representative of affection, renewal, and the idea of seizing the moment. With their delicate vines and cheerful trumpet-shaped blooms, they bring a playful and meaningful touch to floral embroidery.

Whether you stitch asters with their layered petals, morning glories with their climbing vines, or combine them, embroidering these September flowers allow their recipient to cherish this fleeting month.

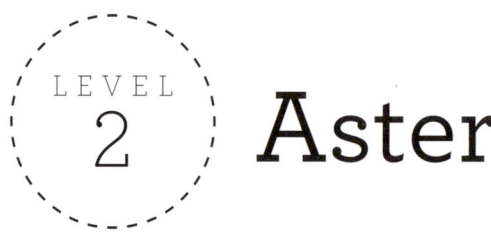

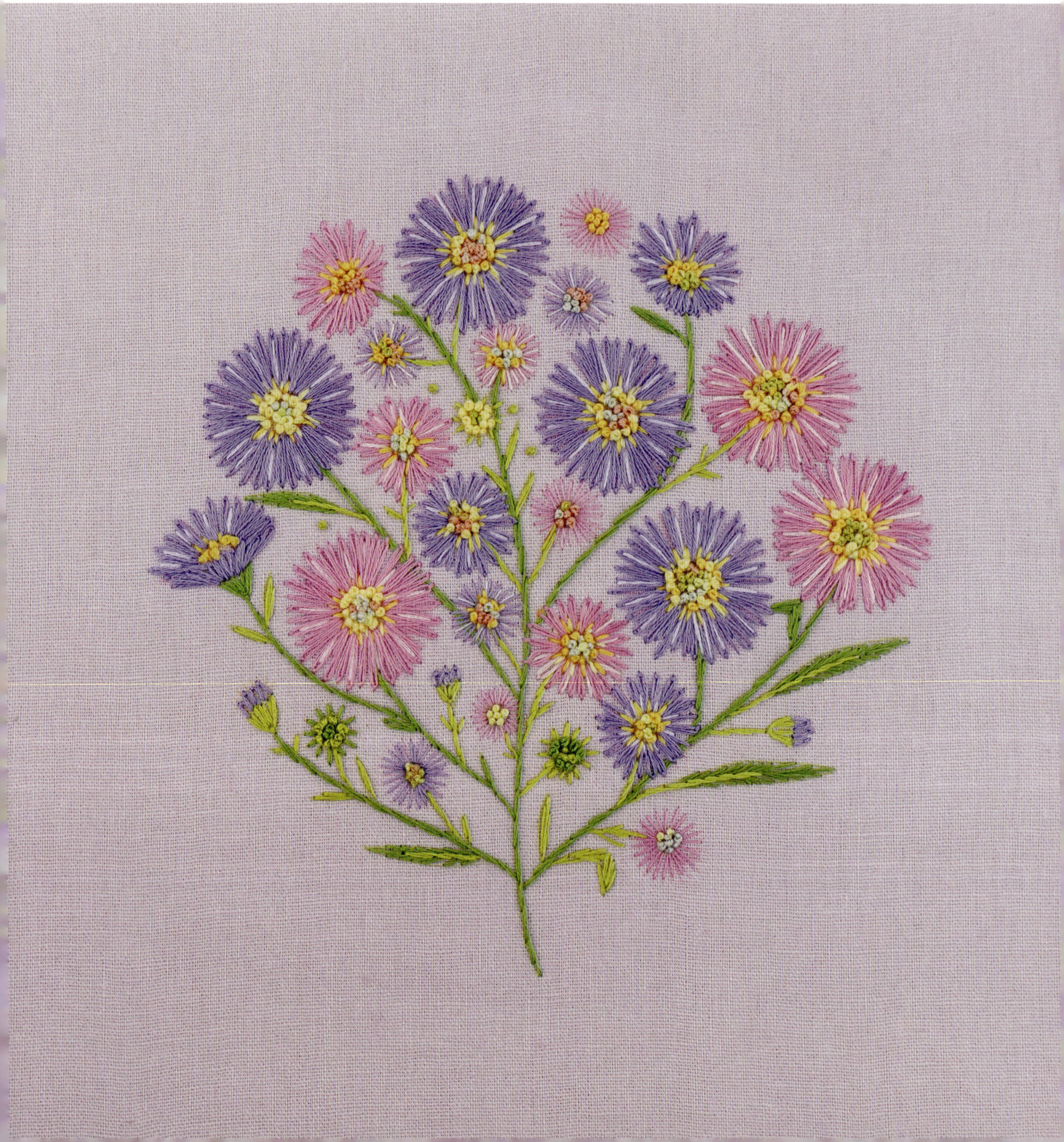

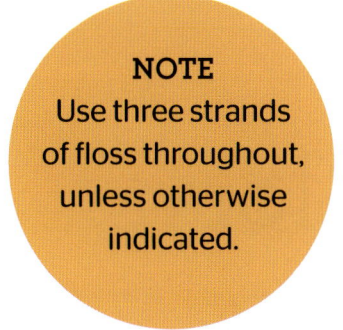

NOTE
Use three strands of floss throughout, unless otherwise indicated.

Thread Guide
DMC Thread Colors

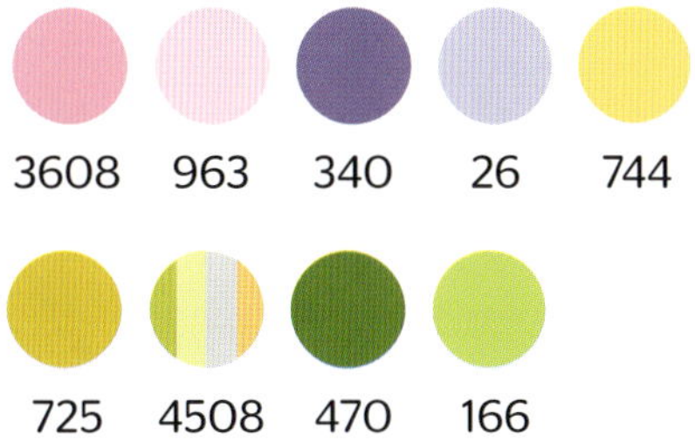

3608 963 340 26 744

725 4508 470 166

Stitches Used
Stitch Guide, pages 13-21

- Detached Chain Stitch (DCS)
- Fly Stitch (FLY)
- French Knot (FK)
- Stem Stitch (STM)
- Straight Stitch (SS)

FLOWER DETAIL 1

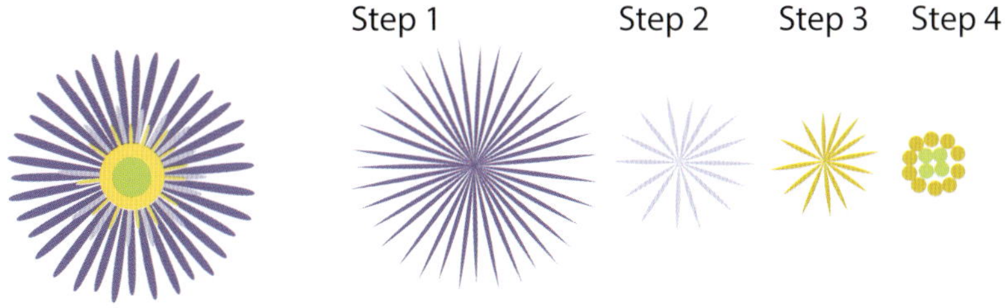

Step 1   Step 2   Step 3   Step 4

FLOWER DETAIL 2

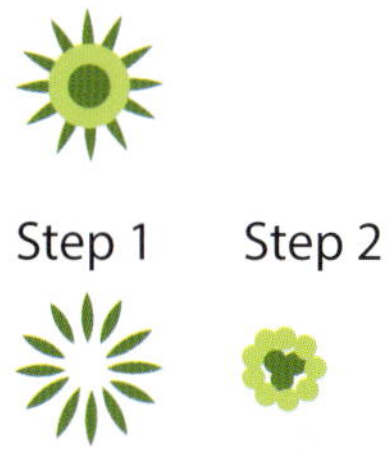

Step 1   Step 2

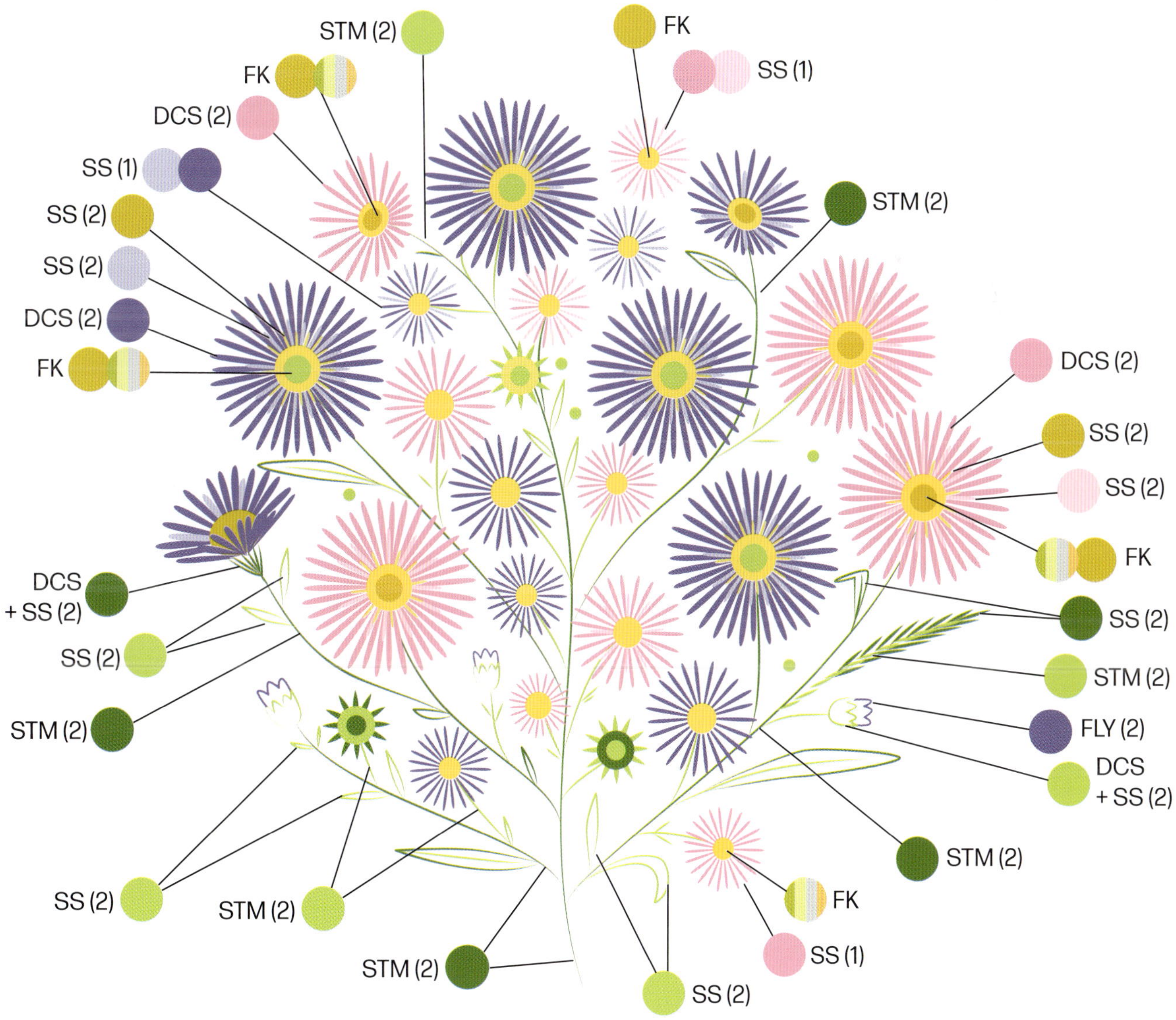

STM (2)

FK

FK

DCS (2)

SS (1)

SS (2)

SS (2)

DCS (2)

FK

STM (2)

SS (1)

STM (2)

DCS (2)

SS (2)

SS (2)

FK

DCS + SS (2)

SS (2)

SS (2)

STM (2)

STM (2)

FLY (2)

DCS + SS (2)

STM (2)

SS (2)   STM (2)

STM (2)

SS (2)

FK

SS (1)

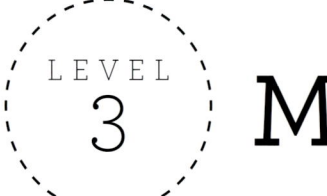

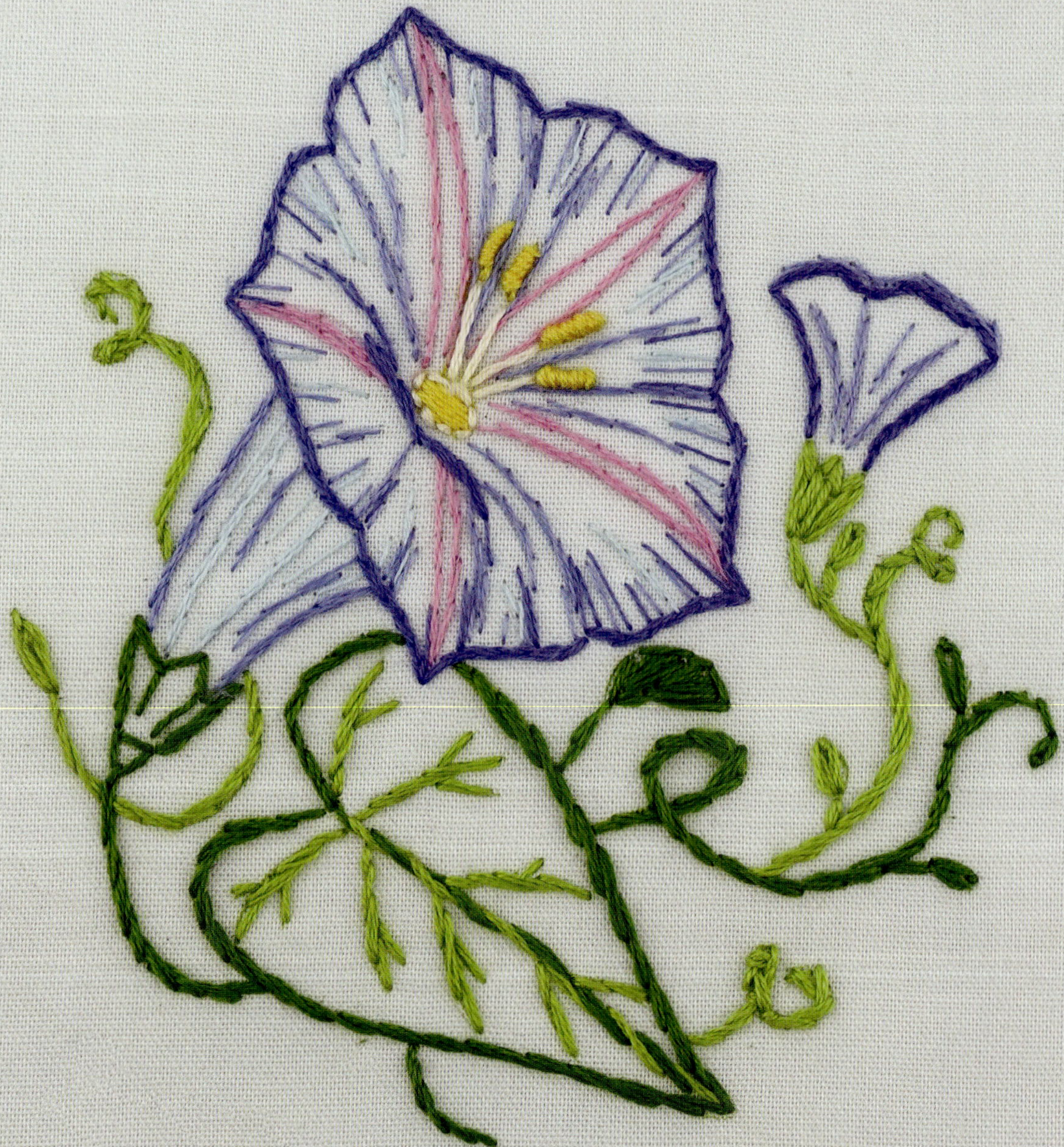

Thread Guide
DMC Thread Colors

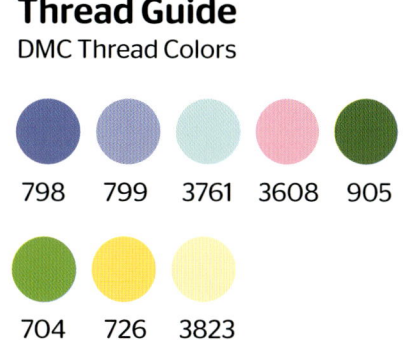

798 799 3761 3608 905

704 726 3823

Stitches Used
Stitch Guide, pages 13-21

- Backstitch (BS)
- Bullion Stitch (BUL)
- Detached Chain Stitch (DCS)
- Satin Stitch (SAT)
- Split Backstitch (SPLBS)
- Stem Stitch (STM)
- Straight Stitch (SS)

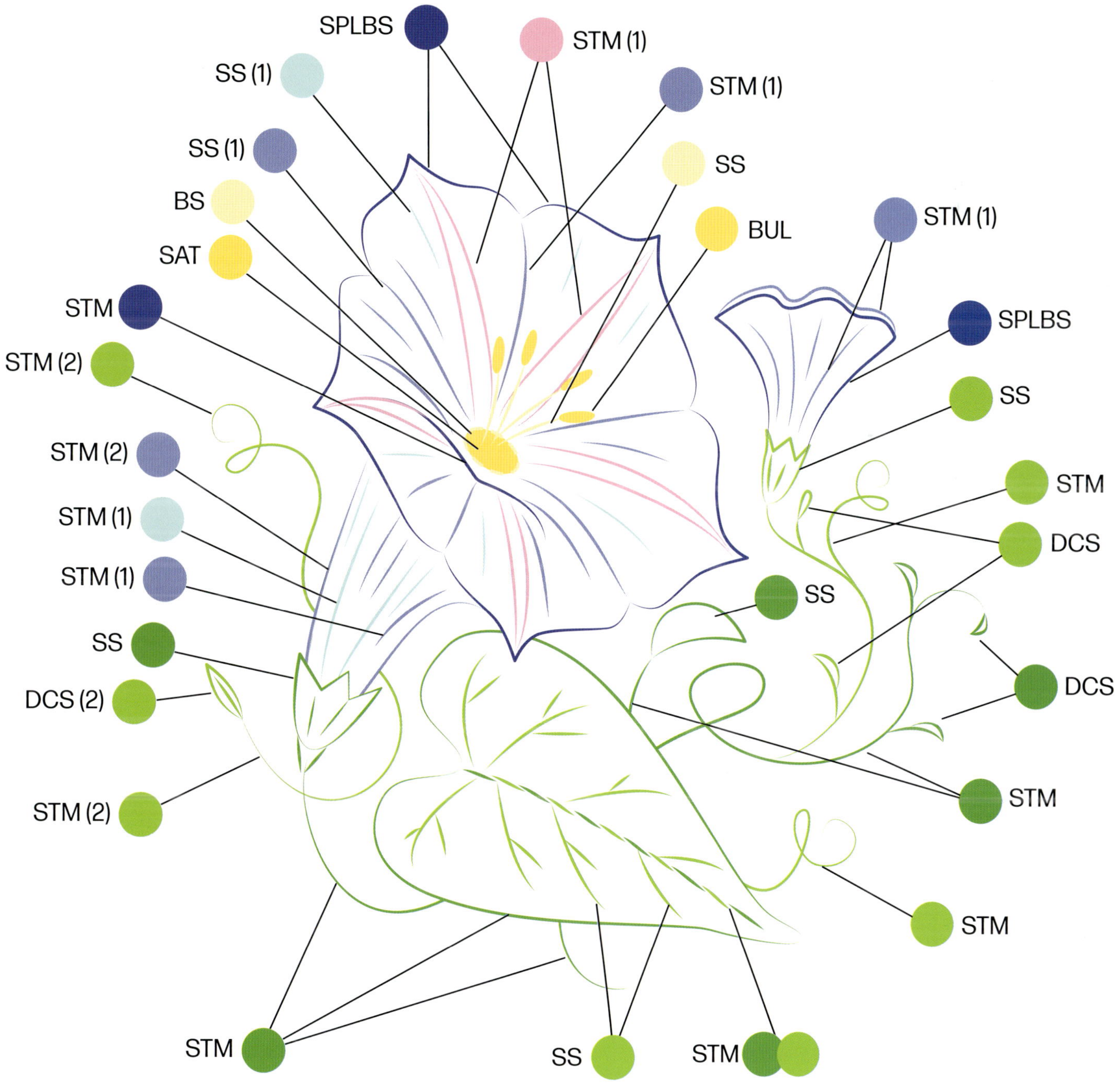

SPLBS
SS (1)
STM (1)
STM (1)
SS (1)
SS
BS
BUL
STM (1)
SAT
SPLBS
STM
SS
STM (2)
STM
STM (2)
DCS
STM (1)
STM (1)
SS
SS
DCS
DCS (2)
STM
STM (2)
STM
STM
SS
STM

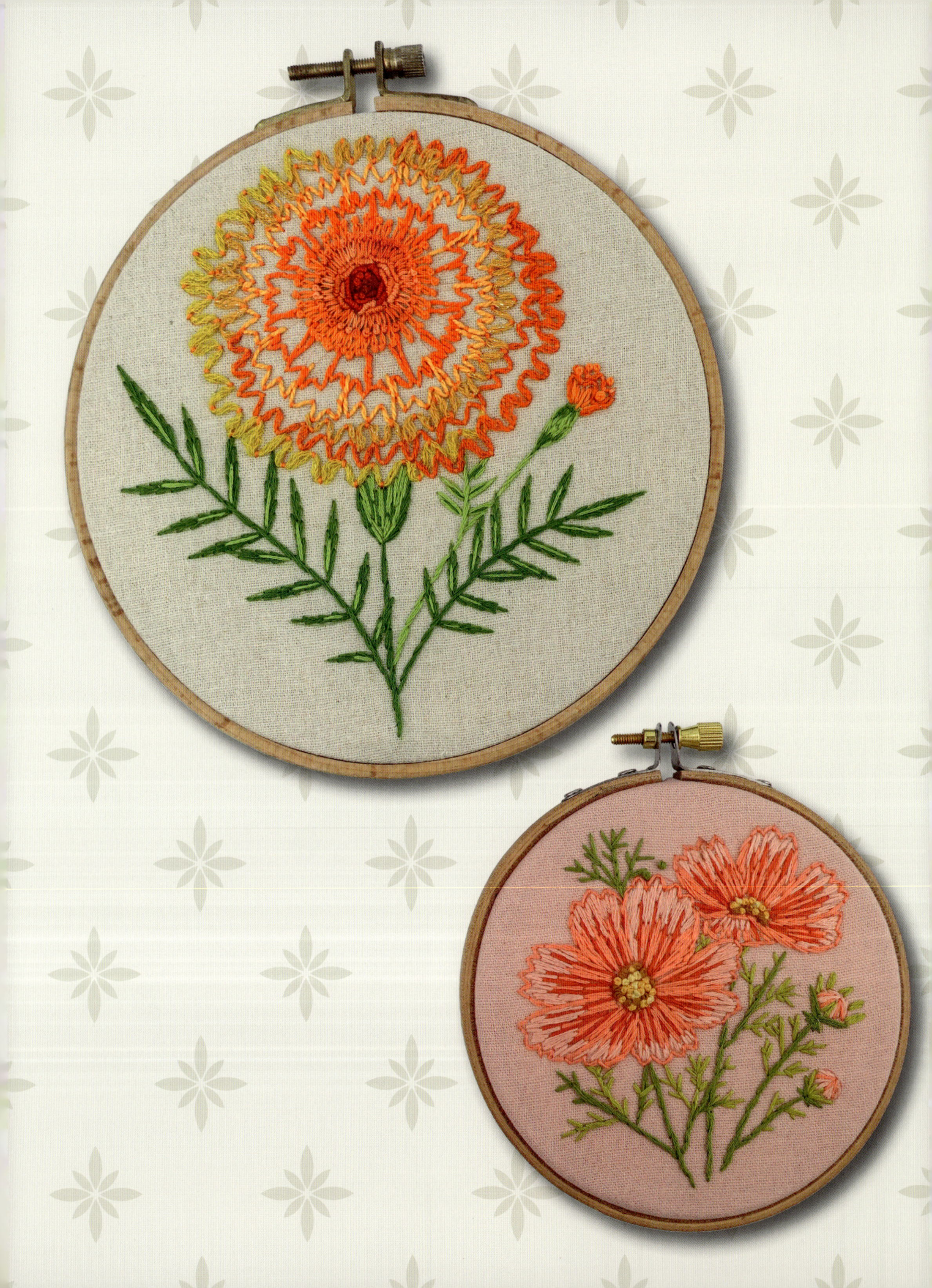

OCTOBER

Marigold and Cosmos

Marigolds and cosmos are hearty blooms and last from the scorching days of summer until the first frosty winter morning.

Marigolds represent warmth, creativity, and positive energy. Their bright colors include orange, yellow, and rust, and symbolize power, strength, and the sun's journey across the sky. In ancient Aztec culture, where they were originally discovered, they were considered a sacred flower because of their use in religious ceremonies and medicinal properties. In *The Language and Poetry of Flowers*, marigolds represent grief and sadness, and were often given during times of mourning to express unity and sorrow. Their bright colors were meant to help ease the pain and grief.

Cosmos come from the same family as sunflowers, asters, and daisies. Their name is derived from Greek word *kosmos*, meaning "order" or "arrangement." In ancient Greece, the cosmos referred to the heavens, the earth, and the underworld, as well as the relationship and balance between mortal humans, gods, and other celestial beings. Cosmos flowers likewise have symmetrical, orderly blossoms. In alignment with that ancient Greek concept, cosmos flowers stand for harmony, peace, love, and beauty.

Gather your favorite sunshine shades of embroidery floss and stitch flowers for October birthdays that celebrate this abundant season!

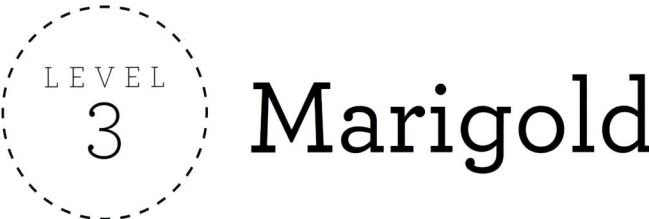

LEVEL 3 Marigold

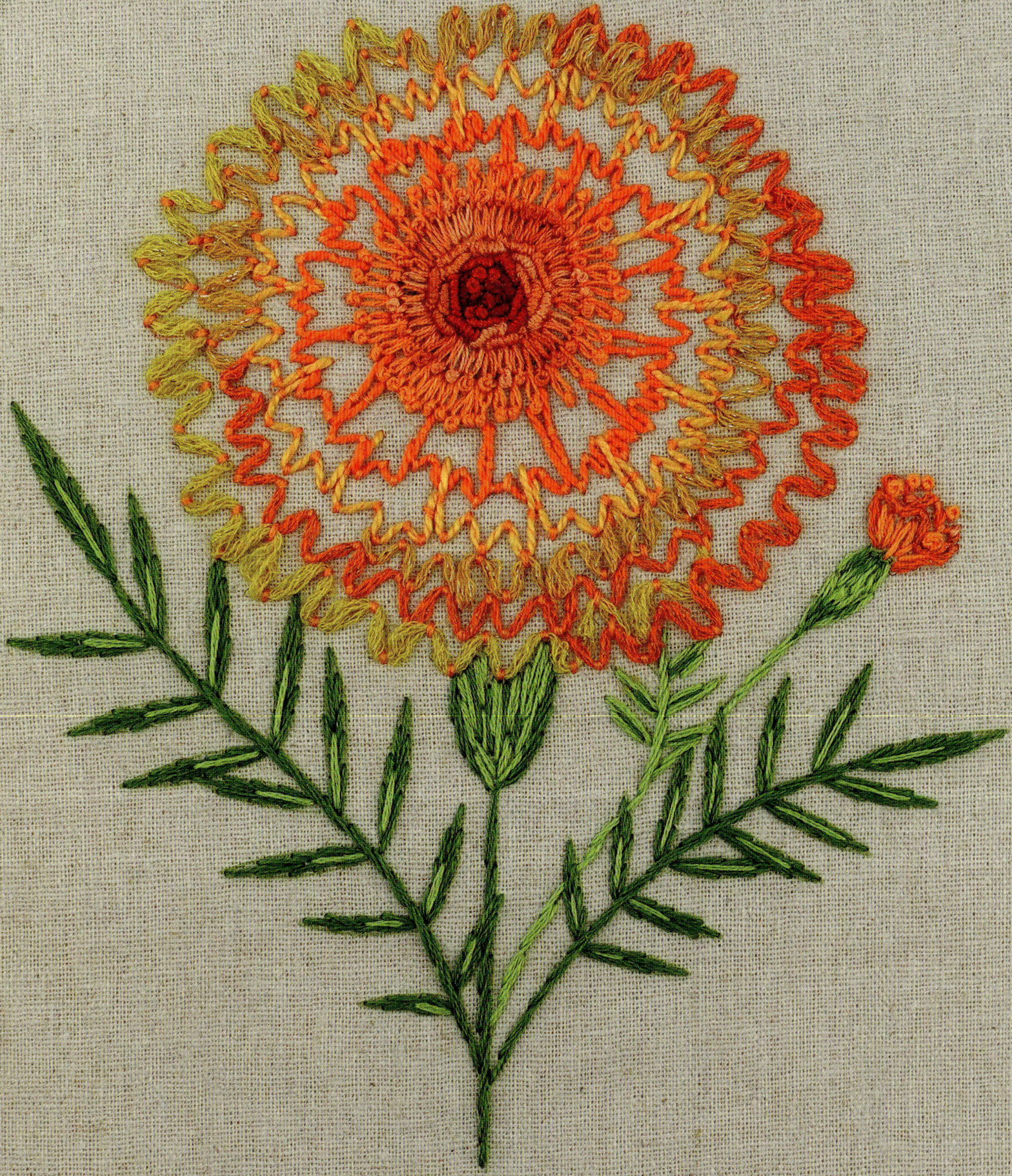

NOTE
Use three strands of floss throughout, unless otherwise indicated.

Thread Guide
DMC Thread Colors

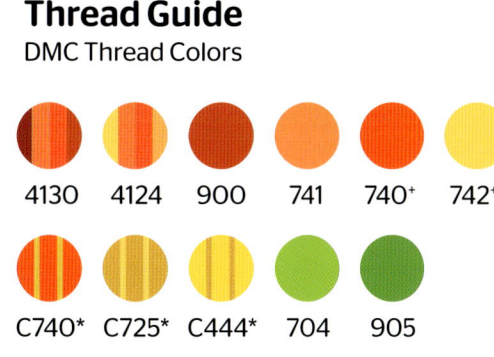

| 4130 | 4124 | 900 | 741 | 740+ | 742+ |

| C740* | C725* | C444* | 704 | 905 |

+ Perle cotton   * DMC Étoile

Stitches Used
Stitch Guide, pages 13–21

- Bullion Stitch (BUL)
- Couching Stitch (CH)
- Detached Chain Stitch (DCS)
- French Knot (FK)
- Stem Stitch (STM)
- Straight Stitch (SS)

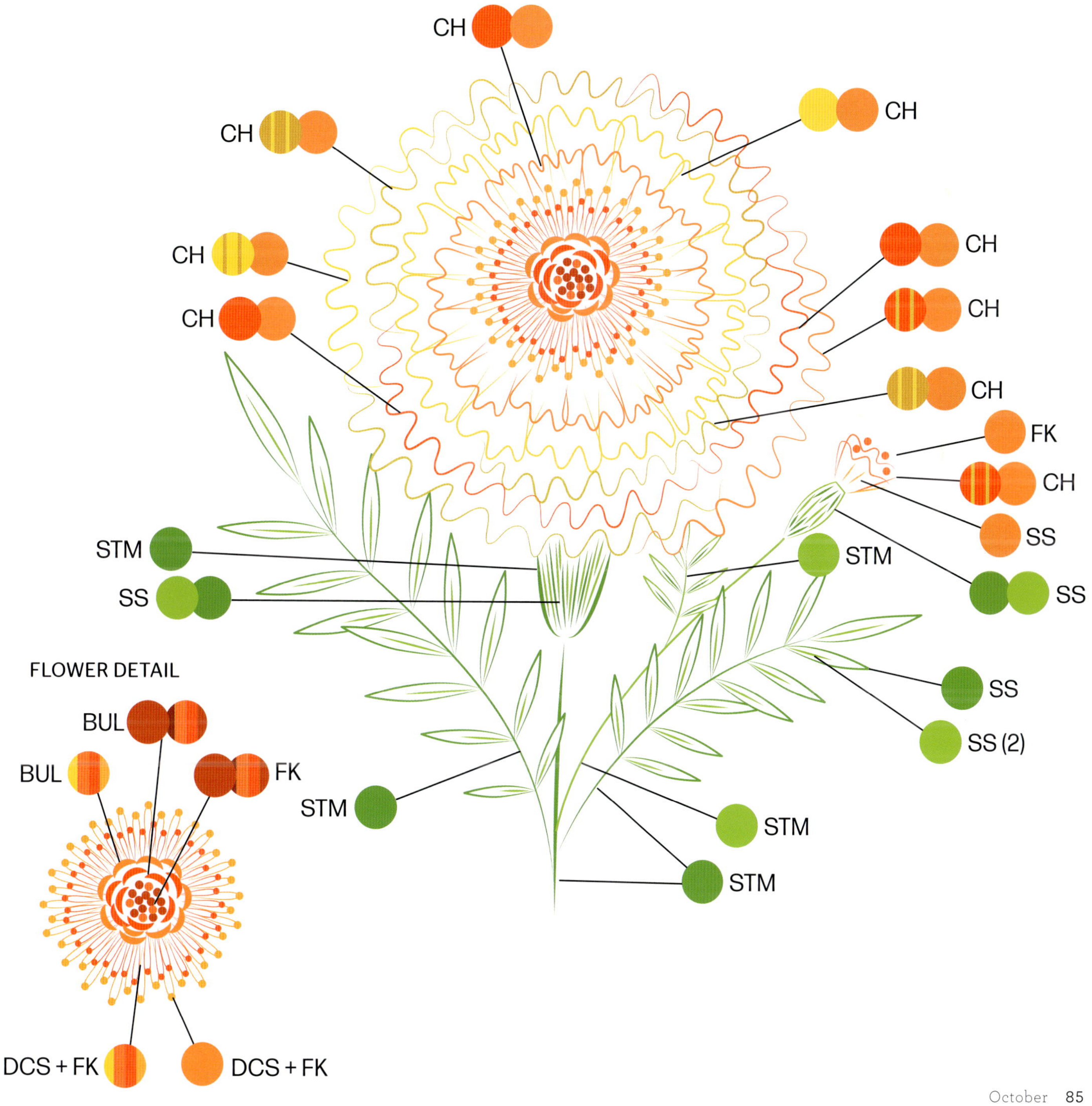

CH

CH

CH

CH

CH

CH

CH

CH

CH

FK

CH

SS

STM

STM

SS

SS

SS

SS (2)

STM

STM

STM

STM

FLOWER DETAIL

BUL

BUL

FK

DCS + FK

DCS + FK

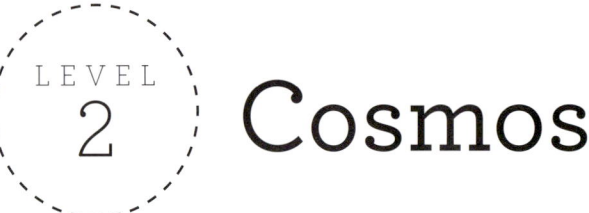

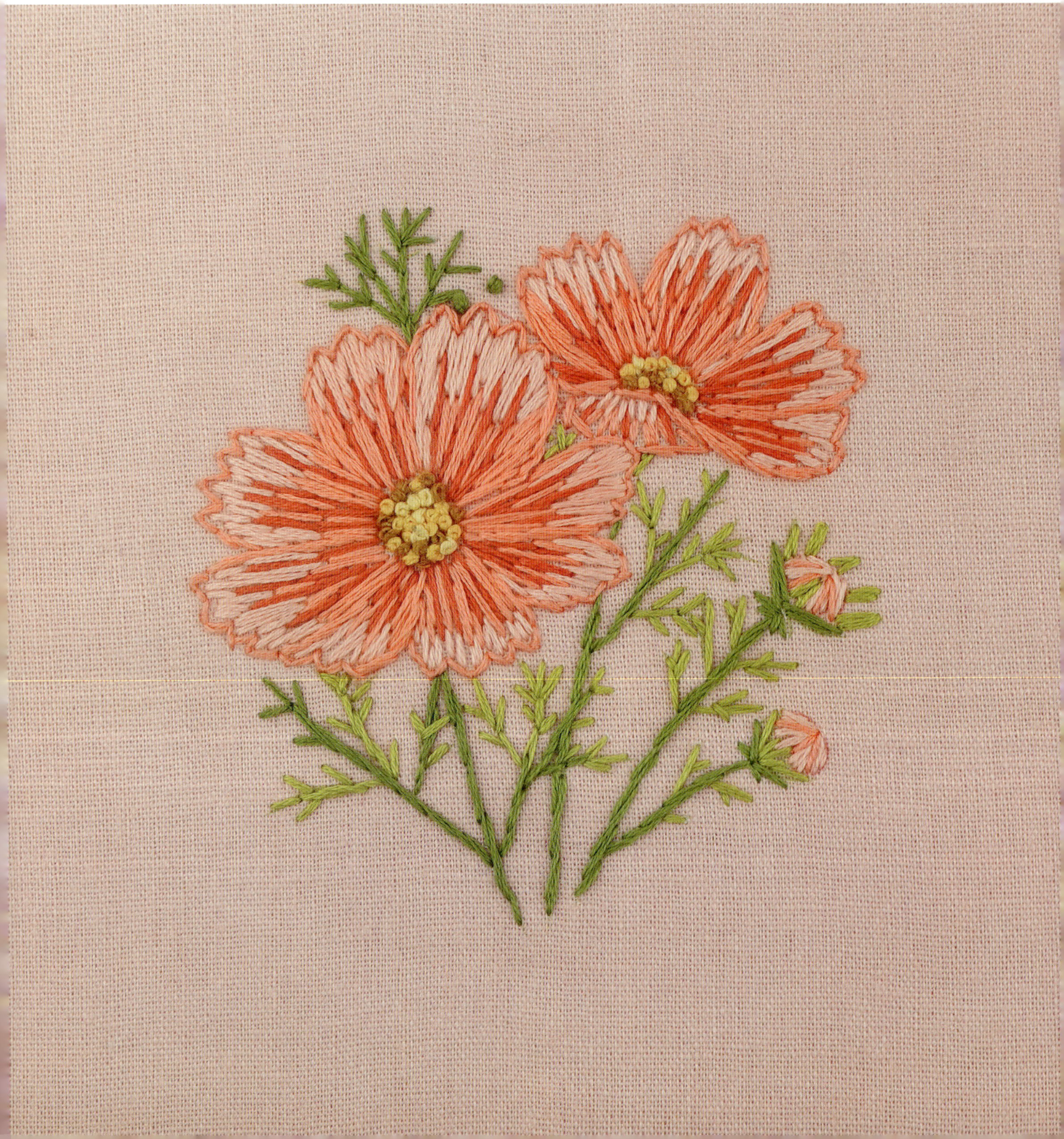

NOTE
Use three
strands of floss
throughout.

Thread Guide
DMC Thread Colors

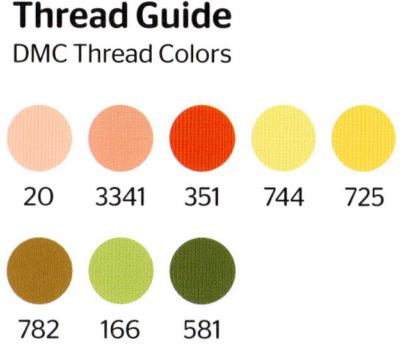

20 3341 351 744 725

782 166 581

Stitches Used
Stitch Guide, pages 13–21

- Fly Stitch (FLY)
- French Knot (FK)
- Shaded Satin Stitch (SHSAT)
- Split Backstitch (SPLBS)
- Stem Stitch (STM)
- Straight Stitch (SS)

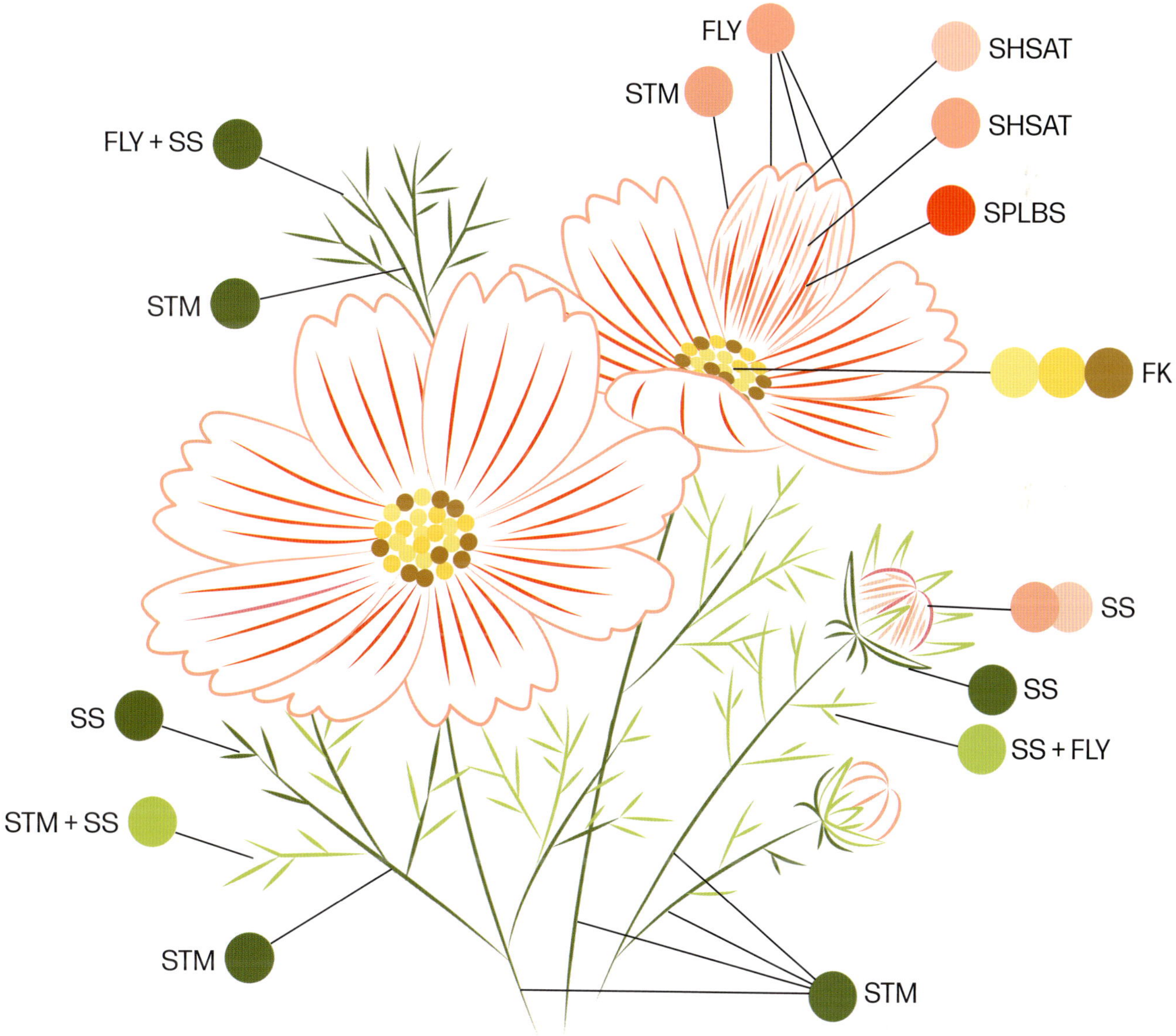

FLY

STM

SHSAT

SHSAT

SPLBS

FLY + SS

STM

FK

SS

SS

SS + FLY

SS

STM + SS

STM

STM

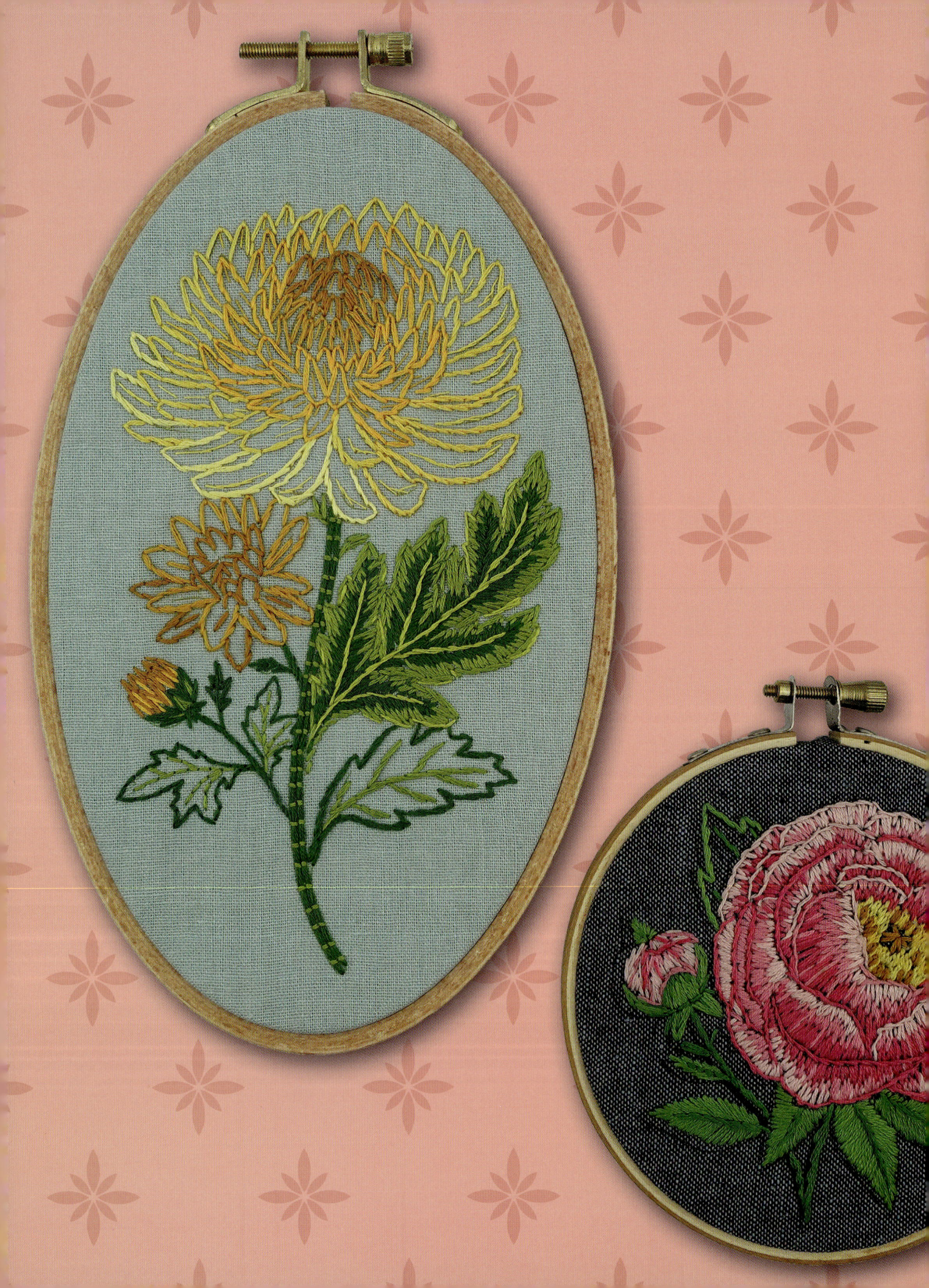

NOVEMBER

Chrysanthemum and Peony

As the calendar turns to November, the late autumn birth flowers for this month are two big, bold blooms with robust symbolism—chrysanthemum and peony.

Chrysanthemums, or mums for short, are the stars of November. The name is derived from the Greek words *chrysos* and *anthemon*, meaning "gold flower." It is a flower that has been significant to many cultures with wide ranging connotations. From health and prosperity in China, to good fortune and longevity in Japan, and friendship and happiness in the United States, the chrysanthemum flower's symbolism is diverse.

The secondary birth flower this month is the lush and fragrant peony. Peonies have been cultivated for more than 4,000 years. The origin of its name is a conflicting story. Some attribute it to the Greek god Paeon, while others think it was named after the flirtatious nymph Paeonia who was transformed into a flower by a jealous Aphrodite. Regardless of how it got its name, its sweet scent has made it a beloved flower with rich symbolism, including wealth, prosperity, honor, and good luck.

The lucky recipient of a stitched bouquet of these meaningful autumnal blooms is sure to be grateful for one of these heartfelt creations.

LEVEL 3

Chrysanthemum

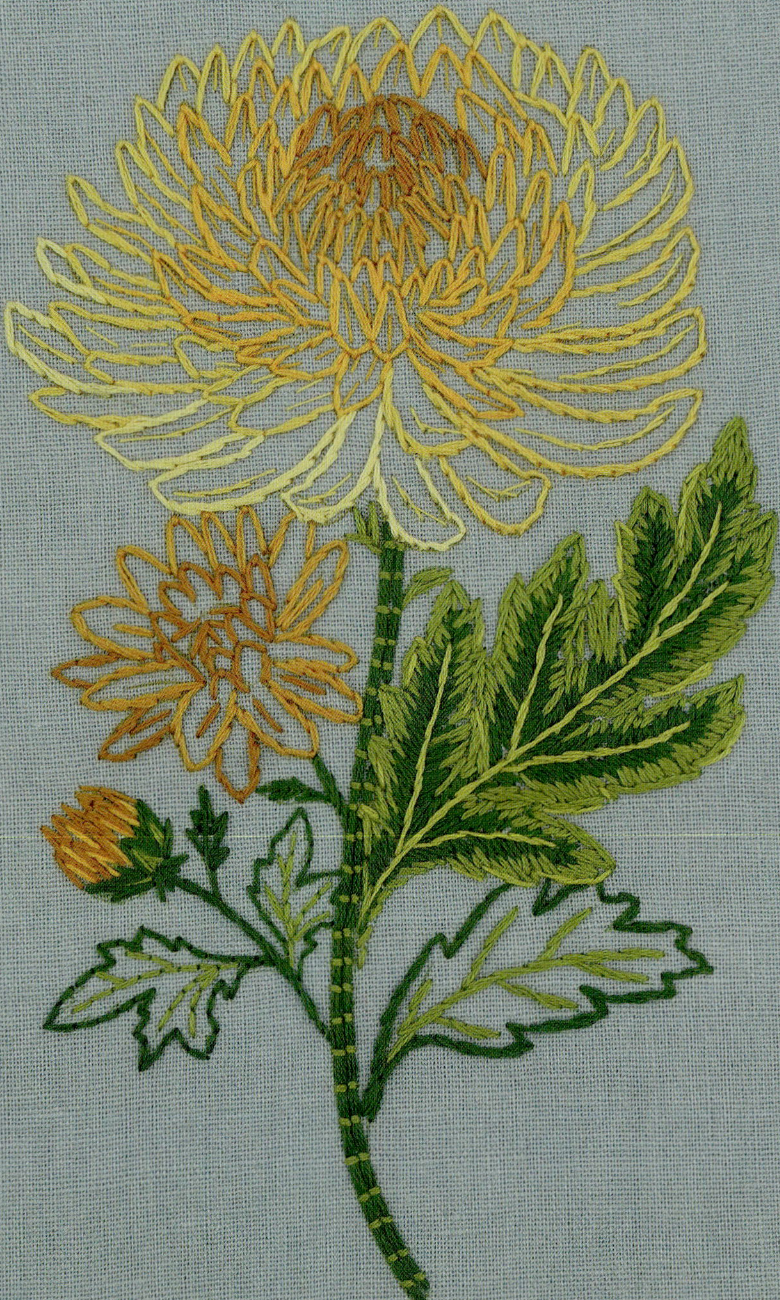

Thread Guide
DMC Thread Colors

986 581 166 782 3820

972 725 744

Stitches Used
Stitch Guide, pages 13–21

- Backstitch (BS)
- Couching Stitch (CH)
- Fly Stitch (FLY)
- Long and Short Stitch (L+S)
- Satin Stitch (SAT)
- Stem Stitch (STM)
- Straight Stitch (SS)

LEAF DETAIL

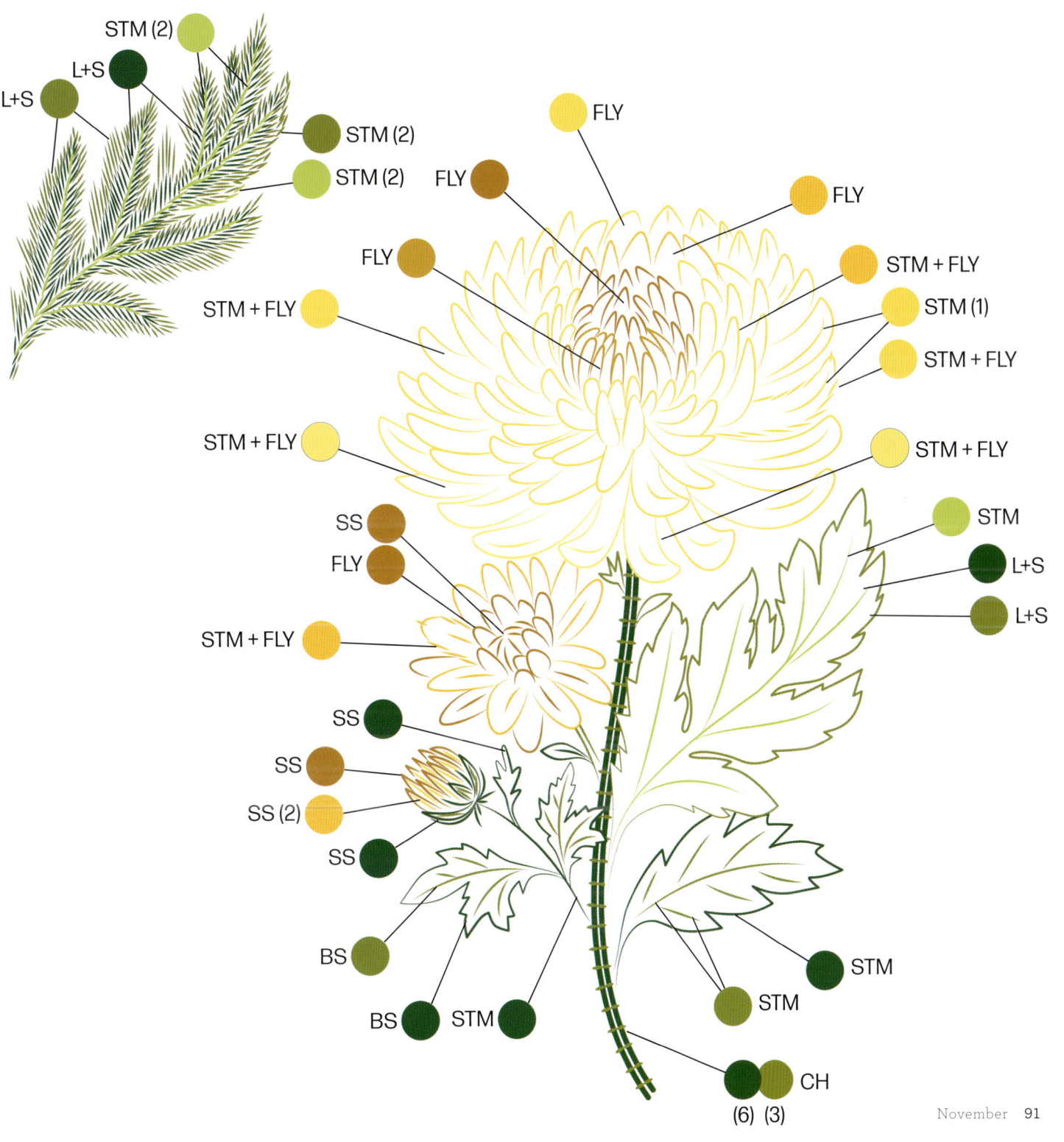

STM (2)
L+S
L+S
STM (2)
STM (2)
FLY
FLY
FLY
STM + FLY
FLY
STM (1)
STM + FLY
STM + FLY
STM + FLY
STM + FLY
STM
L+S
L+S
SS
FLY
STM + FLY
SS
SS
SS (2)
SS
BS
BS   STM
STM
STM
CH
(6) (3)

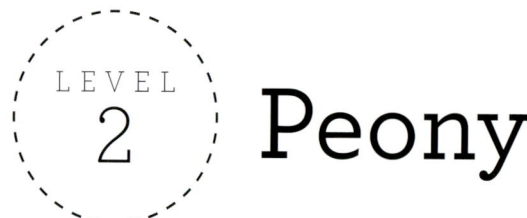

LEVEL 2 Peony

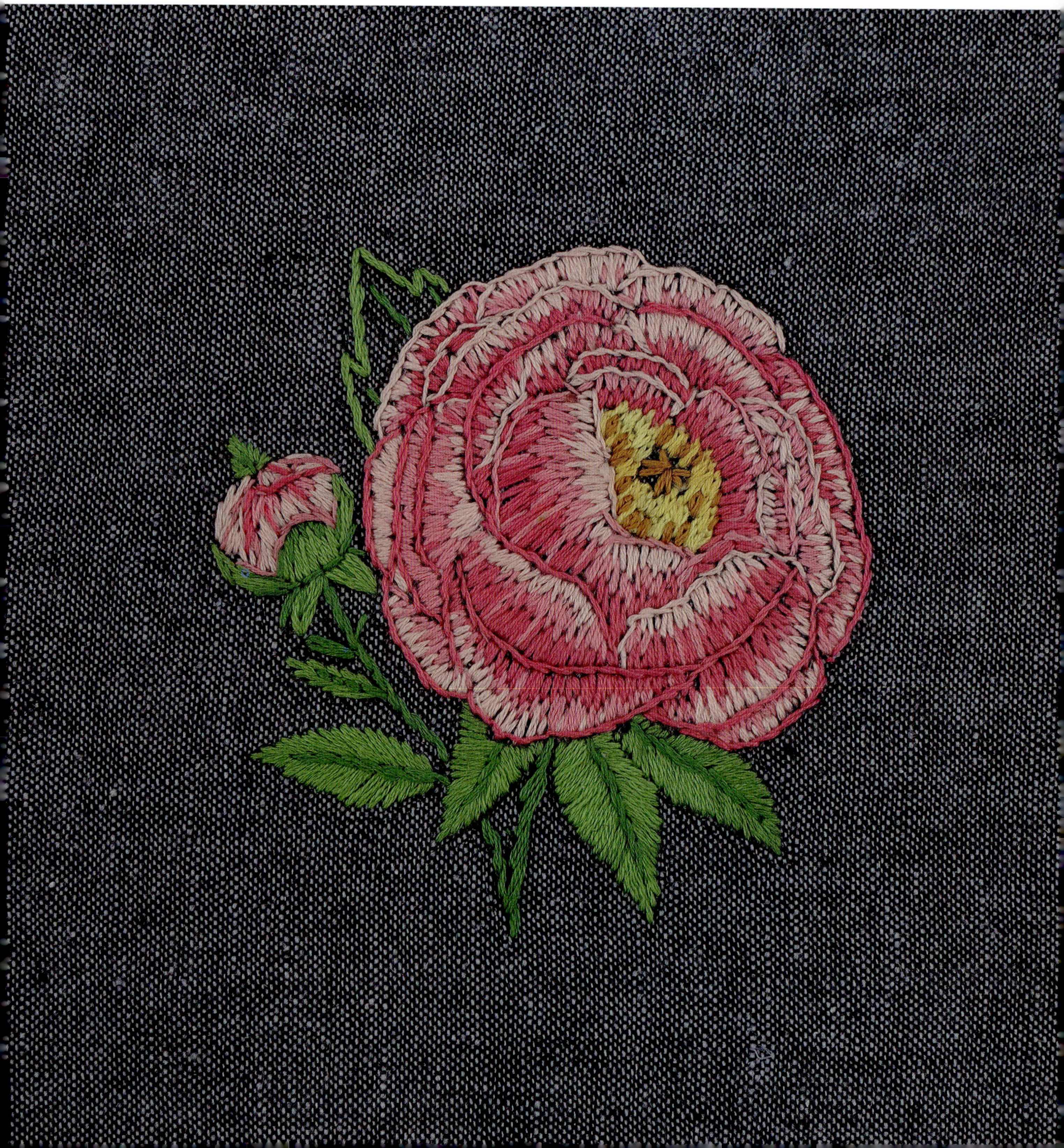

Thread Guide
DMC Thread Colors

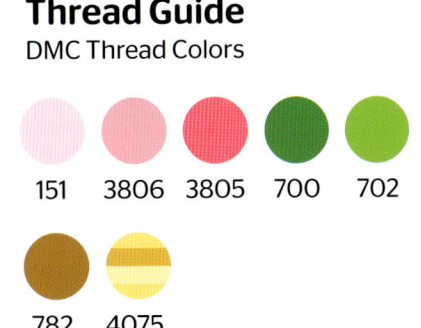

151 3806 3805 700 702

782 4075

Stitches Used
Stitch Guide, pages 13–21

- Backstitch (BS)
- Detached Chain Stitch (DCS)
- Leaf Stitch (LF)
- Long and Short Stitch (L+S)
- Satin Stitch (SAT)
- Stem Stitch (STM)
- Straight Stitch (SS)

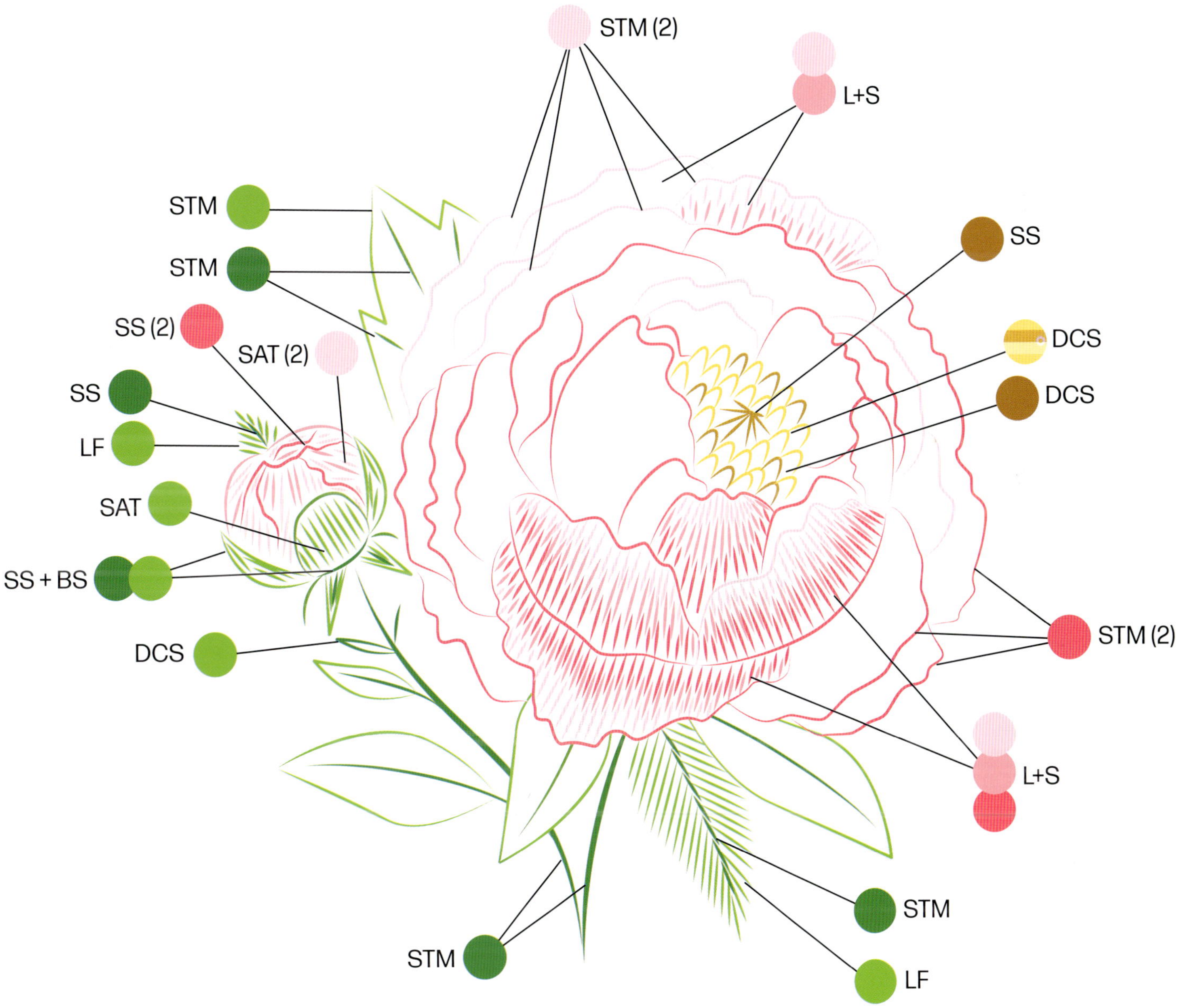

STM (2)

L+S

STM

STM

SS

SS (2)

SAT (2)

DCS

DCS

SS

LF

SAT

STM (2)

SS + BS

DCS

L+S

STM

STM

LF

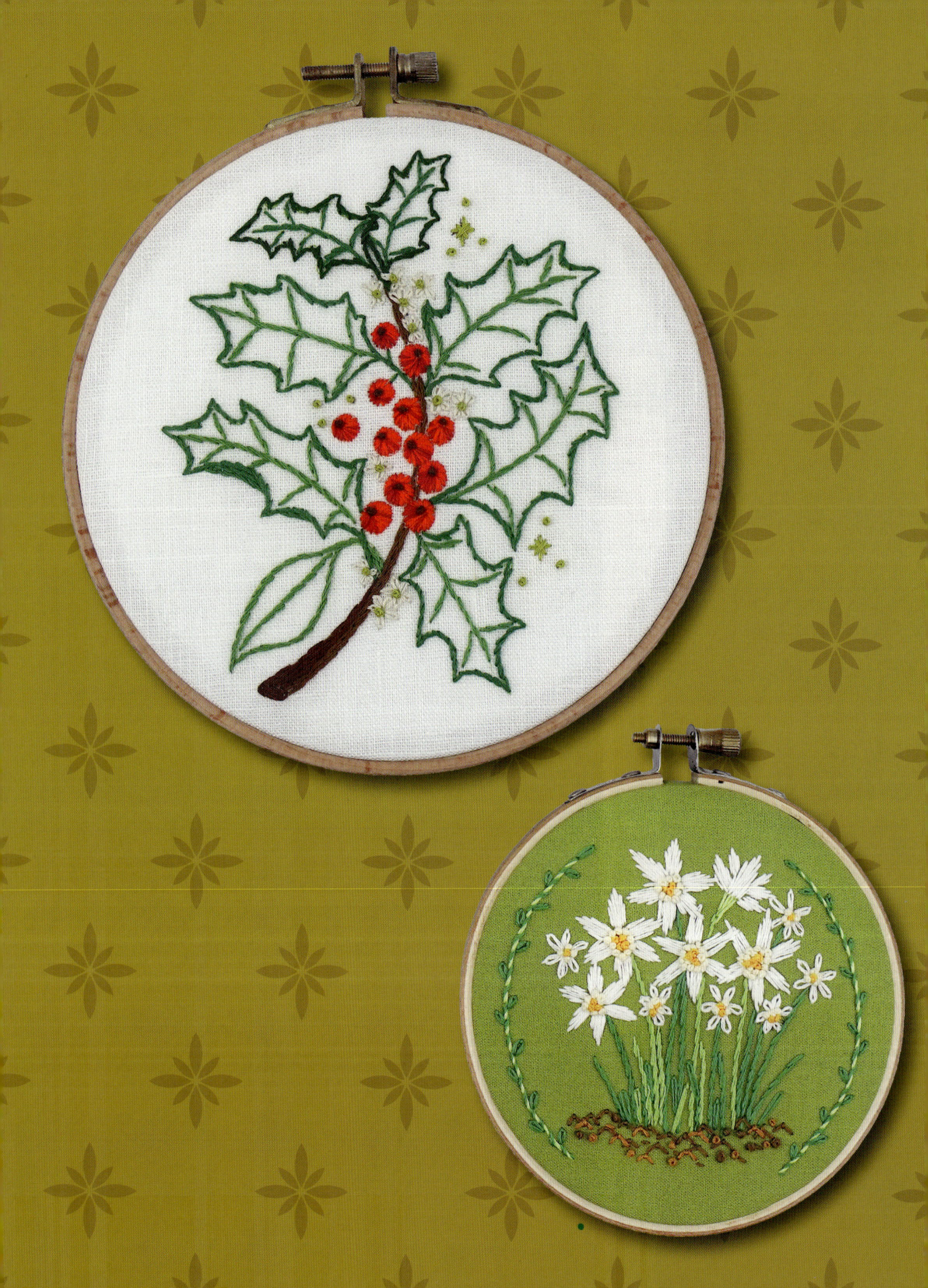

DECEMBER

Holly and Narcissus

The final month of the calendar closes with two quintessential holiday flowers—holly and narcissus.

Holly is native to North America and their leaves and berries are an important source of winter food and shelter for birds and wildlife. The myths and legends that surround its glossy green leaves and bright red berries tell how holly has come to symbolize protection and an ability to provide shelter. In Christian traditions, it's said that holly's thorny leaves hid and protected the baby Jesus from the cruel King Herod and his men. Pagan legends say that holly is refuge for sprites and fairies and can be used to ward off evil.

The variety of narcissus known as paperwhites, are in the same family as daffodils. Able to survive and even thrive year-round indoors, the paperwhite narcissus is December's secondary birth flower. Some believe these dainty white flowers got their name from the Greek word *narke*, which means "numbness," and could refer to how the entire plant is toxic to humans and animals. Other lore suggests that narcissus gets its name from Greek mythology and the young man Narcissus who fell in love with his own reflection. *The Illustrated Language of Flowers* (1858) includes a stanza about the narcissus flower from English romantic poet Percy Bysshe Shelley's "The Sensitive Plant" and led to the Victorian-era belief in the flower as a symbol of egotism. Today, they've evolved to symbolize unconditional love, good wishes, and faithfulness.

Not only are these embroidered flowers the perfect gift for December birthdays, but they'd make a wonderful present for anyone who relishes the holiday season.

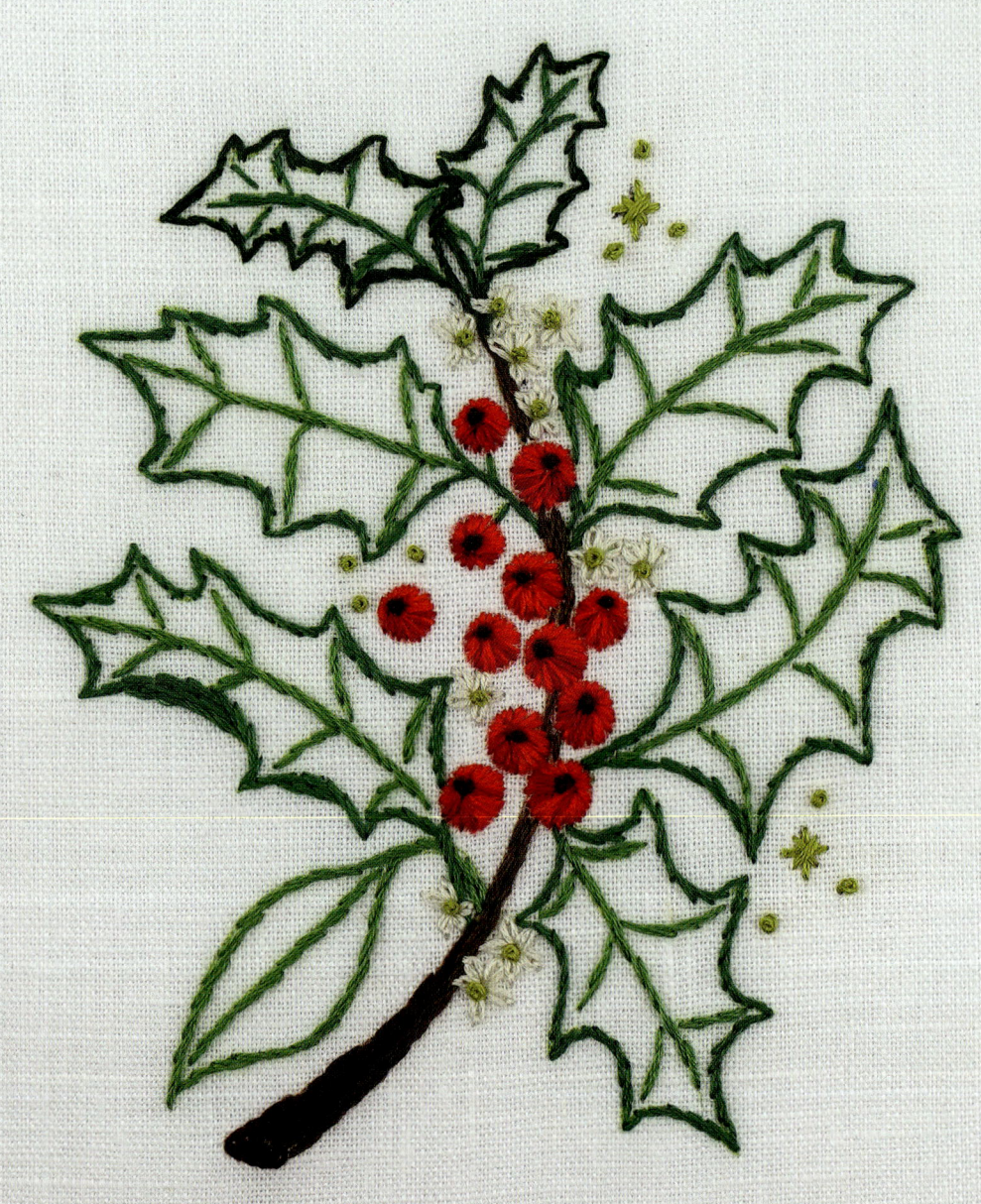

NOTE
Use three strands of floss throughout.

Thread Guide
DMC Thread Colors

986	700	702	166	606
321	869	801	Ecru	

Stitches Used
Stitch Guide, pages 13–21

- Backstitch (BS)
- Detached Chain Stitch (DCS)
- French Knot (FK)
- Satin Stitch (SAT)
- Star Stitch (STR)
- Stem Stitch (STM)

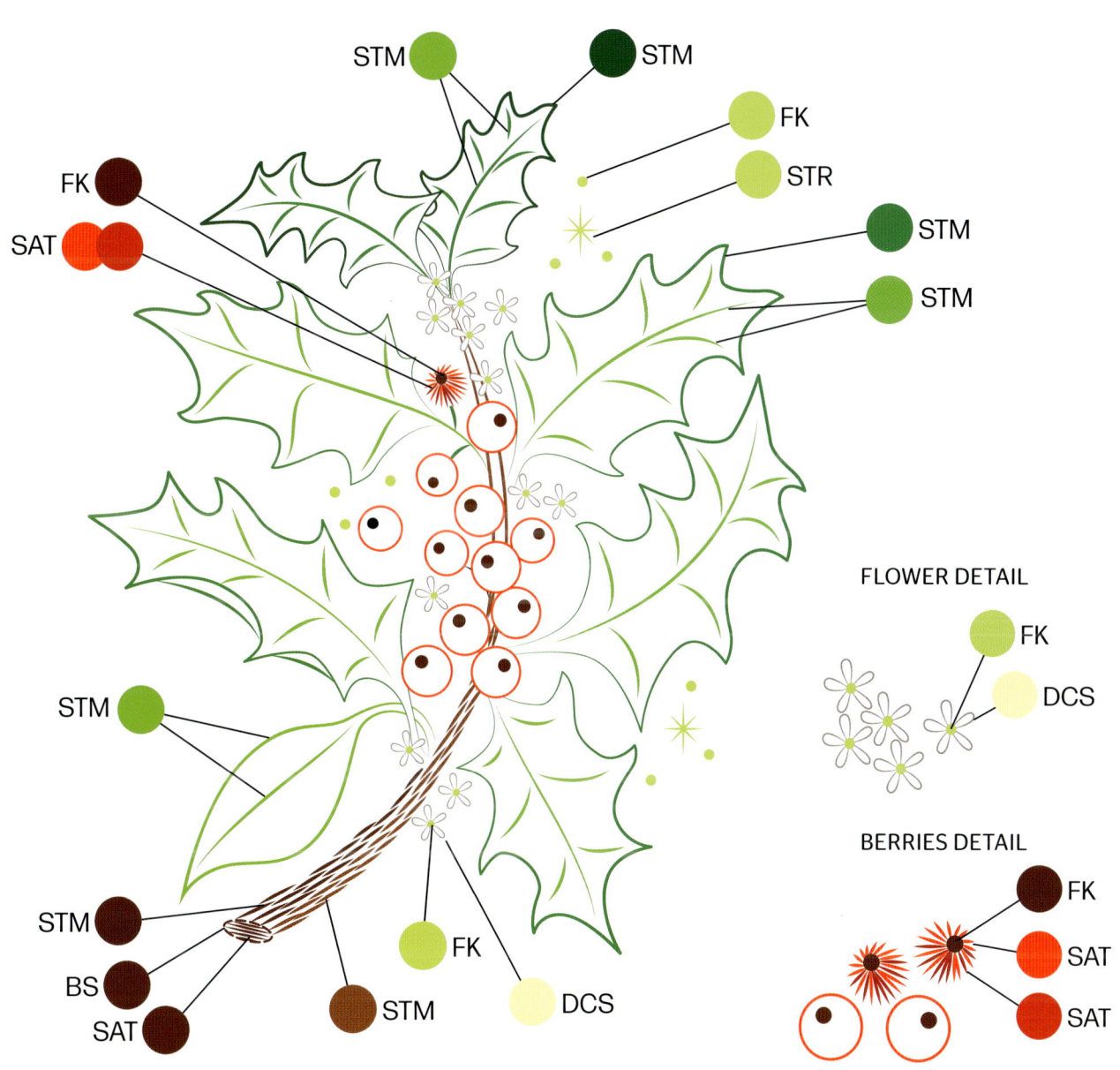

FLOWER DETAIL

FK
DCS

BERRIES DETAIL

FK
SAT
SAT

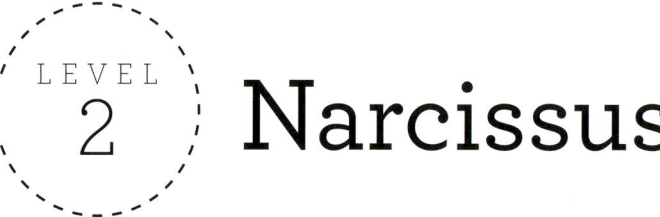

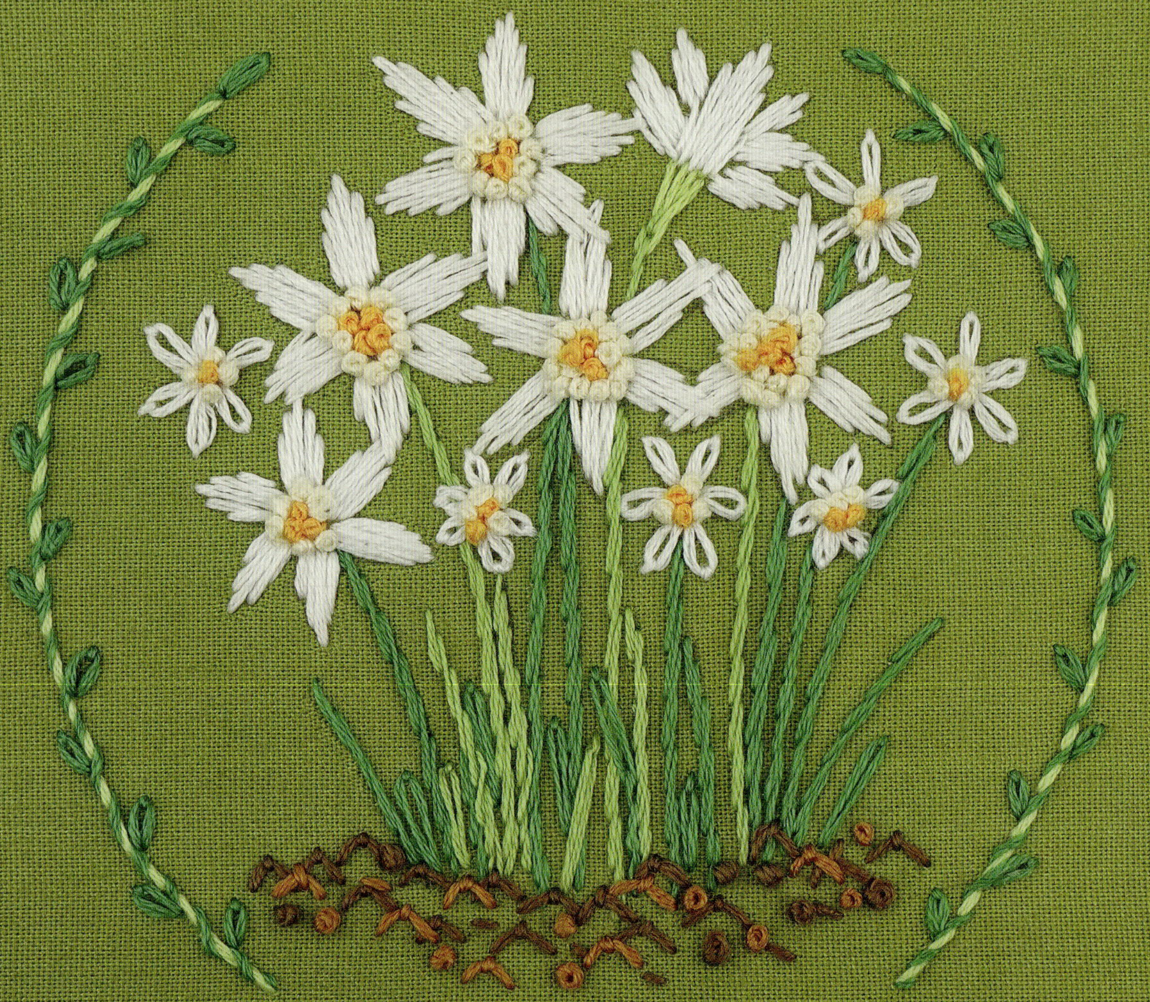

Thread Guide
DMC Thread Colors

Blanc   3823   972   782   869

16   704   701

Stitches Used
Stitch Guide, pages 13-21

- Detached Chain Stitch (DCS)
- Fly Stitch (FLY)
- French Knot (FK)
- Satin Stitch (SAT)
- Stem Stitch (STM)
- Whipped Backstitch (WBS)

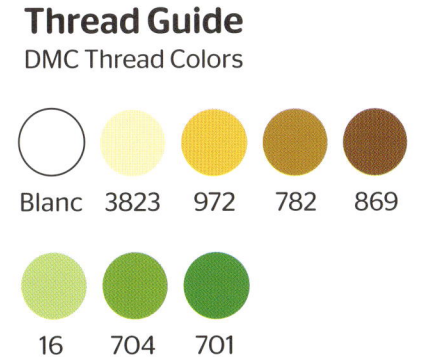

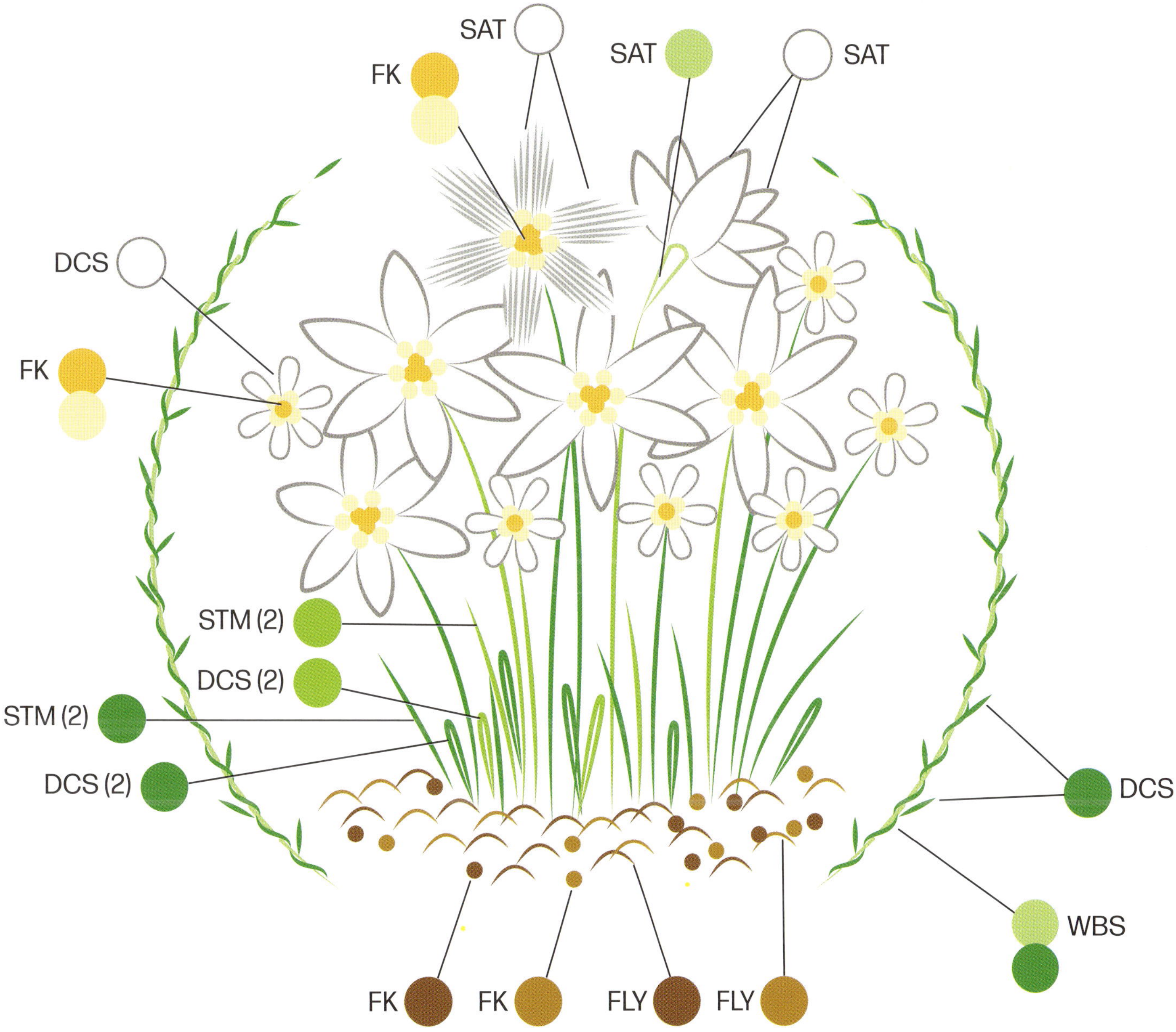

SAT   SAT   SAT

FK

DCS

FK

STM (2)

DCS (2)

STM (2)

DCS (2)

DCS

WBS

FK   FK   FLY   FLY

BONUS DESIGNS

Personalizing the embroideries in this book can be as simple as adding a few ladybugs, or a butterfly or two fluttering around the flowers. In this section, you'll find a variety of bonus motifs to enhance your designs. It doesn't take much to add an extra bit of personality!

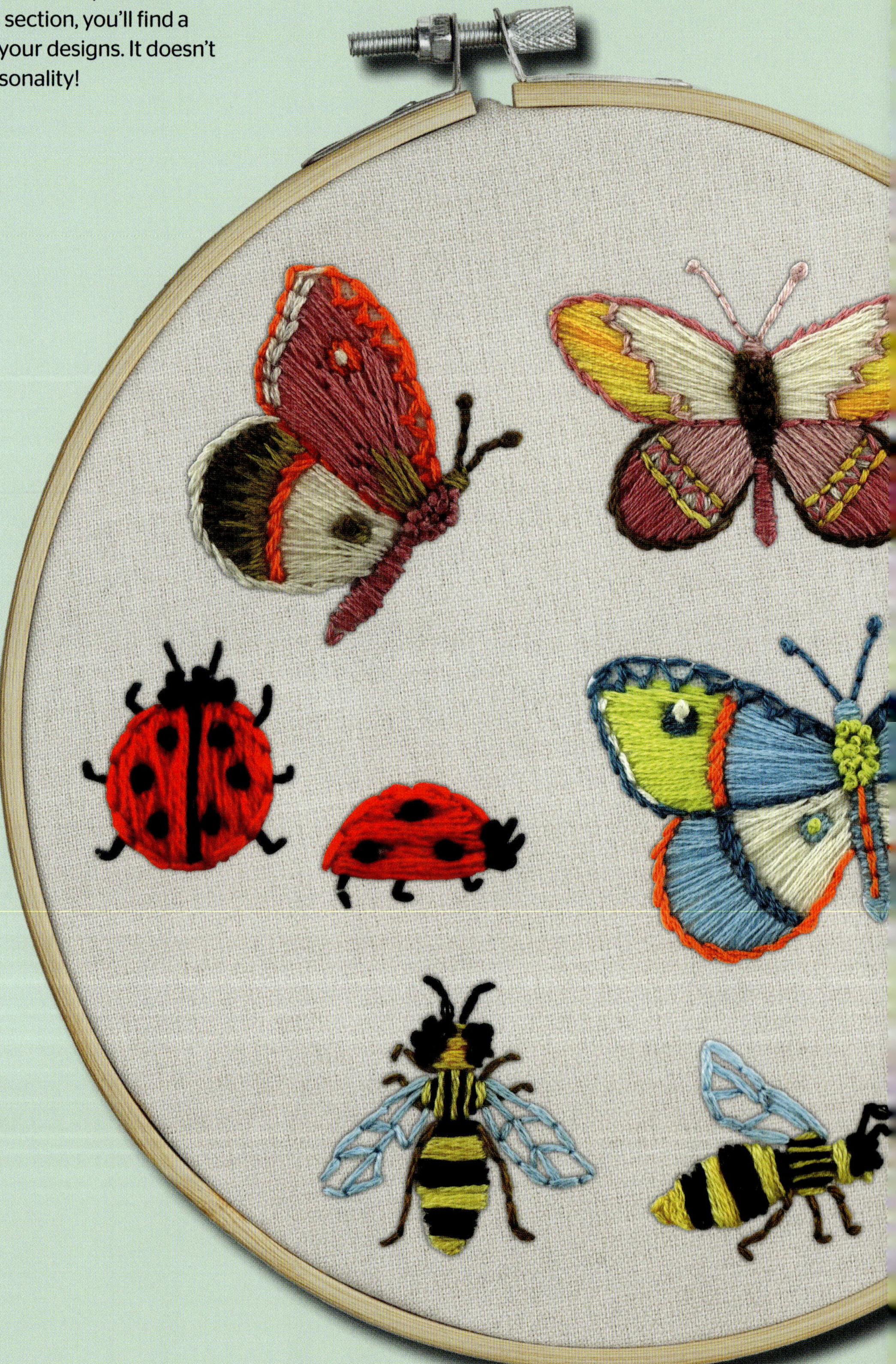

Thread Guide
DMC Thread Colors

●	666	●	310
●	721	●	869
●	4075	●	833
●	12	●	Ecru
●	955	●	3809
●	703	●	3766
●	904	●	778
		●	3688

Stitches Used

See the Stitch Guide on pages 13–21 for step-by-step instructions to these and other stitches.

- Backstitch (BS)
- Detached Chain Stitch (DCS)
- French Knot (FK)
- Long and Short Stitch (L+S)
- Satin Stitch (SAT)
- Split Backstitch (SPLBS)
- Stem Stitch (STM)
- Straight Stitch (SS)

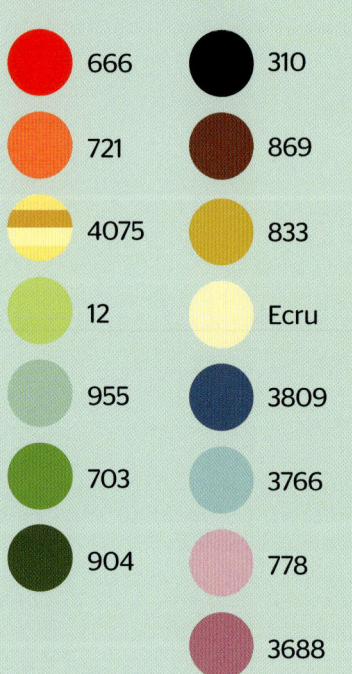

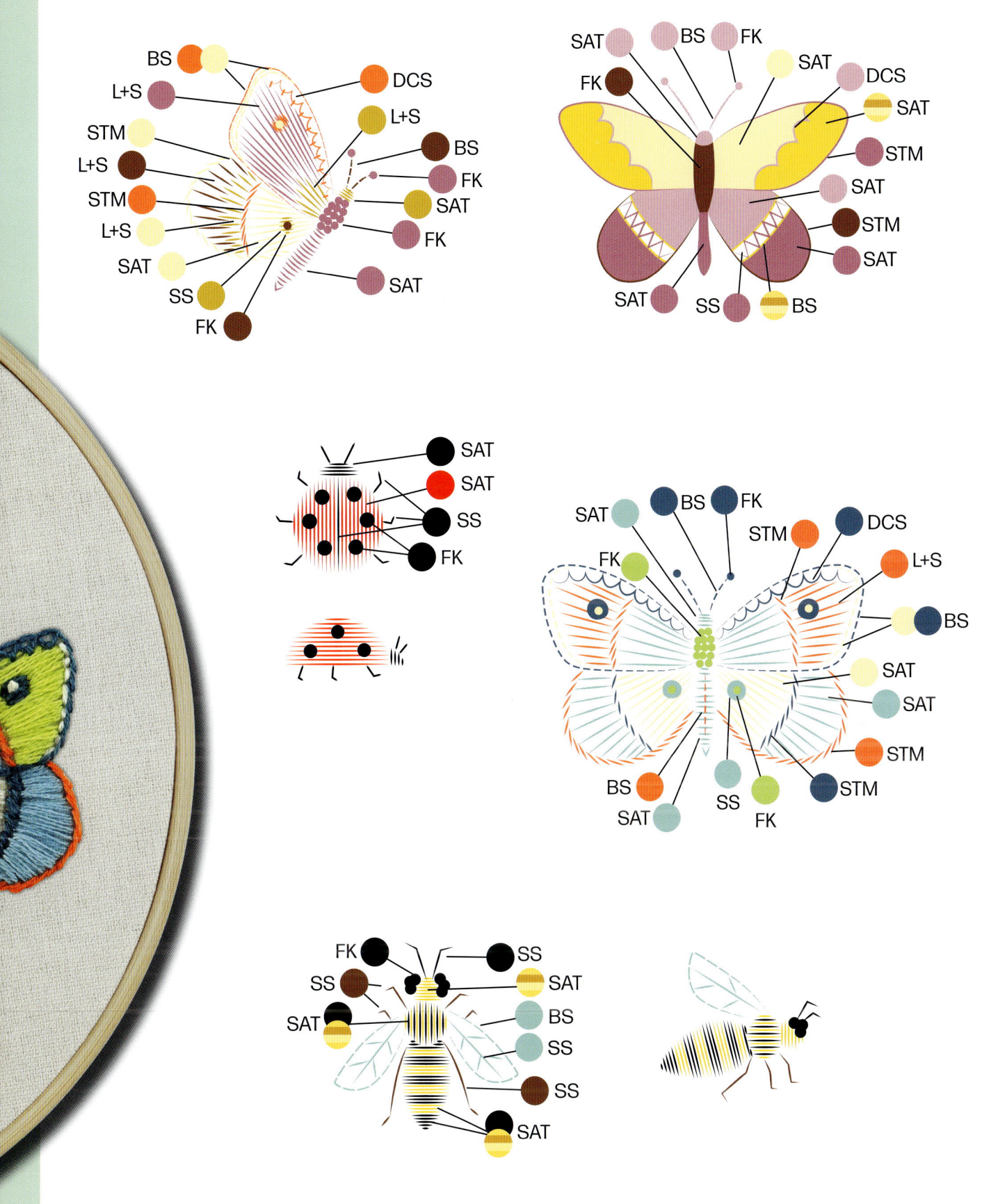

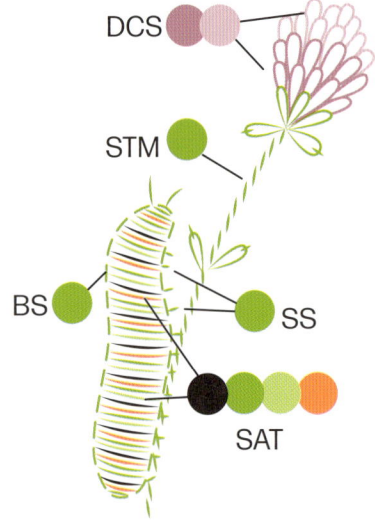

DCS

STM

BS

SS

SAT

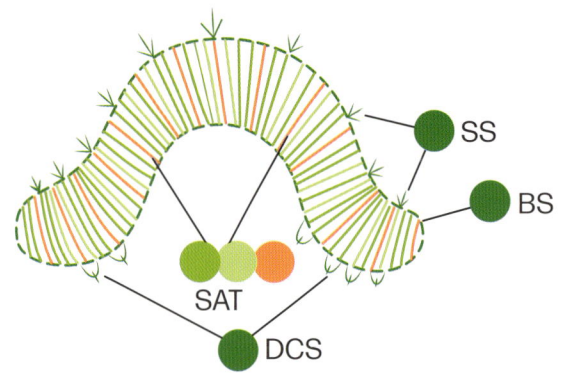

SS

BS

SAT

DCS

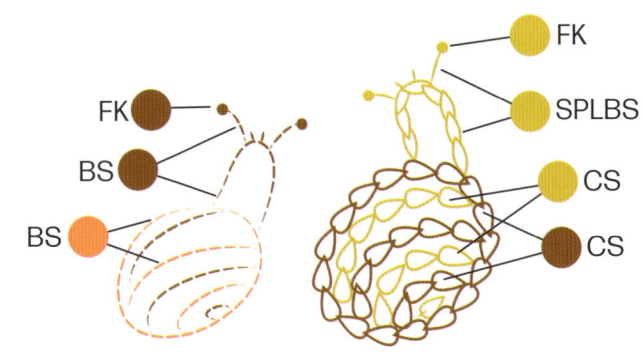

FK

BS

BS

FK

SPLBS

CS

CS

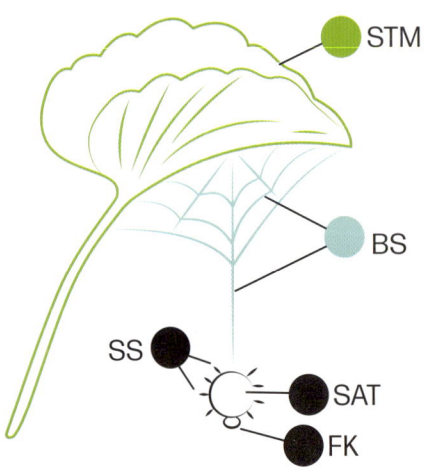

STM

BS

SS

SAT

FK

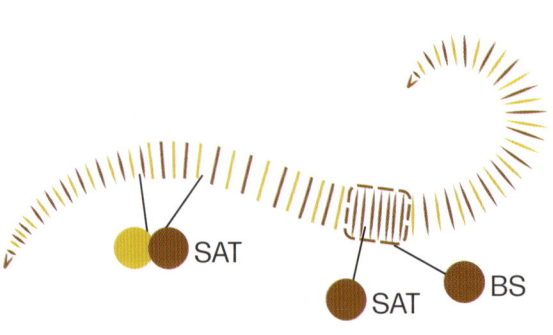

SAT

SAT

BS

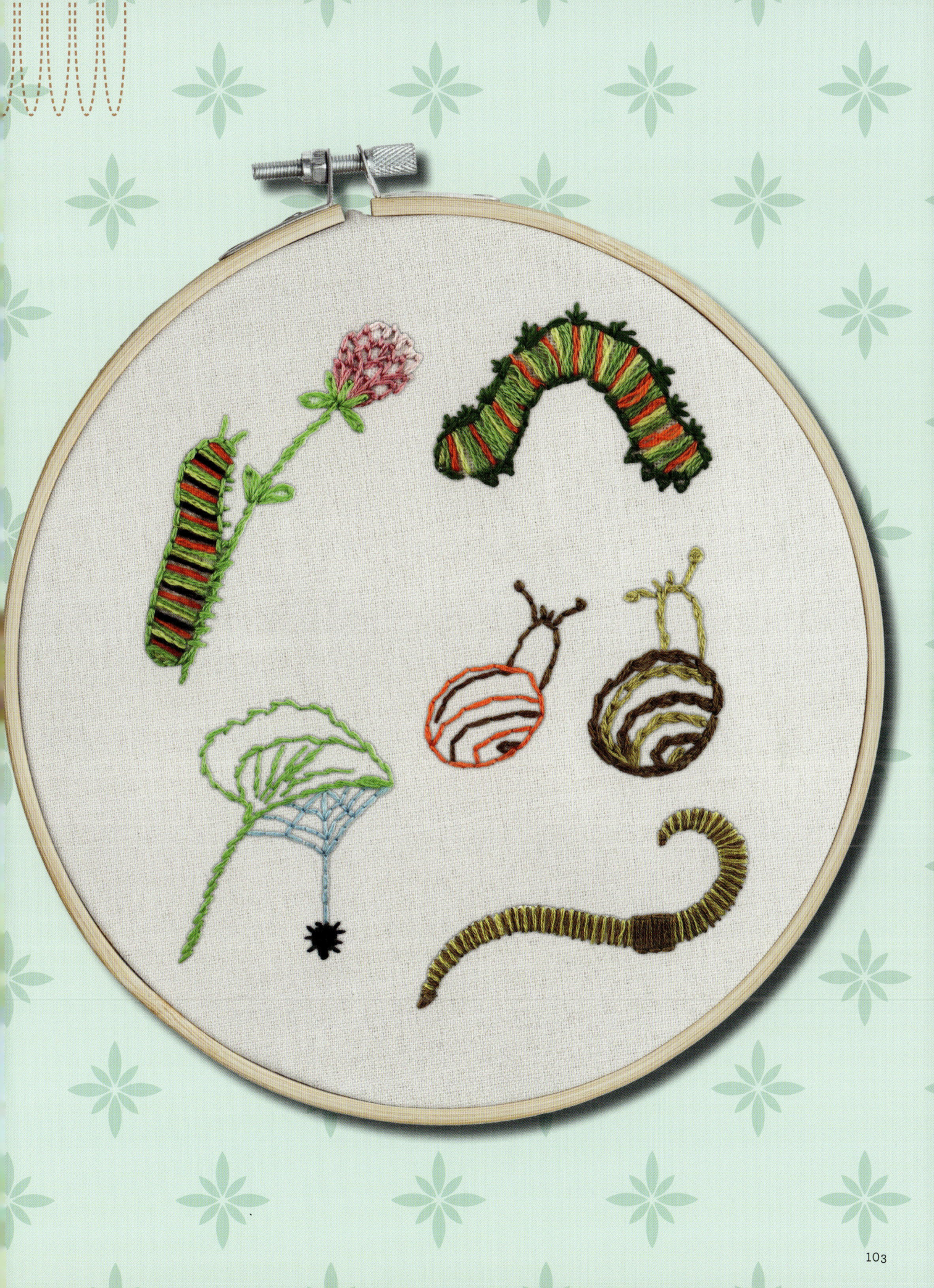

PROJECT TEMPLATES

The templates on the following pages have been sized to fit 4" to 6" (10 to 15 cm) hoops depending on the flowers. The primary flower for each month is shown in a 6" (15 cm) hoop, and the smaller, secondary flowers are in a 4" (10 cm) hoop. To scale the template to a custom size, use the QR code provided or visit **quarto.com/files/BirthFlowerEmbroidery** to access a printable download.

CHANGING THE SCALE

When adjusting the scale of a design to fit your needs, there are a few things to consider. In most cases, you can simply print the template at a larger or smaller percentage. However, some situations may require a bit more effort and planning.

- Reducing a very complex design could mean that you will need to simplify it by reducing the number of flowers or details that you stitch.

- Enlarging a simple design might require you to use six strands of thread instead of three. You might also need to add more stitches to the design to fill it in.

- You can break any design apart and stitch just a few flowers. Use tracing paper and a pencil to play with the layout you want before stitching.

Scan the QR code with your smartphone to download printable templates.

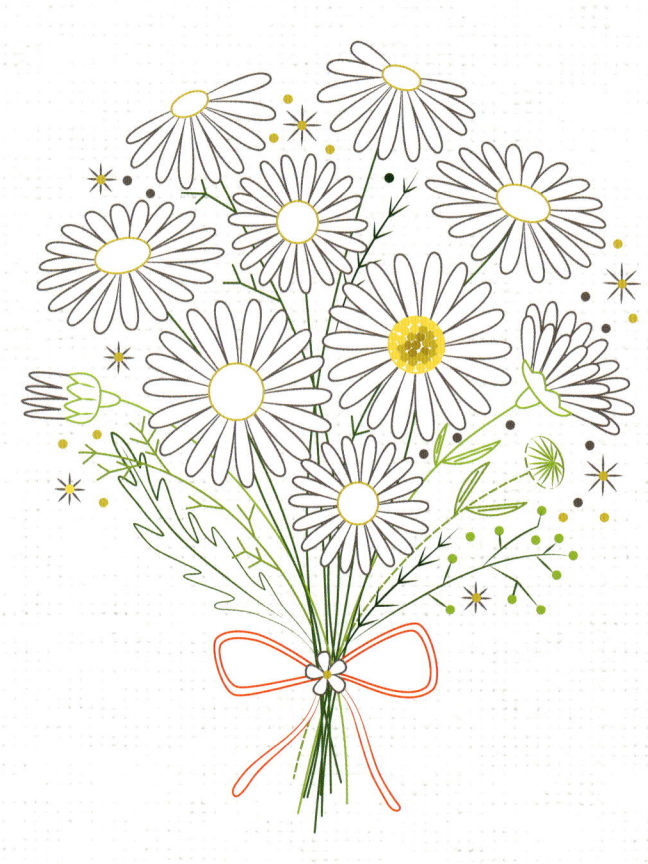

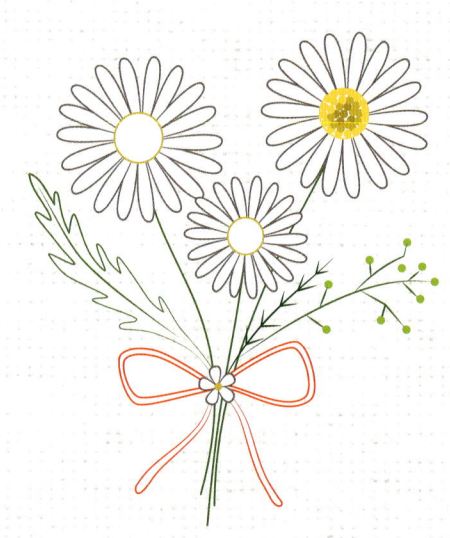

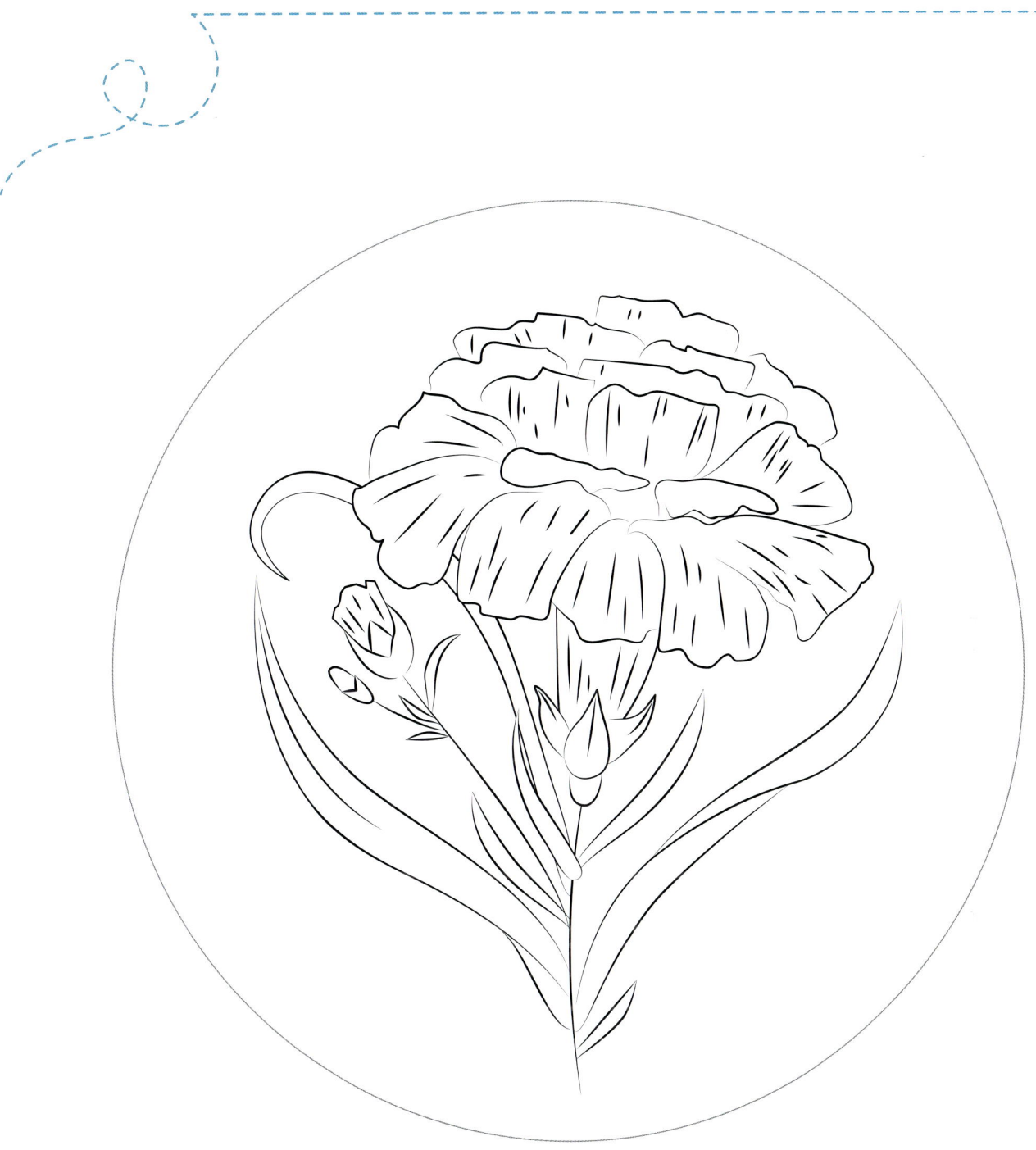

JANUARY
CARNATION

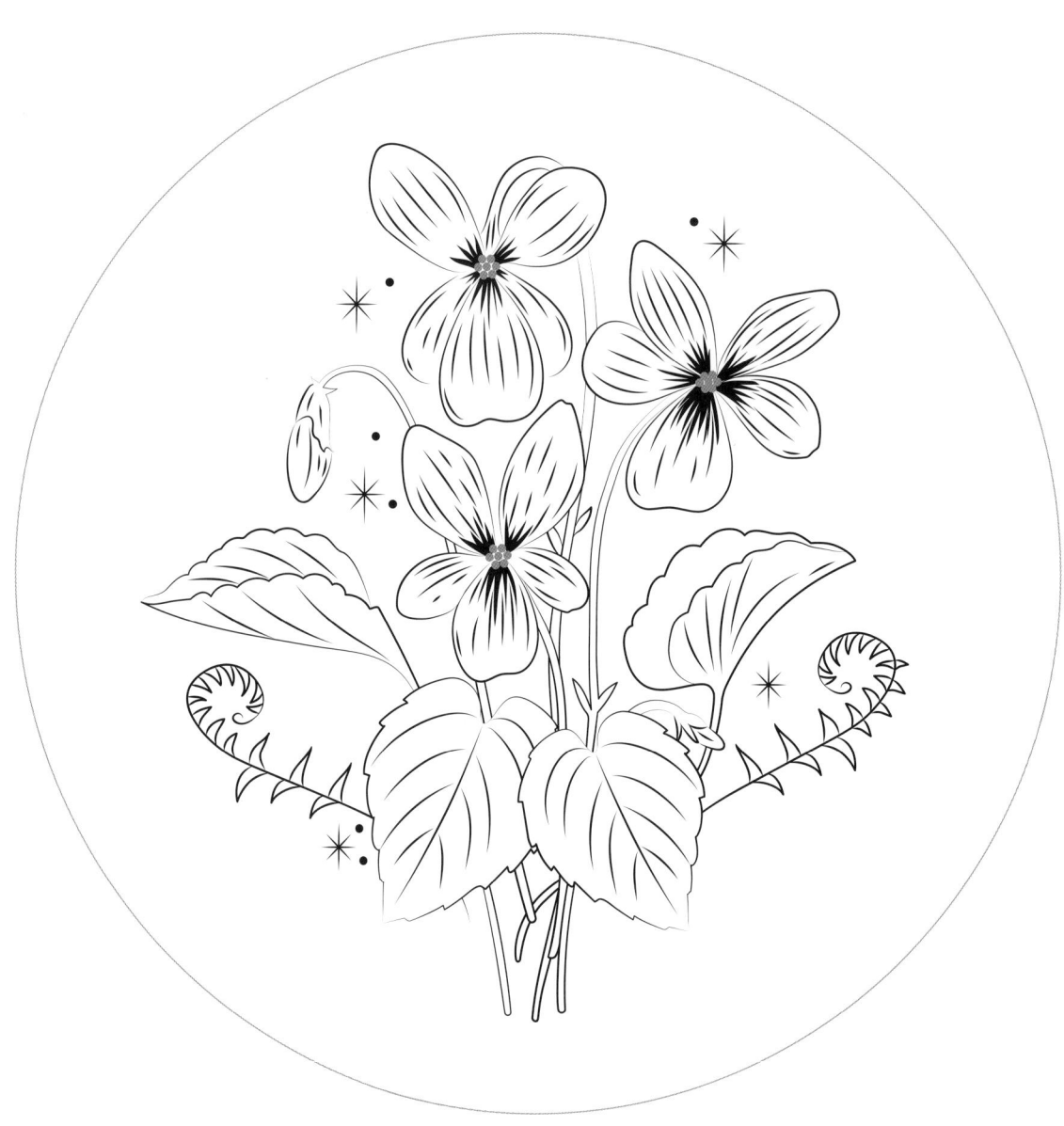

FEBRUARY
VIOLET

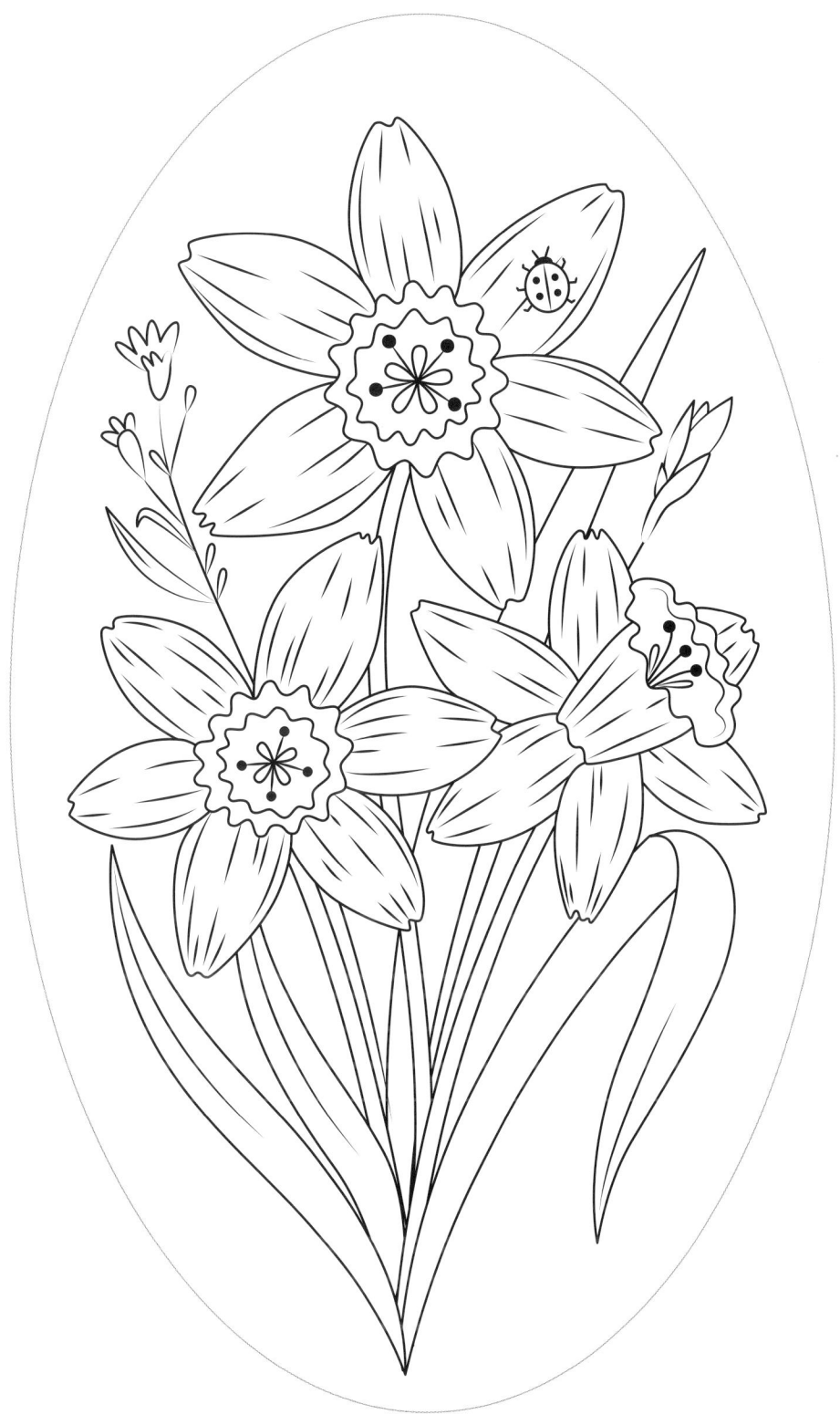

MARCH
DAFFODIL

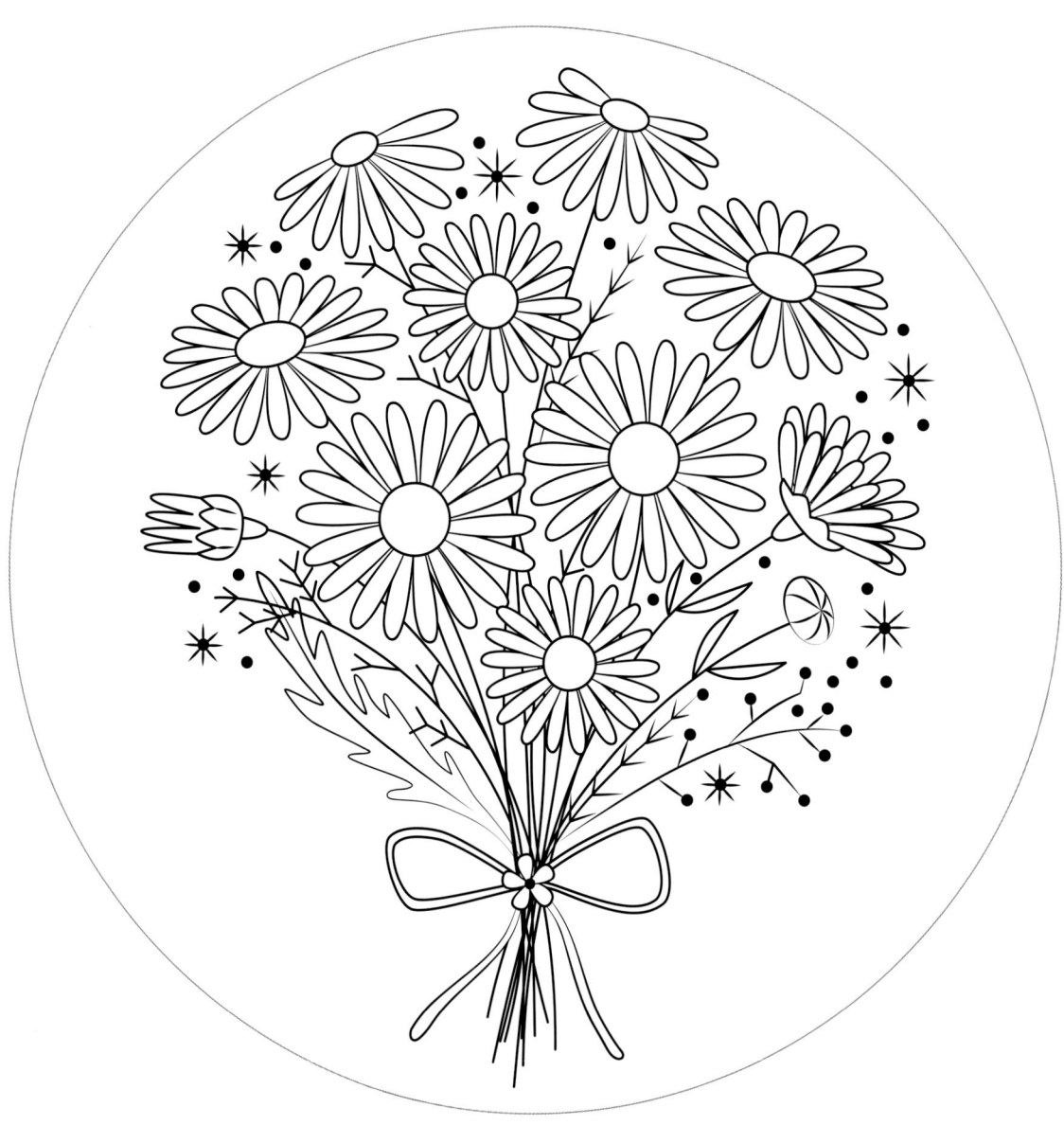

APRIL
DAISY

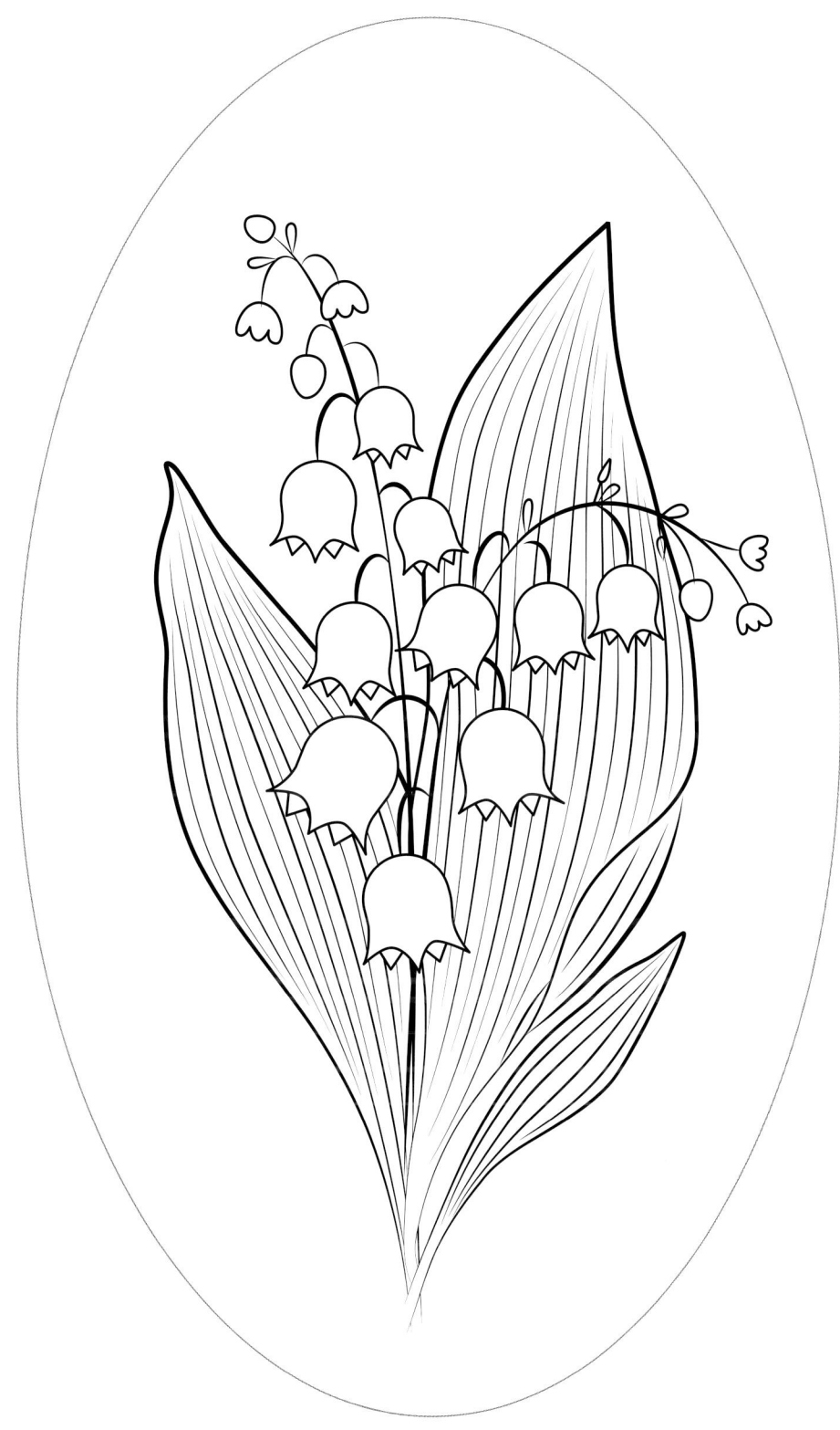

MAY
LILY OF THE VALLEY

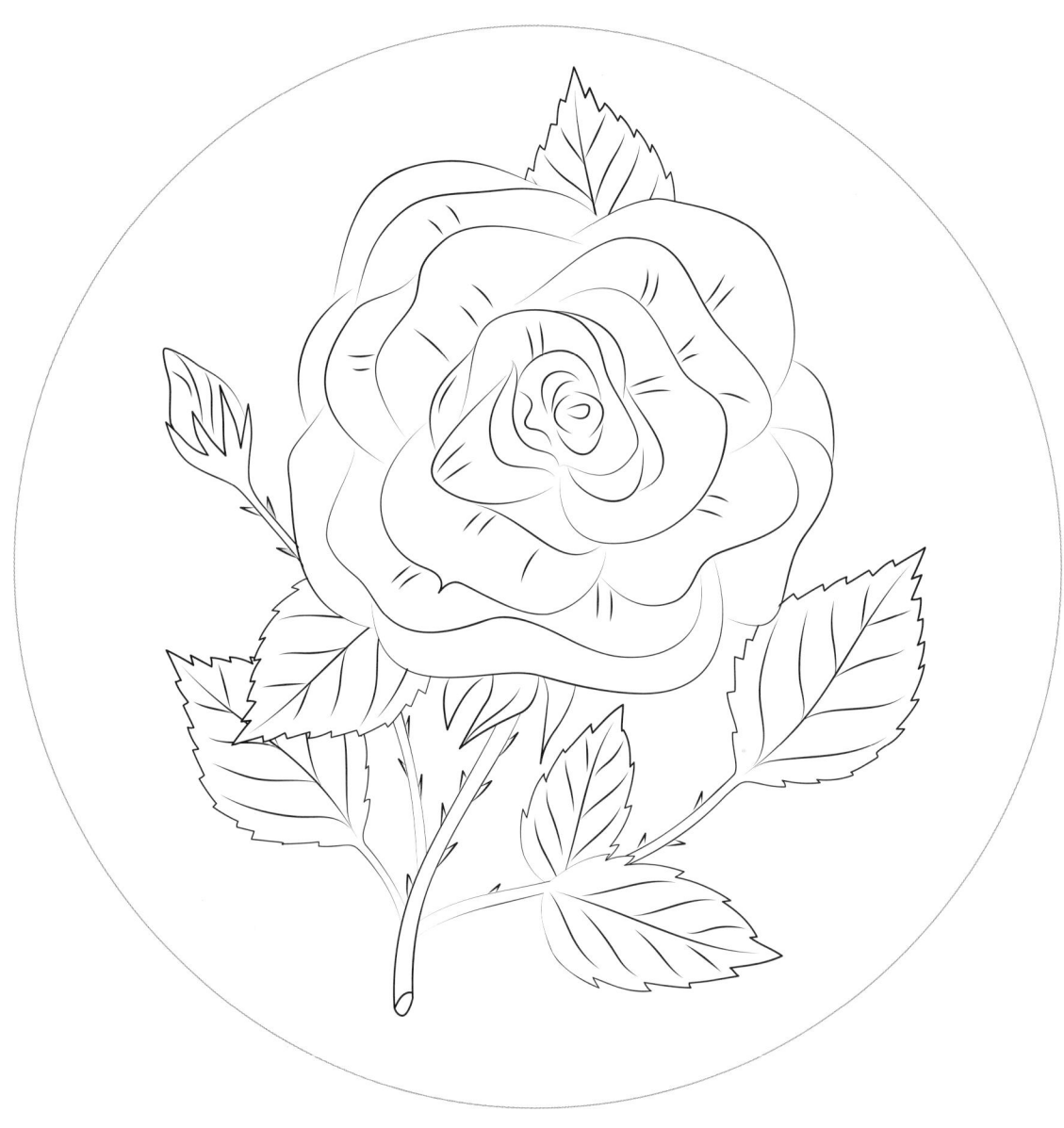

JUNE
ROSE

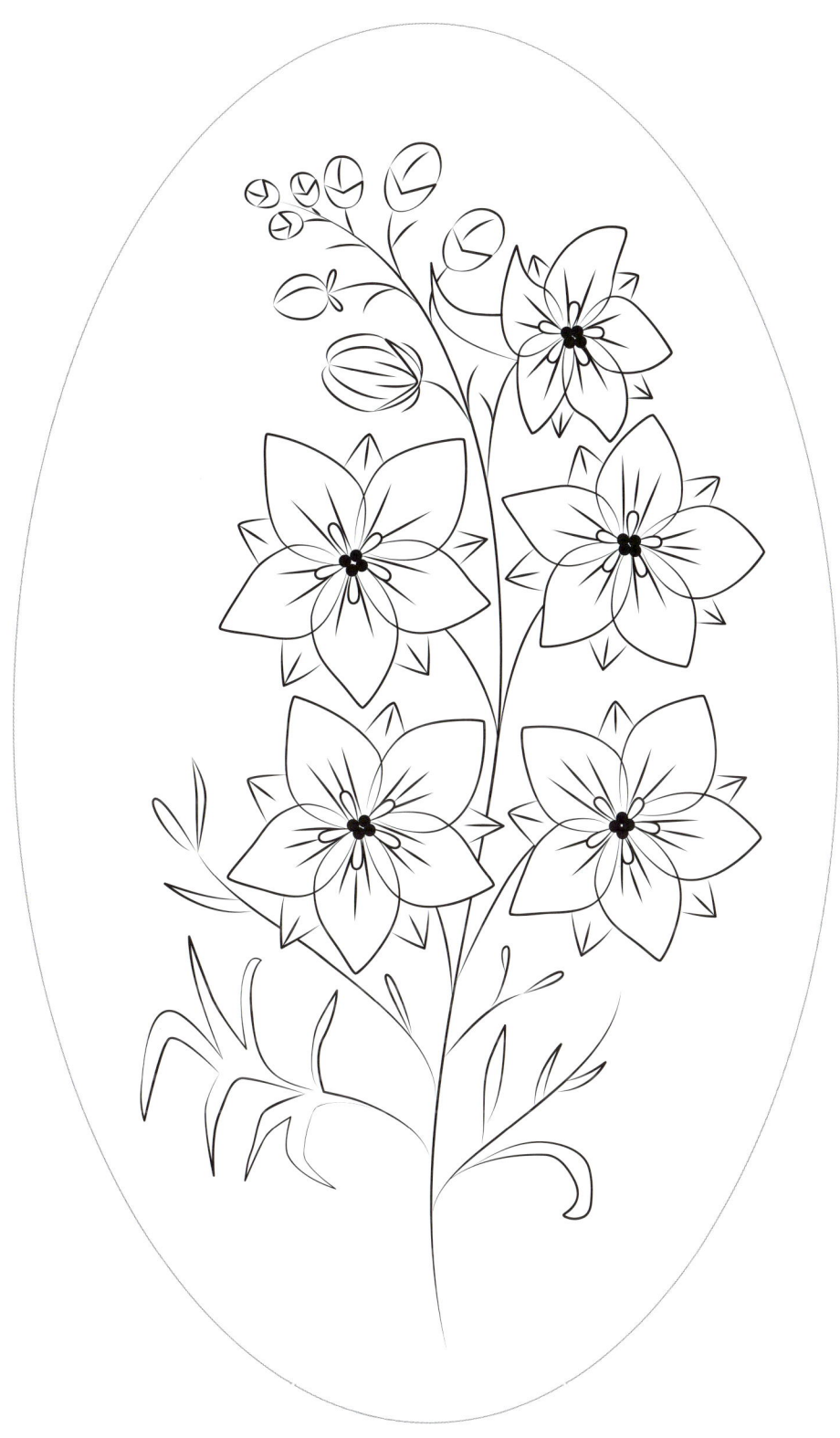

JULY

LARKSPUR

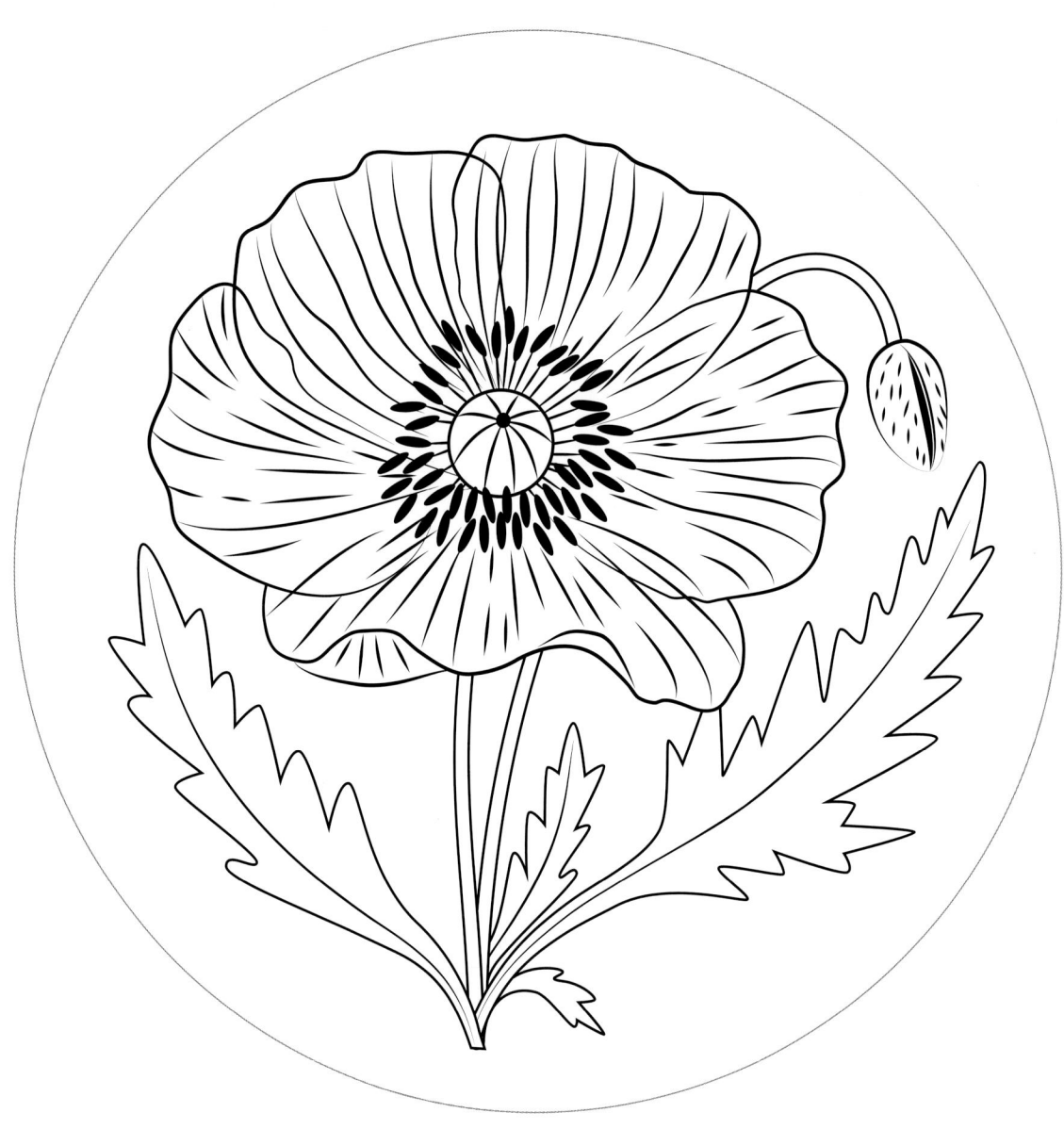

AUGUST
POPPY

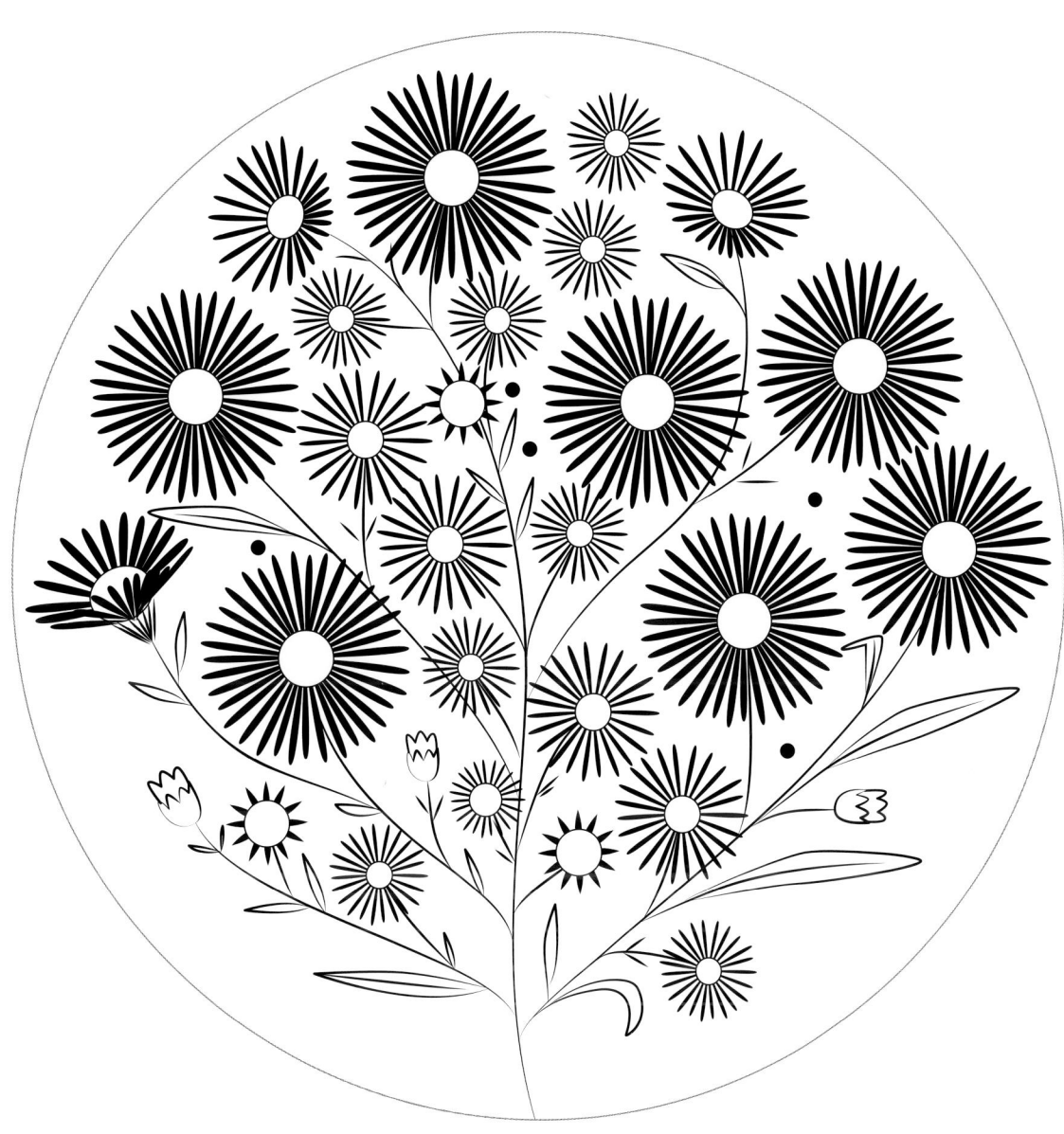

SEPTEMBER
ASTER

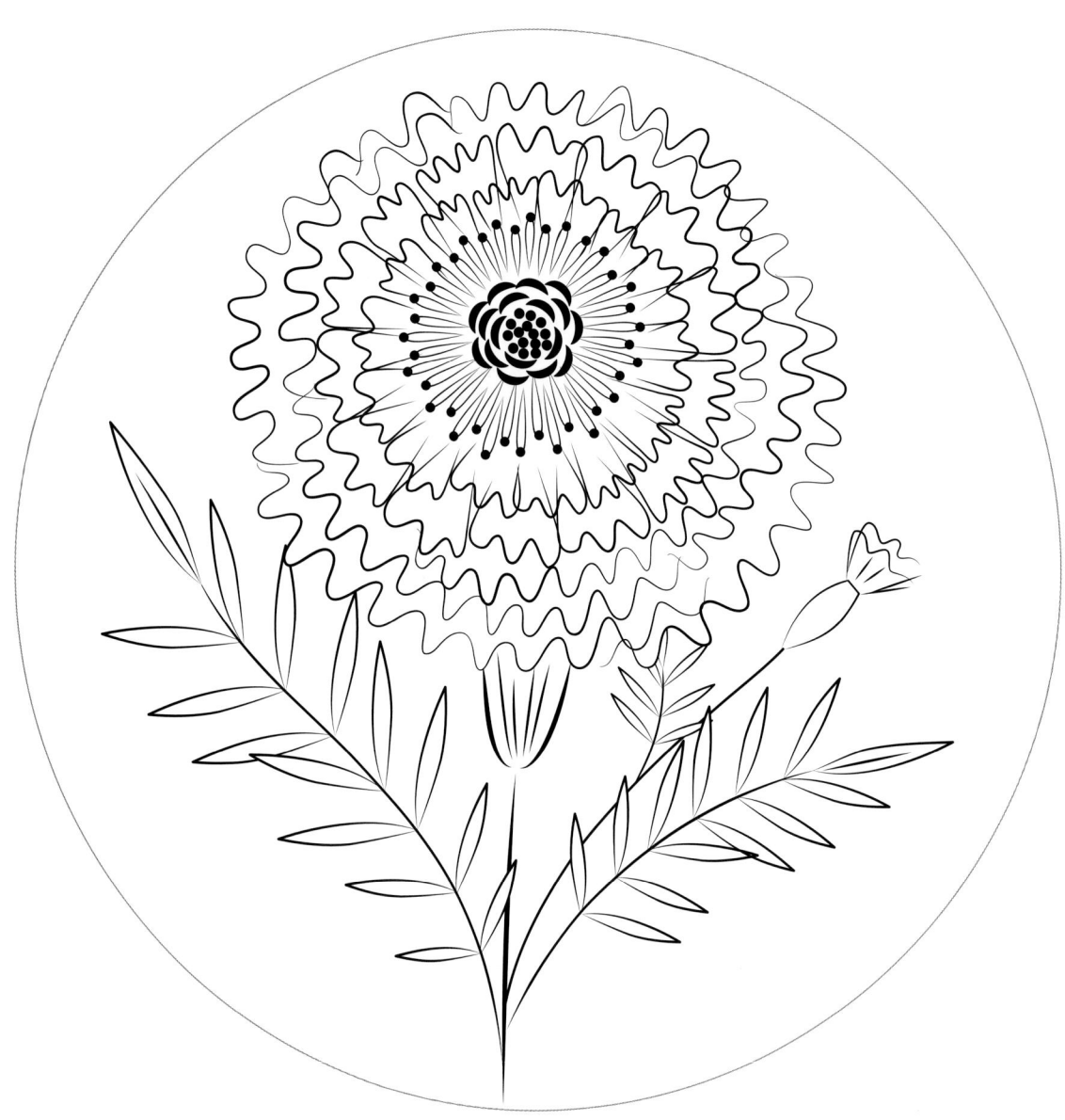

OCTOBER
MARIGOLD

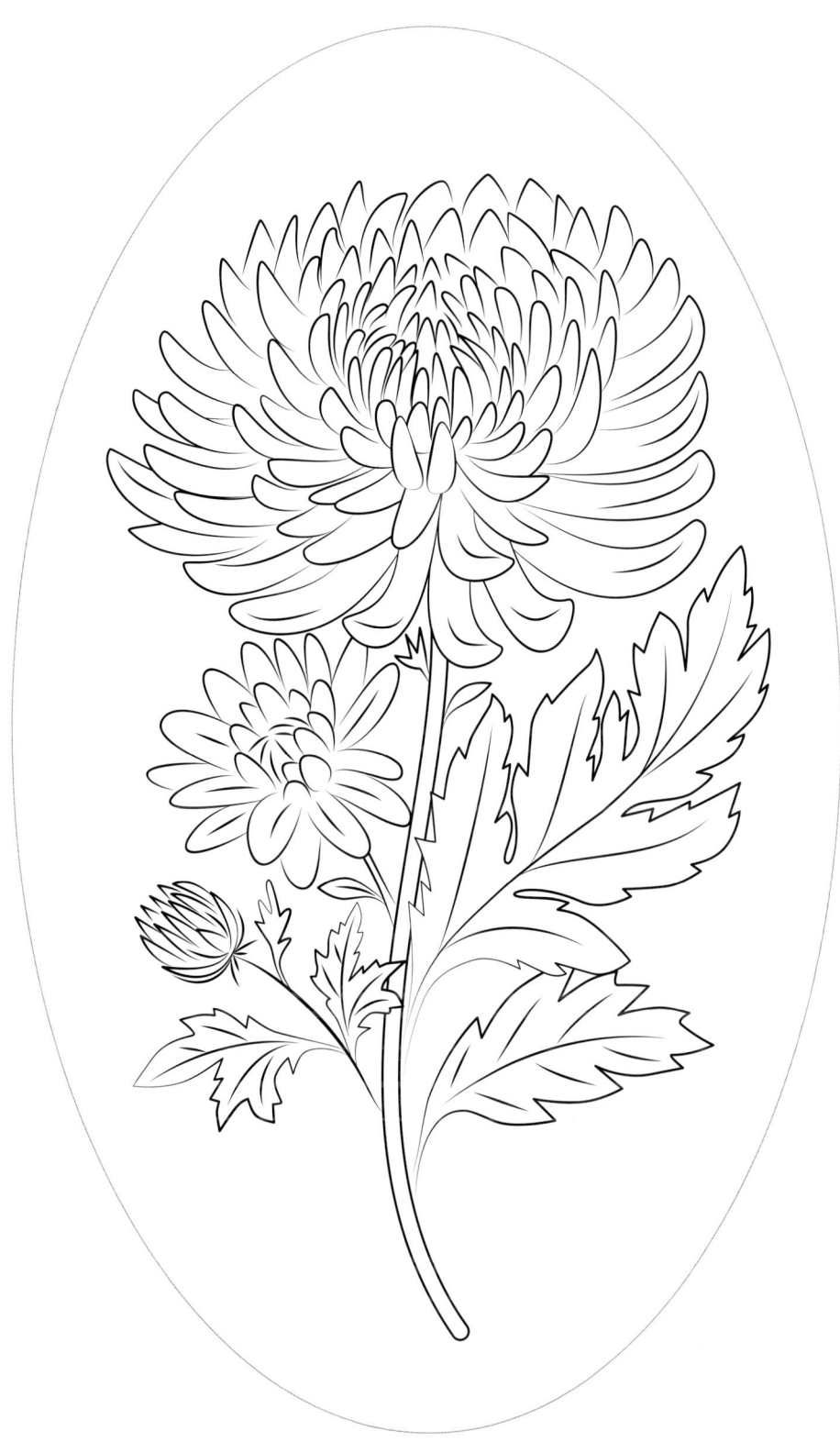

NOVEMBER

CHRYSANTHEMUM

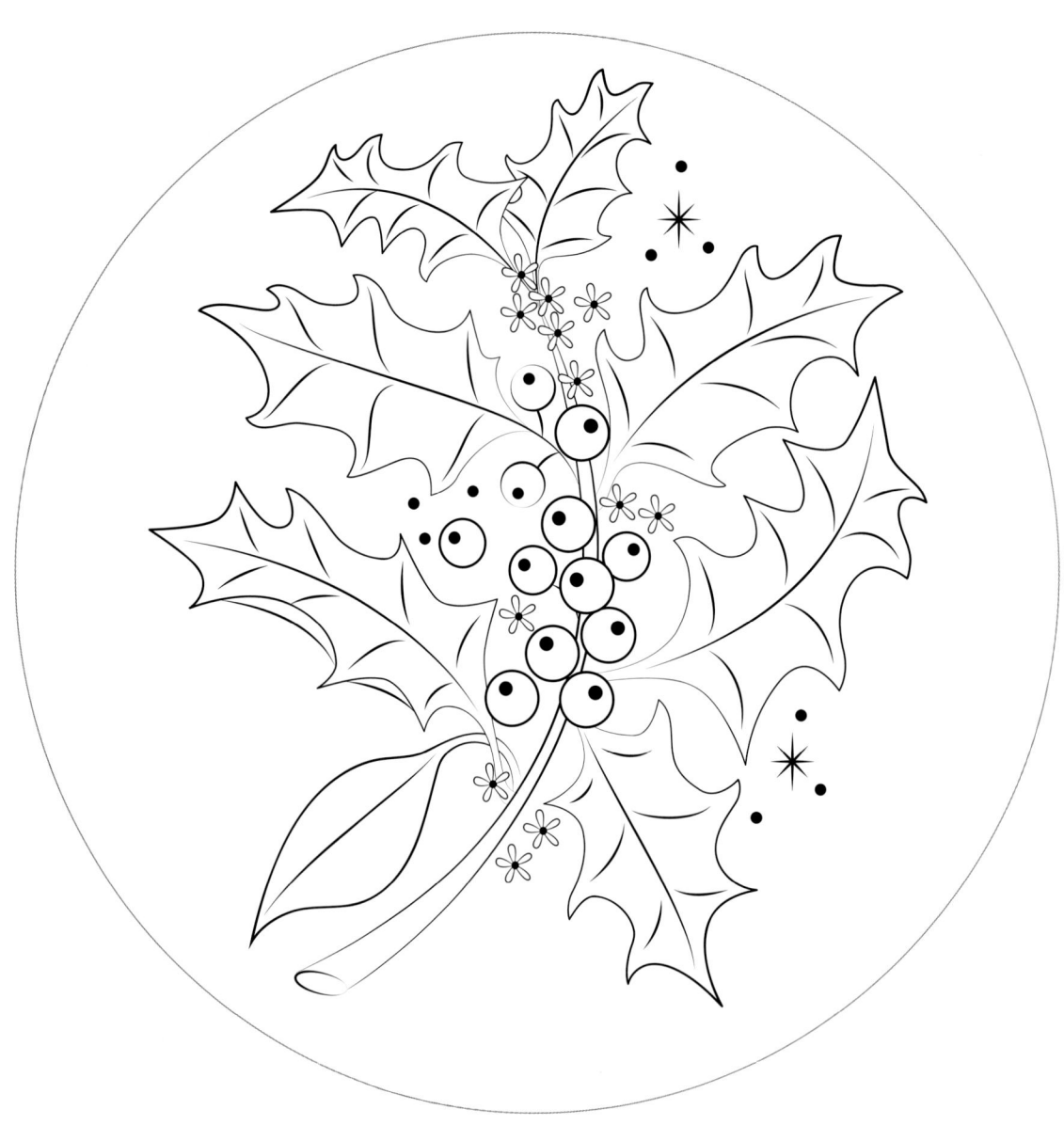

DECEMBER
HOLLY

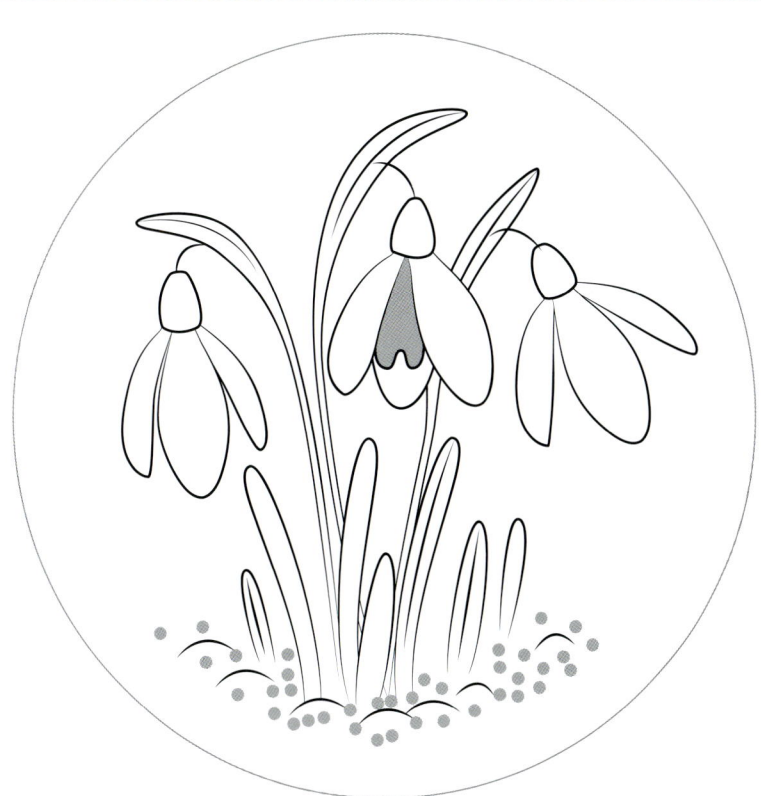

JANUARY
SNOWDROP

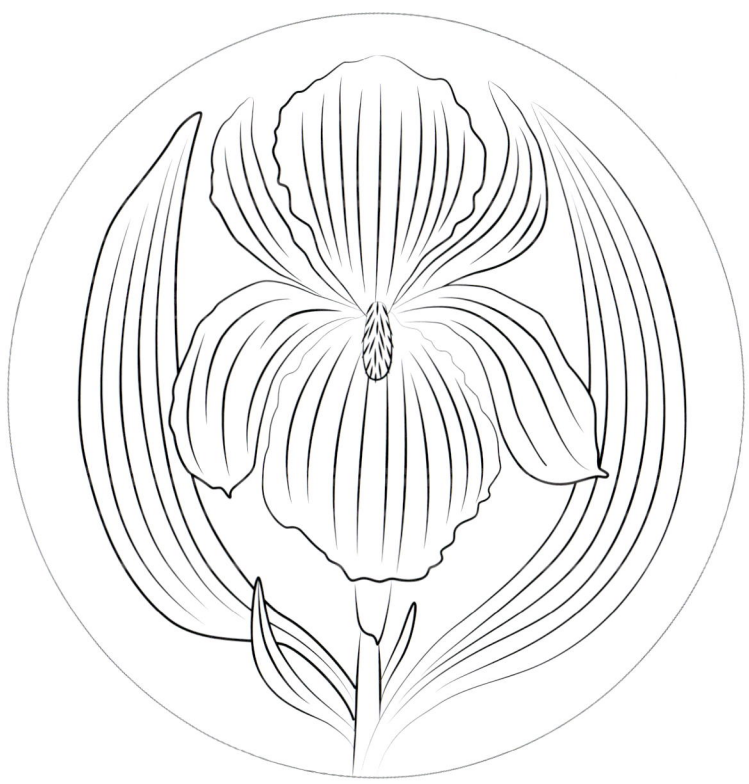

FEBRUARY
IRIS

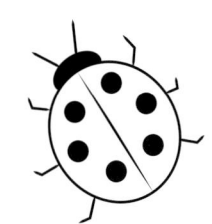

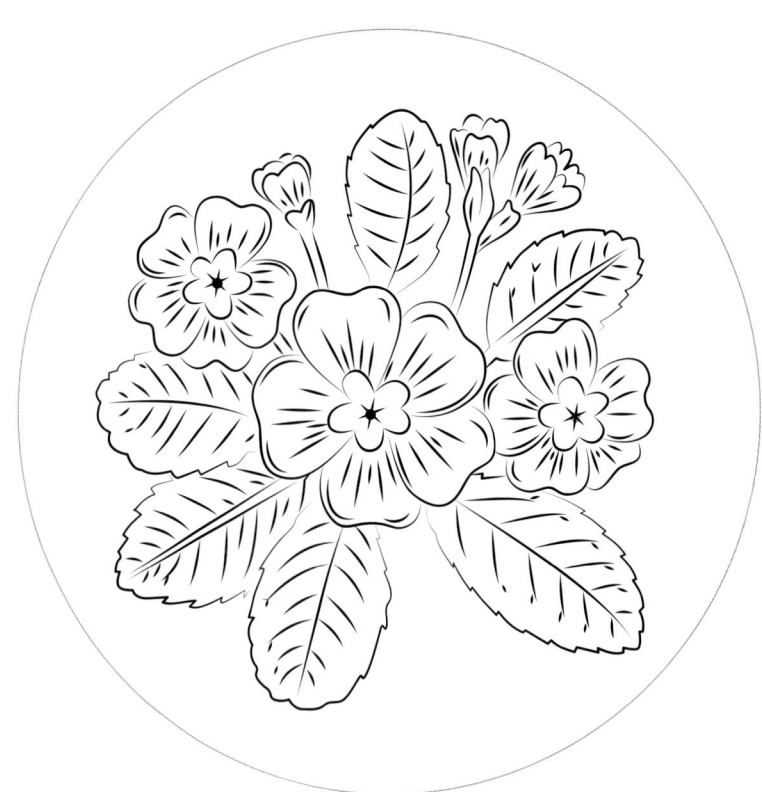

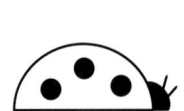

FEBRUARY
PRIMROSE

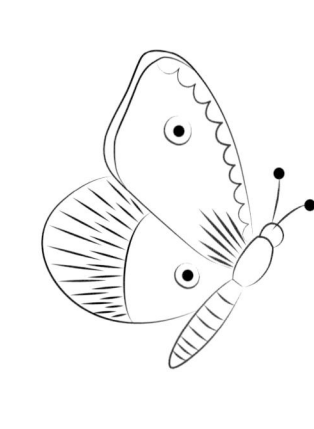

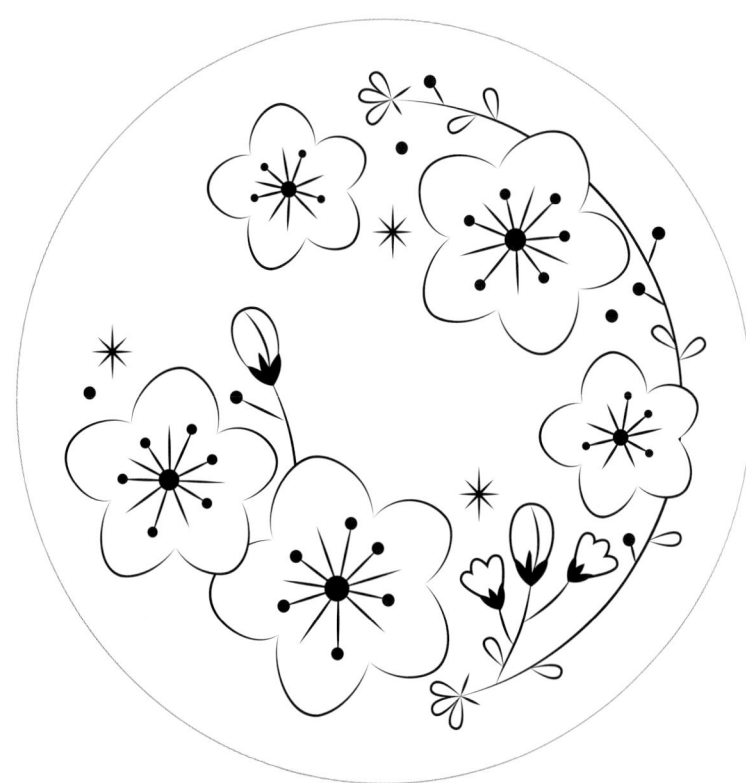

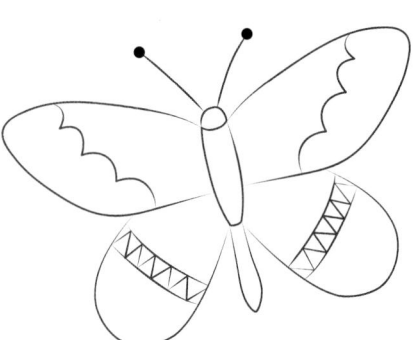

MARCH
CHERRY BLOSSOM

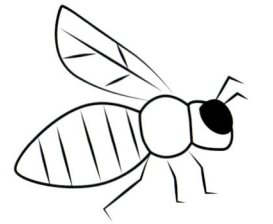

APRIL
SWEET PEA

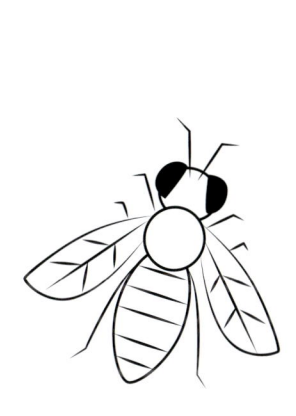

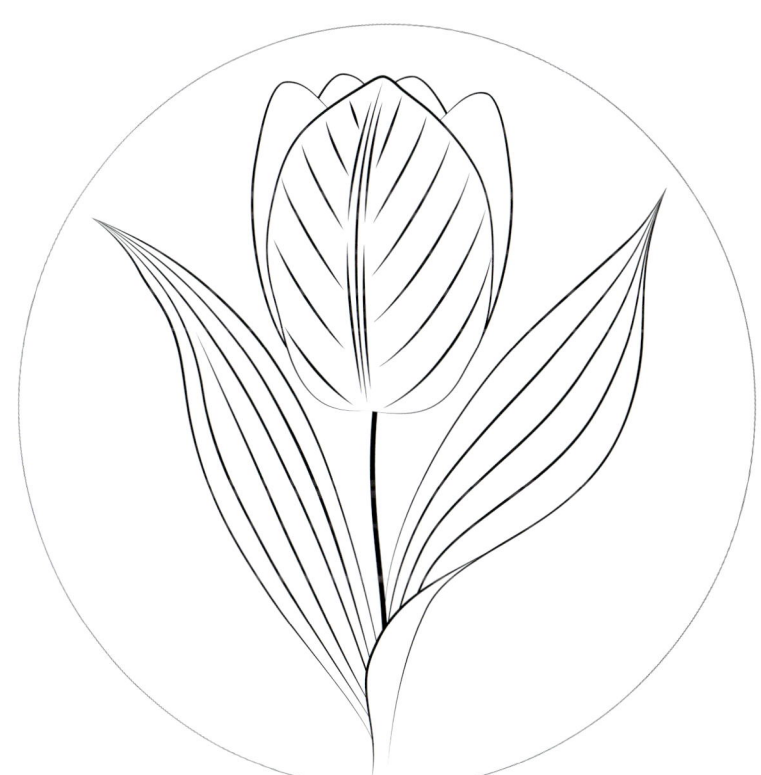

APRIL
TULIP

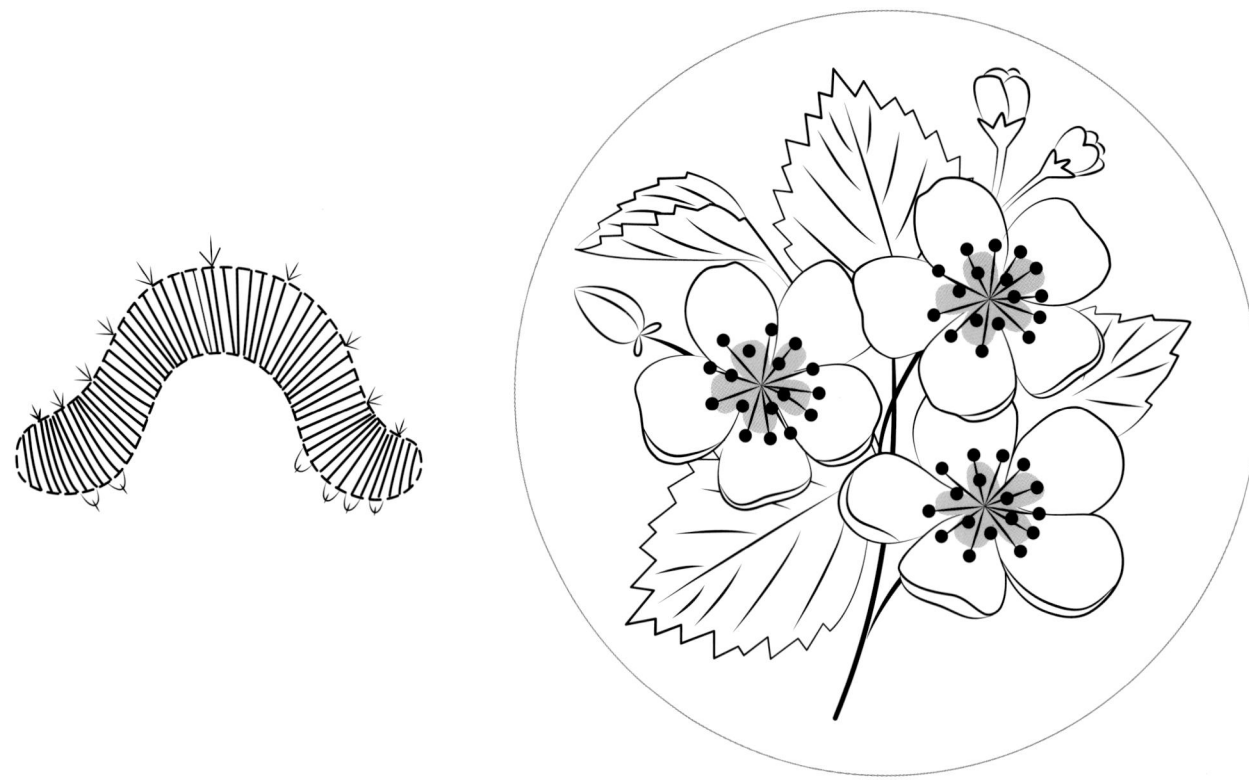

MAY
HAWTHORN

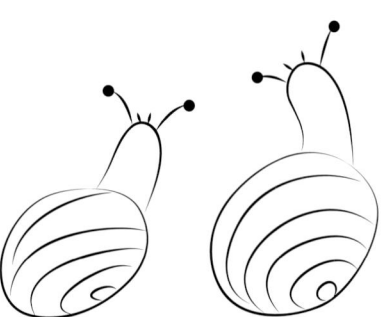

JUNE
HONEYSUCKLE

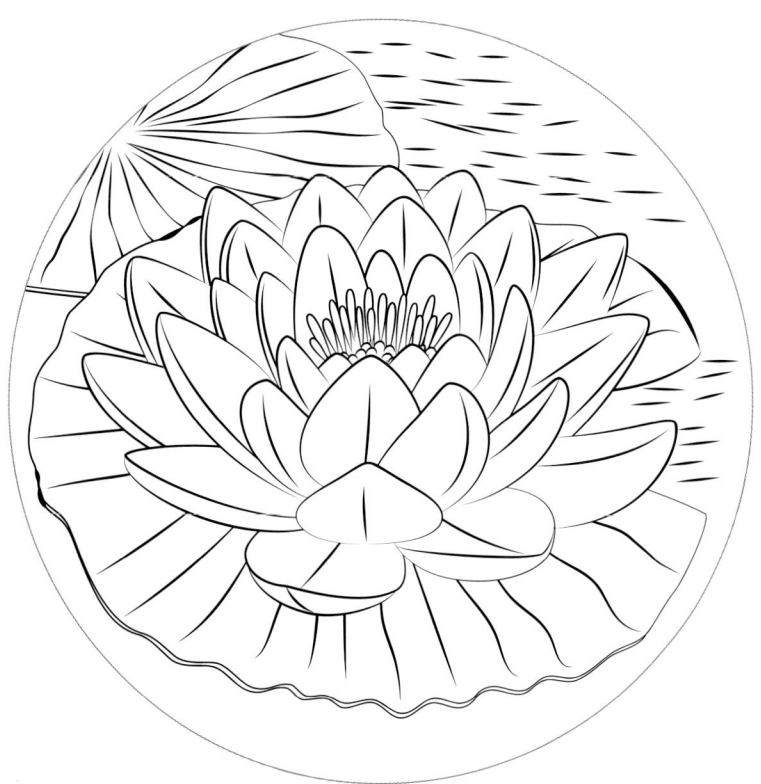

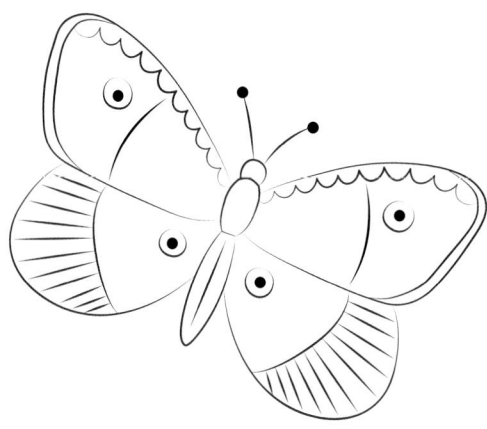

JULY
WATER LILY

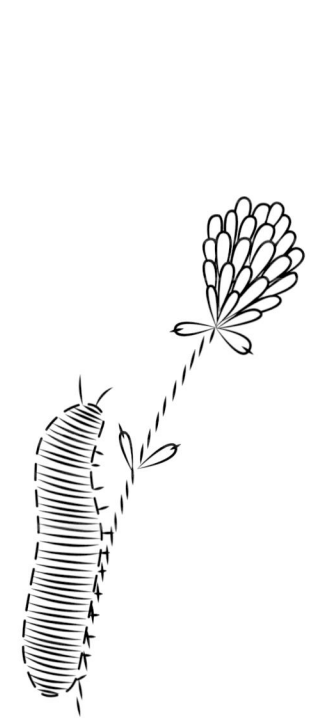

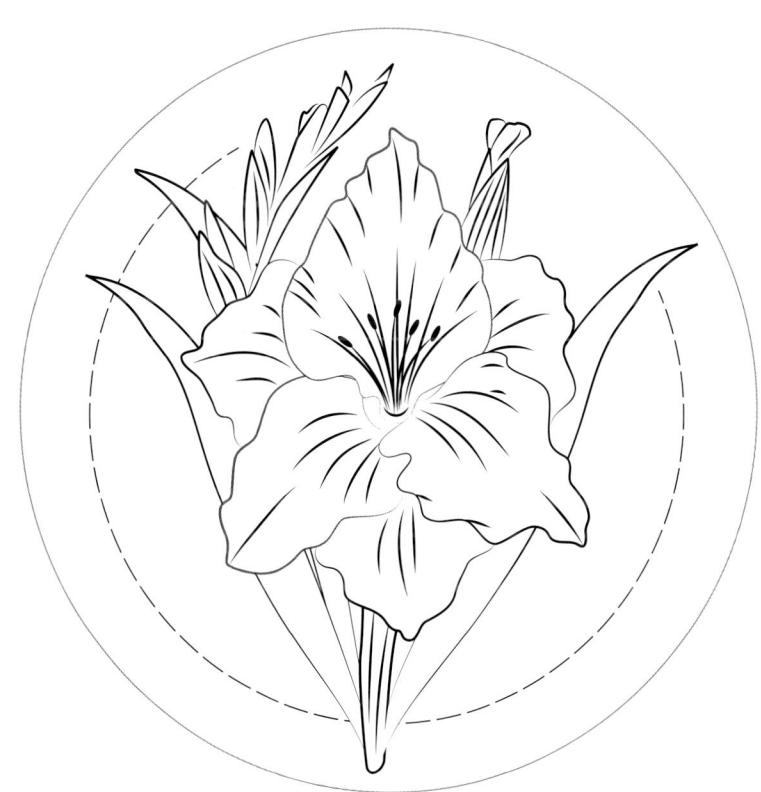

AUGUST
GLADIOLUS

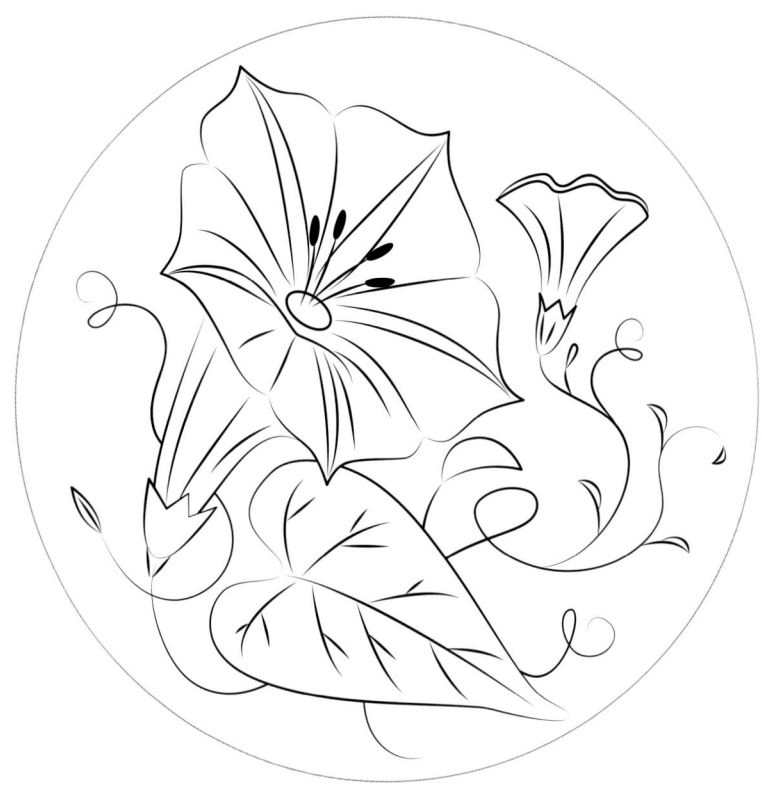

SEPTEMBER
MORNING GLORY

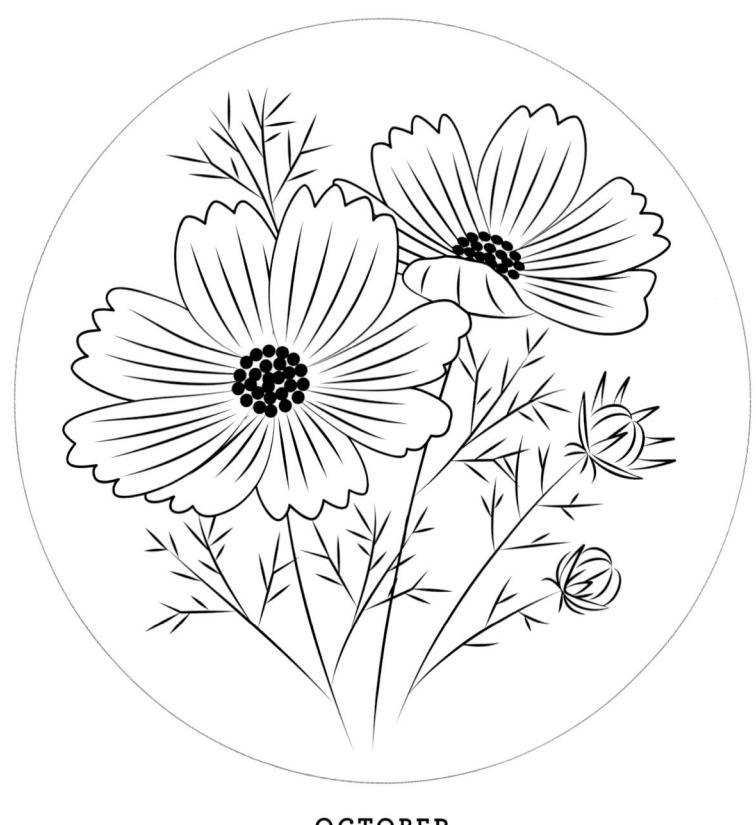

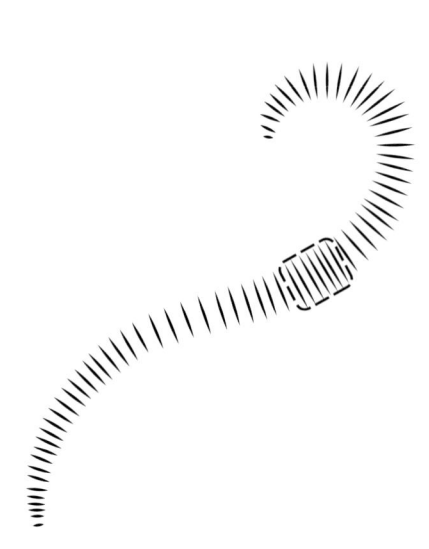

OCTOBER
COSMOS

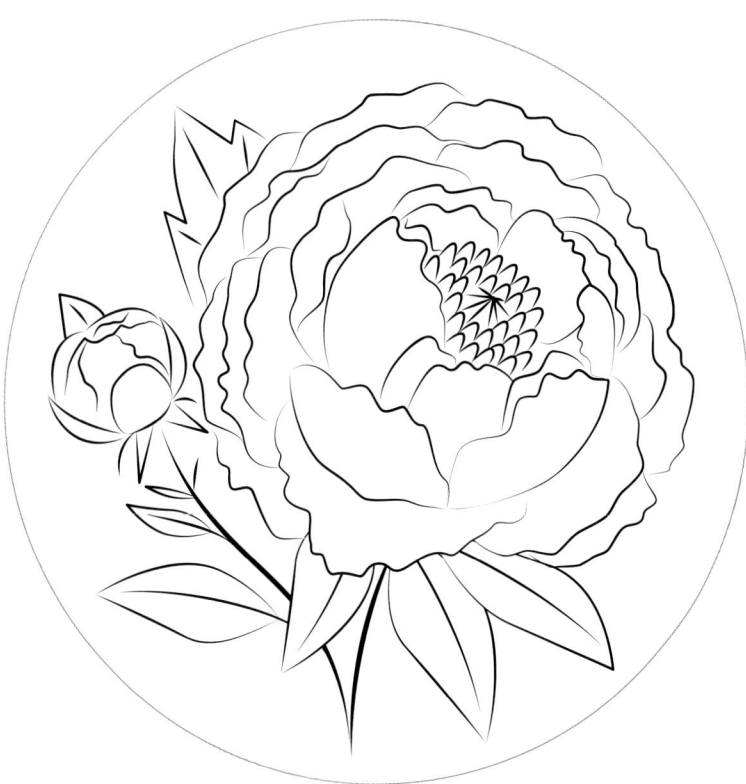

NOVEMBER
PEONY

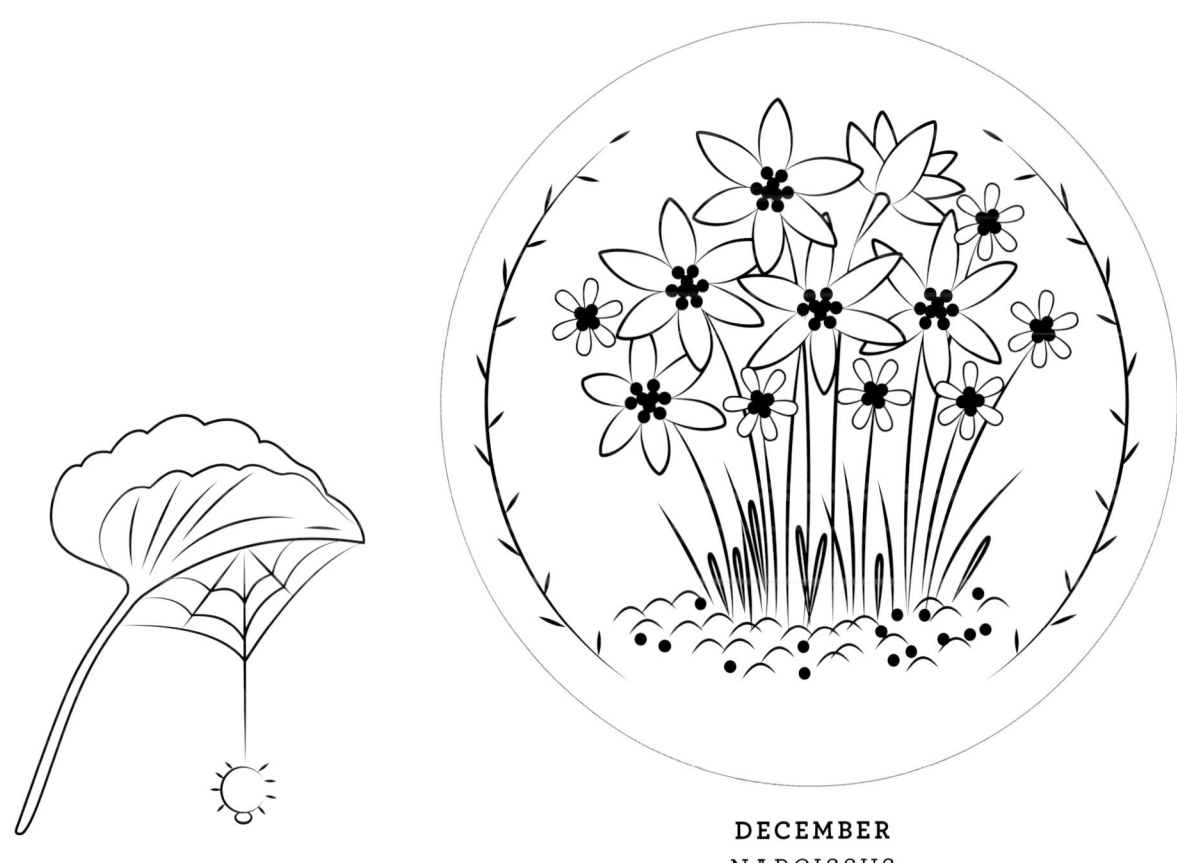

DECEMBER
NARCISSUS

RESOURCES

ESSENTIAL TOOLS

merchantandmills.com

handicraft.com

jjneedles.com

michaels.com

123stitch.com

yarntree.com

firemountaingems.com

sulky.com

fabricdepot.com

THREAD AND FLOSS

dmc.com

purlsoho.com

kreinik.com/store

etsy.com

ebay.com

OTHER MATERIALS

modernhoopla.co

pellonprojects.com

johnbead.com

warmcompany.com

sulky.com

pilotpen.us

shopartograph.com

dickblick.com

sublimestitching.com

BOOKS

The Complete Language of Flowers: A Definitive and Illustrated History (Wellfleet Press, 2022)

quarto.com/books/9781577152835/the-complete-language-of-flowers

The Illustrated Language of Flowers (London, New York, G. Routledge & Co., 1858)

biodiversitylibrary.org/item/264613#page/1/mode/1up

The Language of Flowers: An Alphabet of Floral Emblems (London, Edinburgh, New York, T. Nelson and Sons, 1857)

publicdomainreview.org/collection/the-language-of-flowers-an-alphabet-of-floral-emblems-1857/

The Language of Flowers, with Illustrative Poetry (London, Saunders & Otley, 1841)

archive.org/details/languageflowers00s/mode/2up

The Language and Poetry of Flowers (New York, Derby & Jackson, 1858)

archive.org/details/languagepoetryof00adamiala/mode/2up

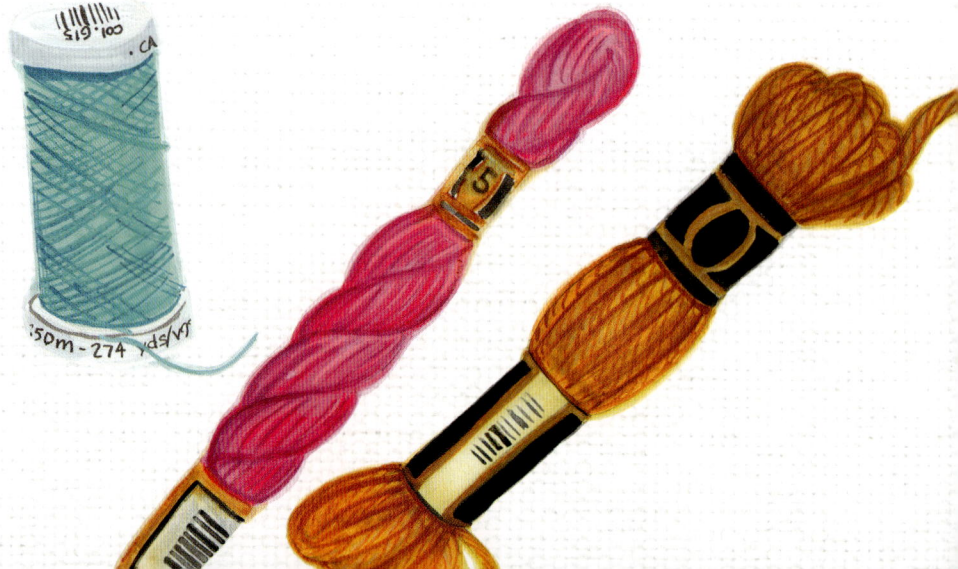

ABOUT THE AUTHOR

AMY L. FRAZER is an illustrator and embroiderer living and working in Portland, Oregon, where the trees are greener and the forests are for everyone. A multidisciplined craftsperson, Amy has a deep appreciation for all things made by hand. Through her work she captures the beauty of the world around us, adding personal touches through mark-making. Amy believes that embroidery is a means to bring people together, building community and fostering connections where previously none existed.

Amy holds a BFA from the Columbus College of Art and Design (CCAD) and has a strong foundation in drawing and illustration, but considers herself a lifelong learner. A self-taught embroiderer, Amy teaches workshops with local craft shops and arts and nature organizations with a focus on florals and iconic Portland bridges. With extensive experience in product creation working at companies such as Galerie au Chocolat, Old Navy, and Nike, she enjoys designing objects as well as the prints and colors that adorn them.

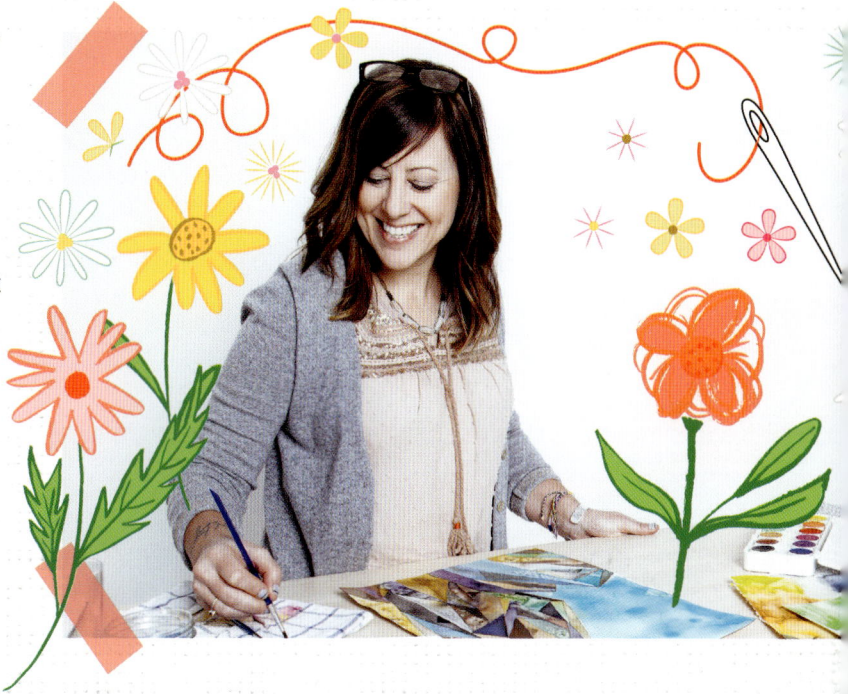

Her artwork has been featured in *Stationery Trends* magazine, the *UPPERCASE Encyclopedia of Inspiration: Stitch-Illo*, Uncommon Goods, the Hudson Valley Seed Company, and on the popular Portland Trail Blazers gameday poster series. Amy's products are sold through her stationery and gift company, Keller Design Co., to retailers across the US.

Amy's inspiration for this book was the floral tattoo she got after researching the birth flowers of herself, her granny, and her mom. Amy was surprised to learn that each month has not only one representative flower but in most instances two and sometimes even three! She found the flowers that best represented her mom, granny, and herself; three generations of women that are strong, kind, and creative. Her birth month, February, has three flowers: violet, primrose, and iris. Amy's grandmother always had violets growing in her room, and the sight or smell of these instantly transports her back in time and connects to the early memories of childhood. Flowers hold the power to create connection to memories, to loved ones, to nature, and to a world beyond our senses.

Amy lives in Portland with her boyfriend, Matthew, and their two rescue dogs, Duke and Josephine, who love to wrestle. Their bags are always packed for the next adventure to the mountains, the sea, or a fun city to explore together.

You can see more of her artwork at amylfrazer.com or on Instagram @amylfrazer. Amy's stationery and gifts can be found at kellerdesignco.com or on Instagram at @kellerdesignco.

INDEX

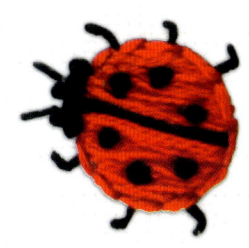

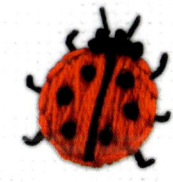

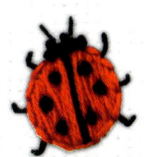

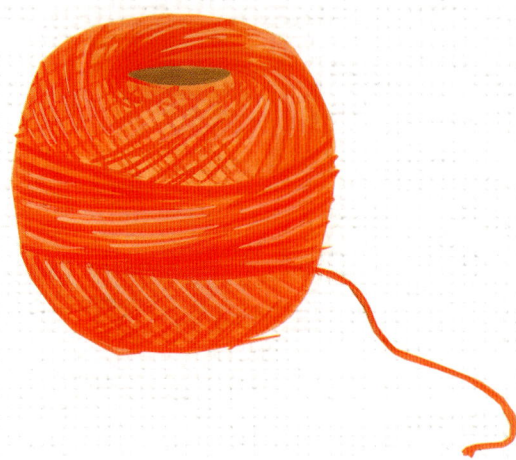

Quarto.com | WalterFoster.com

First Published in 2026 by Walter Foster Publishing, an imprint of The Quarto Group,
100 Cummings Center, Suite 265-D, Beverly, MA 01915, USA.
T (978) 282-9590 F (978) 283-2742

EEA Representation, WTS Tax d.o.o.,
Žanova ulica 3, 4000 Kranj, Slovenia.
www.wts-tax.si

Walter Foster Publishing titles are also available at discount for retail, wholesale, promotional, and bulk purchase. For details, contact the Special Sales Manager by email at specialsales@quarto.com or by mail at The Quarto Group, Attn: Special Sales Manager, 100 Cummings Center, Suite 265-D, Beverly, MA 01915, USA.

30 29 28 27 26   1 2 3 4 5

ISBN: 978-0-7603-9344-4

Digital edition published in 2026
eISBN: 978-0-7603-9345-1

The content on pages 8–10 and 13–21 was previously published in *Empowered Embroidery* (Walter Foster Publishing, 2021) by Amy L. Frazer.

Library of Congress Cataloging-in-Publication Data available

Cover design: Samantha J. Bednarek, samanthabednarek.com

Printed in Guangdong, China TT072025